The Biblical Approach to Alcohol

The Biblical Approach to Alcohol

By
Stephen M. Reynolds
Ph. D.

CONTENTS

APPENDICES

ABOUT THE AUTHOR

STEPHEN M. REYNOLDS has a Ph.D. degree from Princeton University where he worked in Biblical and oriental languages under the teaching of Drs. Henry S. Gehman, Philip K. Hitti, and Harold H. Bender. After receiving this advanced degree he has spent years in adding to his knowledge and skills in the field. He has worked for a time in archaeology under Dr. William F. Albright.

He has written monographs on difficult Bible passages which have been published in *The Journal of Biblical Literature, The Westminster Theological Journal, Zeitschrift fur die Neutestamentliche Wissenschaft, The Reformation Review* and elsewhere. He contributed together with other faculty members of Gordon-Conwell Theological Seminary to the translation of the *New International Version* of the Old Testament, and his written articles in *Baker's Dictionary of Ethics* edited by Dr. Carl F. H. Henry. All he seeks is that this book be read with genuine open minds by sincere seekers of the truth.

PREFACE

Not long ago I was led to study the teaching of a body of Christians with a view to membership. Much of what I found was wholesome and refreshing, but one tenet which was new to me was a constitutional rule which had not been in force until recently.

> Mutual help in a holy life and maintenance of the truth being one design of church fellowship, that individuals may be saved from the ruin wrought by intemperance, and that a testimony may be borne against this sin, and against the temptations thereto, the followers of Christ should totally abstain from the manufacture, sale and use of intoxicants as a beverage.[1]

This had been made less strict in 1980. The new rule says:

> For the preservation of life and because of respect for our bodies as God's creation, we are to be careful in the use of drugs. Christians should avoid enslavement to alcohol, tobacco or any habit-forming drug. The Scripture strongly condemns drunkenness as a sin...
>
> To prevent damage to our neighbor, to provide mutual help in godly living, and to strengthen each other in living a disciplined life it is altogether wise and proper that Christians refrain from the use, sale and manufacture of alcoholic beverages.[2]

Both the earlier and the later rule were new and strange to me, as being part of a church constitution. The later rule was, however, similar to what was commonly taught in churches of which I was a member, but I became aware that there were those who did not agree that "it is altogether wise and proper that Christians refrain from the use, sale, and

---

[1] *The Declaration and Testimony of the Reformed Presbyterian Church of North America*, Chapter XXII, Section 6.

[2] *The Testimony of the Reformed Presbyterian Church of North America* (Adopted August, 1980), Chapter 26.

manufacture of alcoholic beverages." They said that those who are governed by the Bible should condemn and punish drunkenness, but that alcoholic beverages are otherwise praised in the Scriptures. Alcoholic beverages are therefore good. Excess in their use is wrong.

Nevertheless church officers before ordination, installation and licensure are still required to promise "to abstain from alcoholic beverages and habit forming narcotics."

In studying the feeling of members of this church I seemed to sense that this requirement for church officers might be changed, so that officers should not be required to hold to a stricter life than ordinary members, especially since this strict life was thought not to be a Biblical requirement even for officers. My sense of what would happen in this denomination proved to be correct. Will these people be spiritually blessed? God in his own time will provide the answer.

Although I had never belonged to a church with a constitutional requirement of total abstinence, I felt that a change from a stricter to a more relaxed rule on how to live might be a sign of internal decay in the denomination.[3] It has

---

[3] The change, as a study of the Minutes of the Synod shows, did not come about because all, or perhaps any, of those who voted for it did so because they were genuinely convinced that the Bible is intended to encourage a quite relaxed use of alcoholic beverages. Whatever the reason for the change, the freer use of alcohol is fraught with danger. In a sister denomination, for example, which has always considered drinking (without drunkenness) a Christian liberty, a minister has admitted that he is an alcoholic and has sought the prayers of the brethren in this matter and has expressed gratitude for them. There may be cases of a similar nature in churches which totally prohibit the beverage use of alcohol, but these churches could at least be glad that they had not opened the door to what proved to be a downward path for one of their own.

After three years the prayers of these ministers had not been answered favorably. The condition of the man was worse. All Christians should unite in hoping that the prayers of his brother ministers (who are *one-wine theorists*) will

been my experience that a growing laxity in the way people in a church live, leads to doctrinal decay of the fundamental doctrines of Christianity.

I was yet not sure that the Bible taught that total abstinence was a rule for all Christians. I had never been in deep discussion with Christians who believed that it was. I therefore resolved to study the problem with all the tools of learning that a lifetime of theological education, including years of training on a doctoral level in the languages of the Old Testament, had placed at my disposal. The following pages are a result of that study.

The exegetical studies were in part guided by suggestions I found in the writings of Dr. Ernest Gordon and I wish to express my deepest gratitude to him for what he wrote.[4] *He*

---

be answered by his restoration. If their prayers are hindered by their improper thinking that alcoholic beverages are permitted in moderation, Christians who are convinced that they are not permitted to drink alcohol should pray that this poor man and others like him should be relieved of alcoholism. They should also pray that all Christians should come to realize that God prohibits the beverage use of alcohol even in moderation.

When we see a fallen professing Christian ought we not to say, "There but for the grace of God go I"? Why not teach Proverbs 23:31 as a command and not as a rhetorical figure of speech? If we do not begin with a little alcohol we won't end up a slave to this drug. If we preach or write that a little alcohol is a liberty under the Bible, we may have to contemplate the wreckage of people who have listened to us, or read our writings, and who were unable to stop with *moderate* drinking.

If we preach a liberty which is not of God, He may, and probably will, answer our prayers in a negative way. See Proverbs 28:9: "He that turneth away his ear from hearing the law, even his prayer shall be an abomination."

God is continually guiding all branches of the true church with greater or lesser degrees of wisdom. A Christian denomination may make a wrong decision, even though they think they are interpreting the Bible correctly. Their prayers may be hindered (I Peter 3:7). God may wish them to have problems which will lead them to turn back and search the Scriptures more diligently.

[4] Dr. Gordon's *Christ, the Apostles and Wine, An Exegetical Study* is most valuable as an explanation of the Christian total abstinence position. Another, and longer book, *The Wrecking of the Eighteenth Amendment* is an interesting study of how the liquor interests succeeded in their campaign.

being dead yet speaketh. Many of the ideas and arguments are my own, and if they are proved to be wrong I, not Dr. Gordon, am to be blamed. I am, however, rather confident that they cannot be proved to be contrary to sound rules of Bible exegesis. If they are not well received, I will listen to arguments against them. If I am not convinced, I shall conclude that the time is not ripe for their acceptance, and shall say with John Huss, *Mighty is the truth and it will prevail.*

Before Dr. Ernest Gordon had written on this subject his illustrious father, Adoniram Judson Gordon, pastor of the Clarendon Street Baptist Church of Boston had made *an exhaustive study of the whole subject*. As the result of *careful exegetical study* which was published, he was led to abandon *fermented elements altogether*. In this published work he quoted *statements from living rabbis which interdict the use of wine in the Passover services of today*. By *today* we understand, of course, the late nineteenth century.

These quotations are taken from the *Biography* of A. J. Gordon written by his son Ernest B. Gordon, copyright 1896, by Fleming H. Revell (pp. 103-4). A. J. Gordon was the Founder of the still flourishing Gordon College and Gordon-Conwell Theological Seminary.

A. J. Gordon sought out the practice of a distinguished rabbi of his day, namely Rabbi Simeon Reinstein of Boston, who wrote to Dr. Gordon: "The wine which we use at Passover is made from pure raisins, and is unfermented." (*The Watchword*, vol. ix, no. 2, Boston, April 1887, p. 28.)

If anyone doubts that first century Jews and Christians heated grape juice to kill yeast, let him note that the practice of making unfermented wine from raisins may have been used.

ALCOHOL AND CHRISTIAN PRACTICES

There are paradoxes in the Bible about a number of matters. Those professing a form of Christianity, but who deny the inerrancy of the Bible do not consider the solution to the paradoxes important. However, those who believe in the Bible as God's inerrant guide to humanity must search diligently for the truth.

One paradox which has caused great disharmony among Christians is the contradictory statements about what are thought to be alcoholic drinks.

First to be considered is the Hebrew word *yayin*, commonly translated *wine*. The paradox is, what does the Bible tell us to think and to do about this substance? Proverbs 23:31 is commonly understood to say: "Look not on the yayin when it is red" (more properly: *when it makes itself 'red'*).

On the other hand, we have Psalm 104:15, where we read that God brings forth from the earth, *yayin that gladdens the heart of man...*

These two passages from the Bible bring the paradox sharply into view. There are many other aspects to the paradox involving among other things the teaching of our Lord Jesus Christ and His Apostles, and necessitating the study of other words, such as the Hebrew words *shekar* and *tirosh*, and the Greek words *oinos* and *gleukos*.

Before discussing the paradoxes concerning beverages, a brief diversion is proper to clarify the question of paradoxes in general as they occur in the Bible.

One paradox, where two seemingly contradictory statements are put together, is Proverbs 26:4: "Answer not a fool (*kesil*) according to his folly" and Proverbs 26:5: "Answer a fool (*kesil*) according to his folly." Few, if any, respectable commentators have suggested that we solve the problem by taking a half way position, and say that we can indulge with moderation in folly when we answer. No! We should abstain totally from such folly as is condemned in verse 4.

The problem is best solved, as exegetes are more or less agreed, by proposing that the word *kesil,* though identical in the two verses, is in fact used to represent two types of people who are not wise. If, for example, the *kesil* is an unbeliever who ridicules our Lord for making (as he supposes) an intoxicant to give to people who were already drunk, then, if this unbeliever refuses to hear any argument that Christ created a non-intoxicant, we shall not *cast our pearls before swine,* as it were, by continuing a discussion. If we do, we may become like him in folly, as the Bible says. If, however, there is a possibility that we have to do with a different type of *kesil,* with one whose mind is open to sound arguments, we should answer him *according to his folly,* meaning according to the way his particular type of folly deserves to be answered. By doing so, if he is at all reasonable, we may induce him to see weaknesses in the position he has held. Thus he will no longer *be wise in his own conceits.*

The paradox of Genesis 22:1 (*God did tempt Abraham*) and James 1:13 (*God cannot be tempted with evil, neither tempteth He any man*) is to be solved by a careful, soundly exegetical distinction between the word *tempt* in the two passages, Christians are generally agreed on this. They do not say that God's own ethics changed from the time of Abraham to that of James.

The great paradox of James (2:24: *by works a man is justified and not by faith only*) and Paul (Rom. 3:28: *A man is justified by faith without the deeds of the law*) has been a cause of sharp divisions in the church for twenty centuries. This writer believes that John Calvin, after decades of deep study, solved the problem in the sixteenth century. He gave us the solution in his exposition of Ezekiel 18:14-17.

But the paradox of faith, works, and justification must not be taken up at any length in this treatise. It is only mentioned briefly at this point to show how difficult some paradoxes in the Bible are, and how, even when a sound solution is demonstrated, many refuse to accept it and return to old inferior theories which are damaging to sound doctrine and practice.

Notes and Study Questions

There are various paradoxes in the Bible. One such paradox concerns the issue of alcoholic drinks. The Hebrew word *yayin* (commonly translated wine) is both a source of joy and an object of condemnation. Such paradoxes can only be resolved by careful, Biblical study.

What are the two verses cited in this chapter which use the word *yayin*? How do these verses demonstrate the seeming conflict in the Biblical message concerning this word? (p. 1)

What are other paradoxes cited in this chapter? What explanation is given to resolve the apparent conflict? (pp. 1-2)

THE ABSOLUTE PROHIBITION OF PROVERBS 23:29-31[1]

The discussion of other paradoxes to throw light on the paradox concerning drinks alleged to be alcoholic is justified, because it shows how what people believe is often colored by preconceptions, and their preconceptions are often based on desires coming from fallen human nature.

Thus people take pleasure in their sins, and they seize upon a one-sided interpretation of paradoxes to give themselves complacency in these sins, or in struggling half-heartedly against them. A one-sided interpretation of the truth, *a man is justified by faith without the works of the law,* has led to what is called easy-believism and thence to the moral decay of many professing Christians. Similarly a one-sided interpretation of the truth, *Yayin makes glad the heart of man,* may lead men on a course to their destruction.

---

[1] We must not be misled by the idea that an inadvertent glance at wine is a sin. It is the deliberate eyeing of the substance for pleasure that is forbidden. Those who say that because a glance is forbidden, and because it is sometimes impossible not to glance at wine, the whole commandment may safely be ignored are wrong. When looking is punished by God in the Bible we are led to understand that it is a deliberate act of disobedience.

The Biblical Approach to Alcohol

What we must do is detach ourselves from preconceptions when we look at the paradoxes concerning wine. A word which is supposed to denote an intoxicant is in one place treated as God's good gift and in another is strictly forbidden, even to the point that it may not be looked at.

Concerning the paradox of Proverbs 23:31 and Psalm 104:15, an easy solution is to say wine is the same in both passages, and is good if used properly. The passage about not looking on it is then understood to be hyperbolic and not to be taken at all literally. It is true that hyperboles occur in the Bible, but one cannot read Proverbs 23:29-35 without coming to the conclusion that God is speaking of something He loathes as an article for human consumption. There is no suggestion that a good thing which He has given to us to enjoy is in view here. It is viper's poison (verse 32) and the command is not to look on it. We all know television commercials and magazine advertisements do their best to get everyone to look at beautiful representations of liquor and then to drink the products so favorably shown. God says not to gaze at the sparkling stuff. This is a plain command! Bible believers ought to obey this command and not take the opposite course of saying that God has given it for us to enjoy. Ought we to let vipers bite us to enjoy the effect of their poison? God made the vipers, but we should use discrimination about what use we make of their poison.

But wine lovers and even total abstainers who say we must set up no man-made rules for general observance are puzzled by the fact that words which have been translated *wine* and *strong drink* are sometimes permitted for human consumption and are sometimes condemned. It is easy to say that the answer lies in moderation. Of course we should be moderate in all things, particularly in what we put into our bodies, but moderation is not the answer.

If we are told, "do not even look at obscene shows" (e. g. X-rated movies), would we be doing right in saying that the command means to be moderate in our attendance at such performances? Of course not. The Bible has passages which prohibited looking at other particular material things. These examples no longer exist, but the fact that they did exist should make us cautious about accepting the argument that since *no material thing is evil in itself,* a corollary to that proposition is that the Bible never prohibits the looking at or consuming any specific material thing.

For example, Lot and his family on fleeing Sodom were forbidden to look back at that city (Gen. 19:17-26). It is of course true that the material out of which Sodom was made was not evil in itself, but the moral evil which infested the place was such that God placed an absolute prohibition on looking at it. He also put an absolute prohibition on looking at a certain sort of *yayin* (Prov. 23:31). Before discussing what the descriptive phrases in this verse mean, the point must be established that at least some sort of *yayin* is not even to be looked at, no doubt because gazing at something attractive is a first step toward partaking. The prohibition is absolute, like that of looking at Sodom, as the context indicates. We should not resort to saying a passage is hyperbolic when nothing except our preconceptions or selfish desires stand in the way of accepting it in its plain meaning.

The prohibition of Proverbs 23:31 is not properly explained in any other way than *total.* But the next question is, exactly what is prohibited? It is *yayin* with certain descriptive words added which have in subsequent years proved to be hard to interpret, although they may have been perfectly clear to the people of the time in which they were written. The greatest difficulty is in the interpretation of the word *yith'addam.* Most translators and interpreters understand this to mean *it is red.*

The *Septuagint,* being historically the first translation, we would naturally look to as the best guide when we suspect that a semantic shift in language over a period of time has led to a difficulty. But the *Septuagint* translation paraphrases the passage and places a stern warning against *setting thine eyes on bowls and cups* (vessels commonly used in drinking alcoholic beverages). No word suggesting *redness* is used.

As a stream descending into a plain spreads out, the water going in different directions for a while until a channel is cut, after which the water goes in the channel, so translators went in different directions for centuries, until *it is red* was found to be the path of least resistance. Thereafter translators followed this cut channel of least resistance as a matter of course.

The *Septuagint* translators are to be commended for not going this easy, but misleading way. It must have been apparent to them as an easy way out of the real problem. The meaning *when it is alcoholic* for *ki yith'addam* may have become obsolete in common Hebrew in their day. More probably the meaning was clear to them, but they were faced with the difficulty that the Greek language in the centuries before the time of Christ had no words for *to be alcoholic* (used of a drink) or for the noun *alcohol*. The Greeks did not invent words with such meanings until centuries after the *Septuagint* was written. Hence they fell back on a clumsy paraphrase. They did well, however, in not setting the readers' minds in a wrong channel, as though God's concern was in forbidding a drink of a certain color.

Those who translate the Bible into the languages of primitive tribesmen living in the tropics are aware of the difficulty of finding an expression to convey the meaning of *snow*. Such an important concept as *The Lamb of God* is difficult to translate into primitive languages whose speakers know nothing of the *genus ovis*, the animals we know as sheep.

The word *alcohol* is first recorded in English according to the great standard, the *Oxford English Dictionary*, in the sixteenth century. Before that time translators would have had great difficulty in giving readers the idea of an alcoholic drink without a long descriptive passage. Can we wonder that translators, uninspired as they were, took the easy way, and rendered *ki yith'addam* as *when it is red*?

If the meaning of the phrase, *yith'addam* were *it is red*, it could be interpreted to mean do not look on wine when it is made from grapes with such skins as will give it a red color if the skins are allowed to remain with the juice during the initial process of wine making. The idea could then be deduced that if potential consumers were offered a drink with an attractive red color, not clouded with impurities, some of them if they gazed at it would be tempted to drink. An ugly drink, not clear because impure, would not attract and therefore might safely be gazed on by some people.

The idea that what is forbidden are drinks attractive to the eye and that others are tacitly permitted would certainly be unworthy of the Holy Bible. This is because naïve young people and addicts of alcohol would not be deterred from drinking merely because the beverage is less than beautiful as to color. Understood in this way the passage would only restrain connoisseurs of expensive drinks. Such an interpretation is contrary to the whole tenor of verses 29-35. God's revealed will is not to protect only rich hedonists from the woes set forth in these verses. The command is to protect everyone. If something purporting to be Scripture should say, "Look not on a prostitute when she is pretty. Do not ogle an immoral woman if she is physically attractive," we would very properly reject it as not being in agreement with the way the Bible teaches.

But linguistically to understand the words *ki yith'addam*[2] to mean *when it is red* should be rejected. The verbal root *'adom* (a stative verb) is never used in any passage in the Bible concerning *yayin* except in this one (Prov. 23:31), and here it is used in the *hithpael*. It is true that in the *qal* it means *to be red*, but the *hithpael* is a conjugation normally having a reflexive meaning and if it is so used here, the meaning is *it makes itself red*. Next, pushing aside all preconceptions, we must ask ourselves, what does this mean? "Look not on the *yayin* when it makes itself red." The *yayin* is naturally red in color when the grapes are pressed; there is no working of the juice within itself that makes itself red. We must search for the meaning elsewhere.

In discussing *yith'addam* we must note that God does not provide us with an inerrant dictionary of the ancient languages, nor does He usually provide us with an inerrant commentary. Only when one passage of the Bible comments on another have we such an inerrant commentary, and we have none for Proverbs 23:31

What we do have is suggestive, however. In verse 29 of this

[2] Readers not knowing Hebrew and the meaning of the hithpael stem should read the appendix to this paper: "Appendix concerning the word *yith'addam*, etc."

chapter, on the same subject, we have a reference to redness of eye as a result of drinking, or so it has been understood. Since there was no other word in the ancient languages in which the Bible was written for alcohol or for alcoholic beverages, what is more natural than that some characteristic of the result of drinking should be used to designate such beverages? It could be called *red-eye,* referring to the blood-shot eyes of drinkers, or *red-nose,* referring to their noses, and in course of time such an expression could be abbreviated to *red.* Red *yayin* would then mean alcoholic *yayin,* and would not be a mere designation of color distinguishing it from white or rosé wines. The latter may not have existed in the time and place where Proverbs was written, and, even if they did, there would be no sense in permitting them and prohibiting *red* wine.

As noted above *yith'addam* is the hithpael conjugation. This is a reflexive conjugation, so the normal meaning would be *it makes itself red,* and not *it is red,* as most translations render it. As the redness of wines comes from the skin of the grape it is wrong to say that the juice of pressed grapes *makes itself red,* for it is red by nature. If, however, red means alcoholic, the hithpael is appropriate. This is because a microorganism (yeast) on the skin of the grape goes into the grape juice when the grapes are pressed. The product resulting from the pressing, as yet unfermented grape juice, does makes itself alcoholic, the yeast devouring the sugar and excreting alcohol. Therefore it is entirely appropriate to say that *yayin* (originally nonalcoholic) makes itself red (i.e. alcoholic).

It will be demonstrated in a separate place that *yayin* is, in Biblical Hebrew, the appropriate word for the unfermented juice of the grape. But of course it is also appropriate for the fermented juice of the grape. This dual use of the same word is similar to that of the double use of the English word *cider* (either nonalcoholic or alcoholic).

The Talmud (Sanhedrin 70a) quotes Rabbi Isaac as perceiving that *yith'addam* does not speak of the color of the wine, but rather of the unhealthy coloring of the face of the drinking men. The passage is:

> R. Isaac said: "Look not upon the wine, which reddens the face of the wicked in this world and makes him pale (with shame) in the next."[3]

It must be admitted that the meaning *reddens the face* cannot be derived literally from *yith'addam*, but Rabbi Isaac's perception is sound that the redness underlying the word is not a reference to the color of the drink.

Furthermore, another ancient authority, Raba, is quoted in this same section of the Talmud as perceiving that *yith'addam* does not mean *it is red*. Raba said: "Look not upon the wine *ki yith'addam:* look not upon it, for it leads to bloodshed (*dam*)." Concerning this, Rabbi Dr. J. Epstein who translated this passage comments, "(it) is taken as a reflexive of *dam* 'blood.'"[4]

Although this meaning is attractive, it must be regarded as extremely doubtful on linguistic grounds, since, for one thing, the *aleph* in *yith'addam* is unexplained. The wine does not make itself bloody, but makes itself alcoholic. Raba is, however, to be commended for observing that the *hithpael* stem is not to be interpreted as though it were a simple *qal*, as do most translators

---

[3] Socino Edition, p. 476.

[4] With reference to the reflexive sense of *yith'addam*, a sense which Raba noticed and made use of in his exegesis, it is interesting to observe that most translators and commentators ignore it. Most of them say the meaning is *when it is red*, or as in the Latin Vulgate *quando flavescit* (when it turns golden). The Ladino or Judaeo-Spanish version published by the American Bible Society is outstanding in that it correctly brings the reflexive meaning into the translation, although it misses the deeper meaning, *when it makes itself alcoholic*. This version renders the expression *quando se invermizisi*. I am indebted to Professor Karl D. Uitti, John D. Woodhull Professor of Modern Languages, Princeton University, for explaining on the basis of Old Spanish linguistics the difficult word *invermizisi*. The meaning as established by Professor Uitti is *when it turns itself into a red, scarlet color*.

As for the Vulgate, Jerome's translation, is there some reason for his choice of the unusual word *flavescit*? By rejecting the usual translation *when it is red*, he may have used a word which suggested inebriation in the type of Latin he used. The proof of this is not readily at hand, but what we *do* know is that he advised total abstinence from intoxicating wine.

and commentators.[5]

In Proverbs 23:31 the two phrases commonly translated by such expressions as *when it gives its color in the cup* and *when it moves itself aright* have not necessarily been understood correctly. If they have been translated approximately correctly, they should be understood as attached to the phrase where the drink in question is totally prohibited. Thus we may understand the meaning to be: Look not on the wine when it is alcoholic, *even though* it gives its color in the cup, and *even though* it moves itself aright.

On the other hand, these phrases may refer to the fermentation process. The word translated color (*'ayin*) is said by Brown-Driver-Briggs to have *sparkle* as one of its meanings. This may refer to the effervescence which results from fermentation. The expression about moving itself aright may also refer to the movement of effervescence. Both of the phrases, in that case, would refer to sparkling, effervescent or bubbly (alcoholic) wine.

Notes and Study Questions

When two verses of the Bible seem to conflict, there are dangers in only accepting one verse and ignoring the message of the conflicting verse. The paradox concerning wine in the Bible must be resolved by examining both Proverbs 23:31 and Psalm 104:15. In Proverbs 23:31, the command concerning wine is not to look at it. The phrase *ki yith'addam* (*when it makes itself red*) is to be understood as *when it makes itself alcoholic.* The Hebrew word *yayin* can mean both alcoholic and nonalcoholic grape juice (commonly distinguished by wine and grape juice respectively in

[5] It is not strange that alcohol at one period in the history of the Hebrew language should be named for a color (red) which is not the color of alcohol itself. The English (and international) word alcohol is derived from the Arabic *al-kohl*, which refers to a black preparation used by women to darken the edges of their eyes. All scholars are agreed on this. It is no more strange that alcohol should once have been given a name derived from the color red than that it should be generally known by a name derived from a black substance. Alcohol is in fact colorless.

modern English). In Proverbs 23:31, *yayin* is clearly an alcoholic drink.

How is the substance *yayin* described in Proverbs 23:32? (p. 4)

Why is the believer commanded not to even look at the *yayin*? (pp. 4-5)

What is the significance of the Greek language not having a word for alcohol in the time of the *Septuagint* translation? (p. 6)

Is white wine omitted from the prohibition of Proverbs 23:31 because it is not red? (pp. 7-8)

What is the process by which grapes become alcoholic wine? What is the role of yeast and sugar in the process? (p. 8)

What modern English word is given as a parallel example of how *yayin* can be both alcoholic and nonalcoholic? (p. 8)

IS PROVERBS 23:31 ONLY A COUNSEL OF MODERATION

The idea has been expressed that *'al-tere' yayin ki yith'addam,* which means *look not,* followed by an expression the meaning of which is explained elsewhere, is not a prohibition of the use of alcohol as a beverage, but is only a command not to overindulge in the same. Thus *The Living Bible* (which is not a translation but a paraphrase) has: "Don't let the sparkle and the smooth taste of strong wine deceive you." Presumably this could be understood to mean that if one partakes in a way he considers moderate he is not being deceived, and is therefore keeping the commandment.

But *'al-tere'* means *look not* or *don't look,* as all who have studied Hebrew are agreed. The idea of being deceived is no more in this verse than it is in *'al-tedabber* (do not speak) in verse 9, *'al-tasseg* (do not remove) in verse 10, or *'al-timna'* (do not withhold) in verse 13. In none of these passages do translators, commentators or paraphrasers bring out any idea of not being deceived. It is not in verse 23 either.

'al tere' is the same type of prohibition as *'al-tabbet 'achareka* in Genesis 19:17. In all of these examples *'al* before a verb in the jussive makes a prohibition. The command not to look back (to Sodom) was no doubt given to Lot because to look back might lead him to return to his home and to yield to the temptations with which the place abounded. If Lot had understood the prohibition of Genesis 19:17 as those who made the *Living Bible* seem to understand the same type of expression in Proverbs 23:31, he might have said, "This means don't let the attractions of Sodom deceive you. It does not mean that I must take the prohibition literally. I may look at Sodom, return there and enjoy its pleasures. It is enough that I refrain from being deceived by Sodom and the Sodomites."

But Lot's wife learned that *don't look* was not intended to be taken as a mere figure of speech. There is no reason to believe that *don't look* in Proverbs 23:31 is to be treated any more lightly than *don't look* in Genesis 19:17. To look at alcoholic wine often leads to a desire for it, the desire leads to drinking a little, and drinking a little may lead to drinking much and then to utter ruin. God intends those believers who read the Bible with discernment to stop even the first tendency to this downward course. Therefore we have this command.

Notes and Study Questions

The Hebrew words *'al tere'* mean *do not look.* It is used in the prohibition of looking at wine in Proverbs 23:31. When a believer is obedient to this command, he will avoid the deceptively attractive image of the wine, and will remove the temptation to drink it.

Is *The Living Bible* a translation or a paraphrase of the Bible? (p. 11)

Who in the Bible was told not to look upon Sodom? How does this example help believers to see the seriousness of the command in Proverbs 23:31? (p. 12)

What is the process by which disobedience to the command of Proverbs 23:31 could lead to *utter ruin*? (p. 12)

PROVERBS 23:31

It cannot be emphasized too much that it is basic to the argument that alcohol is forbidden as a beverage to everyone, that Proverbs 23:31 be understood in a universal sense. Many brush this verse aside as a mere rhetorical device, but this cannot be sustained because all of the prohibitions can only be understood as a series of solemn commands without rhetorical flourishes.

Strangely, one advocate of the one-wine theory and the idea that alcohol may be taken as a beverage in moderation has come up with the thought that the command not to look at what is commonly translated *wine when it is red* (*yayin ki yith'addam*) is intended only for drunkards. He writes concerning the interpretation I have proposed:

> This passage has to be utterly divorced from its near, far and ultimate context to bear the construction put upon it. The near (immediate) context is extremely clear: the warning and admonition are specifically applied to immoderate abusers of wine. Let us cite the whole passage in demonstration of this:
>
> 29. Who has woe? Who has sorrow?
> Who has contentions? Who has complaining?
> Who has redness of eyes?
>
> 30. Those who linger long over wine, Those who go to taste mixed wine.
> 31. Do not look on the wine when it is red,
> When it sparkles in the cup,
> When it goes down smoothly;
>
> 32. At the last it bites like a serpent,
> And stings like a viper.
>
> 33. Your eyes will see strange things,
> And your mind will utter perverse things,

34. And you will be like one who lies down in the middle of the sea,
Or like one who lies down on the top of a mast.

35. "They struck me, but I did not become ill;
They beat me, but I did not know it.
When shall I awake?
I will seek another drink.

The one-wine theorist continues: "How could a context be any clearer? Here is specifically and carefully described a person to whom the admonition is directed."

This is completely to misunderstand the passage and the whole didactic method of the long section in which this passage occurs, Proverbs 22:17-24:22. Throughout this whole section the one warned is all humanity addressed as an individual by the second person masculine singular pronoun. This is the way God commands all people when He is particularly emphatic and wishes all to obey. Compare the Ten Commandments in which all humanity is addressed as *thou*. A typical commandment is *thou shalt not...*

This one-wine theorist seems to overlook the fact that while drunkards are mentioned prior to verse 31, they are not addressed directly, nor are they commanded to abstain in any place in this section of Scripture. Verses 29 and 30 refer to drunkards, not a single drunkard. A reader of verse 29 in the English where we read *who has woe?* may not notice that it really should be *who have woe?* as the answer in verse 30 shows that drunkards (plural) are these horrible examples. The Hebrew particle *mi* (*who* as an interrogative) has no number.

The point in bringing this out is to show that God in instructing all humanity addresses each one of us as *thou*, a term used to designate a teachable one. Drunkards are not assumed to be teachable and are not commanded to abstain from alcohol in this section. (This is not to say that other parts of the Bible do not give them ground to hope.)

After describing the people steeped in the vice of alcoholism in verses 29 and 30, God returns in verse 31 to command all humanity as a single individual, thus bringing every reader to a close encounter with God.

Then in verses 31-35 God addresses with the same pronoun *thou* the individual whom He sees as not having obeyed the command not to even look at the drug in question. God tells him what He sees him becoming, that is an addict of alcohol, suffering from hallucinations and other ills, sinking into a drunken sleep from which he seeks to arouse himself that he may go back to the drug that has brought him misery. There is no command to abstain or message of hope to the individual in verses 33-35.

The command not to look in verse 31 is not addressed to this miserable addict. In the context of this section of Scripture all of the prohibitions are addressed to a person (*thou*) who is not an addict to the vice described. If we understand verse 22 as only applying to people addicted to despising their mothers, we can say that one who has not fallen deeply into that sin may indulge in it moderately without incurring God's wrath-and so on with moving boundary stones (verse 10), withholding discipline from those under instruction, etc.

This one-wine theorist goes on to speak of "the ultimate context of Scripture which clearly does not forbid the moderate partaking *of aged wine* (Isa. 25:6)..." It is interesting that he cites this passage and calls the drink which God will give to all nations *aged wine*. The words are *shemarim mezuqqaqim*. It is true that some scholars see in *shemarim* the idea of wine that is aged. The idea of lees has for a long time been discerned in this word by many scholars. The word *shemer* (singular of *shemarim*) does not mean *aged* in itself. No scholar thinks it does. If it means lees or dregs the sense of *shemarim mezuqqaqim* would be, as Koehler and Baumgartner understand it, *lees, dregs of wine out of which still clear wine is gained* (by filtering). Wine of this sort might be called *aged* in a loose way. But a major problem is how to fit this into the context. Would God in the great eschatological feast regale the people He loves with wine made by filtering dregs? The idea is out of harmony with the occasion.

There may be some problems about *shemarim*, but Luther's translation of the phrase, *wine in which there is no yeast,* is suitable to the dignity of this feast. It is furthermore to be commended as doing no violence to the root ZQQ from which *mezuqqaqim* is derived. Besides all this it is supportive of the idea that no leaven (yeast) was to be permitted in any sacred feast.

The ultimate authority to which this one-wine theorist appeals is the entire Scripture. Contrary to the one-wine theory, when one examines the entire Scripture he sees that Moses Stuart and Lyman Abbott were right. There are in fact two kinds of wine in the Bible, alcoholic and alcohol free. The one-wine theory is wrong. Appeals to it are without merit. Yet such appeals are made over and over again, often with the assumption that it is an established fact which may not be questioned.

In attempting to prove that it is wrong to argue that Christ could not drink alcoholic wine and fulfill his charge as Priest and King one man wrote:

> First if such methodology were proper, both of these provisions (relative to both priest and king) would witness against our High Priest and King of kings, Jesus Christ. As shown previously, Jesus did partake of wine. Given the integrity of Scripture, this evidence alone exposes the argument's *reductio ad absurdum.*

The fact is there is no evidence anywhere that Jesus ever drank a single drop of alcohol. He drank wine but not alcoholic wine. Wine (*yayin, oinos*) has two meanings in Scripture. Many other words in Scripture have more than one meaning, e.g. *'elohim*. One cannot properly attempt to reduce a sound argument to an absurdity by reasoning in a circle.

Jesus Christ, as sharing with all of us our common humanity, obeyed Proverbs 23:31, as a king He obeyed Proverbs 31:4-5, and as a priest about to offer a sacrifice He obeyed Leviticus 10:9-10. Would that all one-wine theorists would recognize this!

Notes and Study Questions

Proverbs 23:31 cannot be understood as a mere rhetorical device. It is a command, as powerful as the other commands found in Proverbs 23. It is also not just a command for drunkards. The *thou* of Proverbs 23:31 refers to every man, as the *thou's* of the other commands in the chapter refer to every man. The ultimate context of the whole of Scripture does not evidence an acceptance of moderate drinking. Rather, it shows two kinds of *yayin*: nonalcoholic grape juice which is permitted and alcoholic wine which is condemned. The fact that Jesus partook of *wine* evidences that there is a nonalcoholic wine in the Bible, not that it is acceptable to drink alcoholic drinks.

How does the plural reference to drunkards in verses 29 and 30 of Proverbs 23 help in understanding who the *thou* of verse 31 is? (p. 14)

What is the meaning of the Hebrew word *shemer* in Isaiah 25:6? (p. 15)

What Hebrew word of the Bible is given as an example of having more than one meaning? How is that significant for the argument concerning *yayin* and *oinos*? (p. 16)

How are Proverbs 23:31; Proverbs 31:4-5; and Leviticus 10:9-10 significant for determining if Jesus drank alcoholic wine? (p. 16)

IN-DEPTH STUDY OF THE MEANING OF BIBLICAL WORDS

Many not trained in linguistic science and etymological studies will say that of course the words wine and strong drink as used in early English translations, and wine and beer as used in some more modern versions, are accurate translations of the original and that of course they always mean alcoholic beverages. Yet God has never provided that translators should be inerrant. They have worked with more or less aid from the Holy Spirit and this aid has meant that no translation of the Bible which has been put into the hands of believing people is without such truth as may lead to a saving knowledge of Jesus Christ. On the other hand no translation is inerrant, and old errors of translators are from time to time being corrected. Sometimes errors once corrected are revived.

Thus a study of Ugaritic, a language only brought to light in the twentieth century after millennia of being totally unknown, has led many scholars to accept the idea that the preposition *b* may be *from* in the Hebrew of the Bible. This gives a better understanding of a number of passages, of which Psalm 68:18 (verse 19 in Hebrew) is one. The preposition *b*, in the minds of ancient translators meant *in*. The *Septuagint* and the *Vulgate* so translate, giving a very obscure sense. Luther and the King James translators rendered it *for*, but their reasons for doing so are not clear. After the discovery of the Ugaritic language in the twentieth century, scholars, such as Cyrus Gordon and Mitchel Dahood, began to understand it in the sense of *from*, a meaning which can be sustained by linguistic science and which also makes for good sense and ease of understanding. The New International Version (NIV) makes use of this linguistic discovery and renders Psalm 68:18 *you received gifts from men*.

From this we can see that the inerrant Bible may have been misunderstood in the past, and linguistic science, used by believers in the inerrancy of the autographa, may be able to give correct meanings to passages in which people have been groping for the true sense for centuries.

The meaning of *pugme* in Mark 7:3 has, it is believed, been brought to light in the twentieth century,[1] a meaning which is reflected in the *NIV*.

It is entirely possible that the precise meaning of *epiousion* in the Lord's Prayer will be made certain by the discovery of a first century papyrus or some other discovery.

All readers of the Bible in translation must be made aware that not all readings in their favorite Bible translation are necessarily certain. A ruling elder in a Presbyterian Church said that alcoholic drinks are permitted by the Bible because the *NIV* in

---

[1] *Pygme as Cupped Hand, Journal of Biblical Literature*, vol. 85, Part 1, 1966, pp. 87-88. An article by this writer.

Deuteronomy 14:26 translates *shekar* as *other fermented drink*. Now this rendering of *shekar* is better than that of the King James Version (KJV) which is *strong drink*. The scholars in the sixteenth and seventeenth centuries (Luther included) were evidently unaware that distilled beverages ("strong drink") were introduced in the twelfth century, and so, in suggesting that God permitted the purchase and drinking of distilled liquors in the days of Moses, they committed an anachronism.

As proof we may cite the *Encyclopedia Americana*[2] which says:

> All spirits, regardless of their eventual color, come from the still as colorless as the primitive liquor that was distilled from wine and hailed by 12th century alchemists as *aqua vitae* (French *eau-de-vie*, "water of life."). This was described by the 13th century Spanish philosopher Raymond Lully (Ramon Lull) as *"an element newly revealed to man but hid from antiquity because the human race was then too young to need this beverage destined to revive the energies of modern decrepitude."*

Some think distilled drinks were known earlier than Lully thought, but no scholars think they were known to the writers of the Bible. While Lully's idea of the time when distilled liquors became known should be taken seriously, it is to be regretted that he made a serious mistake with regard to what he thought was the good effect of distilled spirits. His glorious death as a missionary martyr should be remembered.

Thus it may be seen that the KJV errs, or at least gives the wrong impression in translating *shekar* as *strong drink*. But is the *NIV*'s translation correct? The citing of this translation to me as though it completely settled all doubts on the problem is somewhat ironic, as I had the honor of working on this translation as a member of a committee engaged in work on parts of the Old Testament. I do not make adverse criticisms of the committee on which I worked, but my experience on this project, hereafter called the NIV, is that at least some human error entered into the final result.

---

[2] "Distilled Spirits," *Encyclopedia Americana*, Danbury, Conn., 1978, vol. 9, p. 188.

An example of what is certainly an error in the NIV, one in which the Committee working on the passage persisted even when the correct translation was pointed out to them, is to be found in I Corinthians 10:29b. The original Greek of this passage indisputably and without variants is to be translated accurately, "why is my liberty judged by another conscience?" This is not a rhetorical question expecting a negative answer, but because people think it is, mistranslations (intended to be paraphrases) have occurred. The word *man's* in italics has been inserted (*KJV*), or an apostrophe with an *s* is added to the word *another* (*New American Standard* and *NIV*). The British Revision of 1885 and the *American Revised Version* of 1901 translated this correctly, and it is to be regretted that later translations have reverted to an old error. Even, if they did not understand the passage, they should not have paraphrased it to set the readers' minds in an interpretation which is not certain.

For a study of this matter see *Another Conscience,* an article by the writer in *The Presbyterian Guardian,* v. 38, No. 3, March 1969, pp. 32-34. A condensed statement of the arguments presented follows: The Greek is *hina ti gar he eleutheria mou krinetai hupo alles suneideseos*. This means: *for precisely on account of what is my liberty judged by another* (that is, a more enlightened) *conscience?*[3] The sense of *for precisely* as a meaning of *gar* is attested in 2 Corinthians 2:9 by Arndt and Gingrich in their article on the word. Verse 30 shows the absurdity of answering the question in the way people usually think it should be answered. Giving thanks for what we partake of does not justify a sin if the partaking is evil. Paul could not have been expecting the answer of his readers that of course if we give thanks for what we consume, our thankfulness justifies the act. Such reasoning would justify drinking to great excess or eating what we steal. The question in 1 Cor. 10:30 ("Why am I evil spoken of for what I give thanks?") is a question posed by one

---

[3] The words *that is, a more enlightened* are of course this writer's and are not intended to be a translation of the original. It is here proposed that they express Paul's meaning. People with different interpretations are of course free to propose and defend them, but they would be in error if they were to say that there are textual variants to *alles*, or that this word may be translated *another's*. For one thing, it is feminine in gender and no woman is in view here.

who persists in eating meat offered to idols when someone questions him about it. He fatuously calls attention to his giving thanks as though that justifies him. The answer is suggested in verses 31-33. If one gives offense in such a matter he is sinning. We should move from an unenlightened conscience, which would permit us to eat things offered to idols in the presence of offended brethren, to another conscience which becomes our own enlightened conscience. Judged by this conscience we would rather suffer want than scandalize one of God's little ones. Incidentally, if we deliberately scandalize one of God's little people, it were better that a millstone should be hung about our neck and we be cast into the sea (Matt. 18:6; Luke 17:2). If we give thanks to God for our supposed freedom to commit a sin, we are using God's name in such a way as to make Him an object of reproach to unbelievers and this is a dreadful thing to do. If we suppose God to be pleased when we thank Him under such circumstances we are sure to be terribly undeceived by Him in His own appointed time. Understood in the way it ought to be interpreted, a Christian is invited to a feast and, not knowing anything about the origin of the food, he eats freely and is right in doing so. Someone tells him that the food has previously been offered to idols. Although he knows the idols are nothing, he also knows that his continuing to eat would wound the conscience of another person. God speaking through Paul, says, *Eat not*. He must cease at once. His liberty is now judged by another conscience of his own, a different understanding of what he must do. As a figure of ridicule Paul introduces a supposed Christian, or more probably he actually knew one, who said, *Surely, I don't have to stop eating if I give thanks for the food?* It is nonsense to suppose that the implied answer is, of course not, if you give thanks, go right ahead. The answer is not implied but stated, *do all to the glory of God* (verse 31). Rom. 14:21 also speaks in answer to this question. "Destroy not him with thy meat, for whom Christ died."

If drinking alcoholic wine were a Christian liberty, it is perfectly clear that God, speaking through the Apostle Paul, does not support the view that a Christian's only obligation to a weaker brother who is offended by his eating or drinking something permitted by God, is to try to convince the weaker brother that he is only exercising his Christian liberty. In Romans 14:21 we read: "It is good not to eat flesh, nor to drink wine, nor to do anything whereby thy brother stumbles, or is offended, or is made weak."

Since eating flesh is a Christian liberty it is to be assumed that the drinking *oinos* is here nonalcoholic *oinos* and is also a Christian liberty. Some believers in the first century may have held to the view of the Rechabites of old that to drink even unfermented grape juice was sinful. In dealing with such we should be very tender with regard to their consciences. If we love them (and of course we should love them), we should stop eating or drinking what causes them to stumble, and then we should show them good scriptural reasons why what we have been doing is a Christian liberty. Paul says to stop is a *good* thing. He does not go so far as to say in this passage that it is a required thing. What he *does* give us in 1 Corinthians 8:13 is his personal promise: *Wherefore, if meat make my brother to offend, I will eat no flesh while the world standeth, lest I make my brother to offend.* If we reassure ourselves with the thought that this promise was only binding on Paul, let us reexamine very carefully the words which go before, that is verses 9-12. Let us likewise remember that Paul under divine inspiration was moved to write: "Join with others in following my example, brothers, and take note of those who live according to the pattern we gave you" (Phil. 3:17 NIV). If we call ourselves believers in the Bible, and call it inerrant, how can we take lightly Paul's example?

Notes and Study Questions

English translations of the Bible have made various errors. One such error can be found in translations of Deuteronomy 14:26. The Hebrew word *shekar* is translated *other fermented drink* by the NIV and *strong drink* by the KJV. The KJV's rendering cannot be accepted, because distilled drinks did not exist until the twelfth century A.D. No drinks were distilled in Bible times.

Another passage which has been translated wrongly is 1 Corinthians 10:29b. It is not *another's conscience* or *another man's conscience,* but simply *another conscience.* With this corrected understanding of the passage, Christians should not feel liberty to do whatever they wish. They must be careful not to be condemned by another conscience and offend other people by using their liberties. Even if drinking alcohol was a liberty God gave to the Christian, which it is not, the Christian should not use this liberty in such a way as to offend others.

What error concerning alcoholic drinks can a Christian fall into when he reads the common English translations of the Bible? (pp. 17-18)

Is 1 Corinthians 10:30 saying that it does not matter what a Christian does as long as he gives thanks to God for it? (pp. 20-21)

THE TIDE OF CUSTOM IN LANGUAGE STUDY

It is very important in all historical language study to know that words change in time so that their meaning or pronunciation or both vary over the centuries. A number of examples touching on words which some people think have invariably meant intoxicants will be discussed in the following pages. Some familiarity with linguistic science is necessary to disabuse ourselves of the idea that if a word means something now it necessarily meant the same thing at another time and place.

John Stuart Mill was not primarily a linguistic scientist, but a philosopher, however something he wrote on semantic shifts (changes in meaning of words) expresses well the idea of how a word may pass from a general meaning to a specific one. He wrote:

> A generic term is always liable to become limited to a single species if people have occasion to think and speak of that species oftener than of anything else contained in the genus.

The tide of custom first drifts the word on the shore of a particular meaning, then retires and leaves it there.[1]

This principle, which can be illustrated many ways in language study, is to be seen working in words which once meant grape juice, either unfermented or fermented, and which drifted into the meaning of fermented grape juice, after which the tide of usage retired. In the following discussion an attempt is made to show how neglect of this principle has led to great confusion.

Notes and Study Questions

Languages have words which change their meanings over time. This is a significant observation which is vital in understanding the argument against drinking alcoholic beverages in moderation. The Hebrew and Greek words which represent grape juice can be understood as either an unfermented or fermented drink.

What kind of shift in meaning did John Stuart Mill observe? (p. 23)

LINGUISTIC SCIENCE AND THE BIBLE

One supporter of the view that the Bible does not command total abstinence from the beverage use of alcohol has a chapter in his book called *The Tyranny of Experts*.[1] His point is that to be ruled by arguments based on medical science and statistics presented by experts in these fields is to be ruled by tyrants. Many nineteenth century advocates of total abstinence attempted to show that alcohol causes crime, immorality and fatal accidents. The people who were determined to be ruled by the Bible only were not impressed. As long as the Bible does not prohibit its use, they

---

[1] *System of Logic*, Book IV, Chapter V.

[1] G. 1. Williamson, *Wine in the Bible and the Church*, Chapter 6.

argued, alcohol is permitted. It causes no evil. Sin alone causes the evils mentioned, and the Christian, understanding that the Bible does not prohibit the beverage use of alcohol, only its abuse, should permit no one to deprive him of the right to use it.

The present writer accepts the idea that Christians should have the Bible as their only rule of faith and practice, but he proposes that the Bible itself, if properly understood, commands total abstinence. To prove this, studies of words in the original languages of Scripture are necessary, and readers are invited to consider the evidence which follows.

Only by taking Proverbs 23:31 in something other than its plain sense can we say that the Bible does not prohibit the looking at (and hence the drinking of) a certain sort of *yayin*. There is no more reason to say Proverbs 23:31 does not mean what it says than to claim that verse 10 of the same chapter is not to be taken literally. I hope that most of us would agree that this verse does not mean that we are merely required to be moderate about moving boundary stones; that we may take one acre from our fatherless young neighbor but not ten! No, do not move a boundary stone to steal one foot of land from anyone! Do not look upon *yayin ki yith'addam*! If commanded not to do so, do not look at Sodom or anything else God forbids!

Notes and Study Questions

Studying the original language is necessary in order to prove the Bible commands total abstinence from alcoholic beverages. Many who have sought to argue for total abstinence only argued on the basis of medical science, statistics, and the sins resulting from drunkenness, such as immorality and vehicular homicide. It is only through sound Biblical study that the moral prohibition to not drink alcohol at all is clarified.

How do those who argue for moderation argue against the fact that other sins result from drinking alcohol? (pp.24-25)

THE HEBREW WORD *Yayin* (Commonly Translated Wine)

Yayin is assumed by many people to be always an alcoholic drink. This is a mistake which has led to much confusion and to much intoxication, which might easily have been avoided. Isaiah 16:10 says: "No treader shall tread out *yayin* in the presses." This obviously means that no treader shall tread out grape juice in the presses, because fermentation is a time consuming process. Therefore alcohol is excluded from the word *yayin* in this passage.

This is enough to establish the fact that *yayin* in the Bible need not be alcoholic. In Rabbinical Literature also *yayin* did not necessarily contain this drug. Sanhedrin 70a of the Talmud says: "Newly pressed wine, prior to fermentation, was known as *yayin mi gat*" (wine from the press).

It is significant that neither of the two words *tirosh* or *'asis,* sometimes thought to have meant grape juice in an unfermented state, are used here. The reason is that neither is appropriate. *Tirosh* is used of an alcoholic drink in Hosea 4:11 and *'asis* is an intoxicant in Isaiah 49:26 and Joel 1:5.

The Talmud in the passage cited above uses the word *toses* for fermentation. It is important to notice that there was no unambiguous, generally recognized word in Biblical Hebrew for fermentation, that is, the production of alcohol in a beverage.

God left a number of clues, of which Proverbs 23:31 is the easiest to understand, but He left a number of things somewhat difficult to perceive as a test of the spiritual perception of Bible readers. One of these was the absolute proof that the Messiah was what He claimed to be and that false claimants to this office were in fact false. The Old Testament gave evidence which ought to have brought Bible readers to the understanding that Jesus of Nazareth was the Messiah, but Jewish leaders failed to read the signs correctly. On the other hand they saw in false claimants what they thought were signs that their claims were authentic; at least a number of them, like Rabbi Akiba, did. He was the principal Jewish teacher at Jaffa, but he accepted the claims of the false Messiah Bar-Cochba, and was executed by the Romans for participating in the revolt of 135 A.D.

In the same way God may have left His true teaching concerning alcoholic beverages with what the undiscerning find to be ambiguities. This may have been with a view of separating the spiritually perceptive (those whose ears are attuned to the true testimony of the Holy Spirit)[1] from those whose perceptions are made dull by some sin which they cherish. Such a separation of those who take advantage of paradoxes in order to indulge their fleshly appetites may be used by God in judging man. As those who fail to show mercy to the least of the King's brethren are condemned (Matt. 25:31-46), even though they had not perceived the relationship between the King and his lowly kindred, it may be that God will judge those who fail to perceive that He is teaching abstinence from intoxicants and not merely a so-called moderation in their use for pleasure or escape. Christ said for the Christian to deny himself (Matt. 16:24). Should the redeemed of the Lord not deny himself the pleasure of taking a poison which, even if taken in small quantity, slows his mental and physical processes? God is always testing even those in the visible church. Some pass the test and others fail, and some of those who fail will not know it until the Last Judgment, even though they thought they were passing, and repeatedly said *Lord, Lord* (Matt. 7:22-23). Some of those who are genuinely redeemed may still grieve the Lord by their failure to be perceptive about denying themselves sensual pleasures.

There is a passage in the Bible which perhaps some people have wrested to their own destruction. It is the last part of the Song of Solomon 5:1, which says: "Eat, O friends; drink, be drunk, O beloved ones." The verb here translated *be drunk* is *shakar*. It

---

[1] In appealing to the Testimony of the Holy Spirit it is necessary to affirm that this testimony is always in harmony with a high doctrine of the inerrancy of the Holy Bible which of course the Holy Spirit inspired. It is necessary to say this because in some Reformed circles it is taught that Reformed Apologetics may be based on what is alleged to be the testimony of the Holy Spirit rather than the Bible as inerrant.

seems that the starkness of the language makes many English translators avoid the rendering which they elsewhere give to *shakar*. The *Septuagint, Vulgate* and Luther translated it in its plain sense, which is the correct thing to do. It is not a true translation to say with the KJV, *drink abundantly*, or with the NIV *drink your full*. These renderings suggest satiety, not joyful exuberance. Whether we regard the Song of Solomon as allegorical, or as typical (with Solomon portrayed as a type of Christ and the bride as a representative of the Church) or as extolling human love, the drunkenness commanded must be understood as a figure of speech. As Segond's French rendering has it, the exhortation is to be drunk with love. Love has some, but by no means all, of the attributes of drunkenness.

In no way does this verse give any support to what some Reformed leaders say, that we may drink intoxicants, but may not become drunk. If the *yayin* is alcoholic and is to be understood literally as a beverage, then we are told to become drunk in the literal sense of the word. The conclusion we must draw is that the *yayin* mentioned in Song 5:1 is nothing physical, but stands for the gracious gift of love which God bestows.

Since *yayin* and drunkenness are both allegorical here, the passage proves nothing about what *yayin* and *shakar* may mean in non-allegorical passages. In non-allegorical passages the insistence that *yayin* and *oinos* are always alcoholic should be resisted.

As Ritchie says:

> If we want to know whether water spoken of is salt water or fresh, rain water or spring-water, it is of no purpose to be told that it is *water*. In this case we should look with a good deal of astonishment at a person who might assure us that there can be no doubt that it is *salt* water, for is it not declared to be *water*? In like manner, when we want to ascertain whether the wine spoken of in the Bible is intoxicating wine, it is no avail to tell us it is said to be wine, and is this not enough to settle the question? Not quite enough, we reply, since we certainly know there are different kinds of wine in the lands of the Bible—some inebriating in their nature and some not. In this case, we

must take the liberty of demanding some proof...[2]

It is to be feared that *wishful thinking* is in control of the minds of those who reason that: (1) "Since some wine (*yayin, oinos*) is alcoholic, and (2) since some wine is recommended for human consumption, therefore, (3) the alcoholic wine which we like to consume is permitted. (Q.E.D.!)"

The doctrine of total depravity teaches us that the human mind is made corrupt by reason of sin. This kind of bad thinking goes out only by earnest and effective prayer. If our thinking is afflicted with fallacy, we should seek relief.

Notes and Study Questions

Though *yayin* is often believed to consistently represent an alcoholic drink in the Bible, Isaiah 16:10 is a clear exception which proves such a belief concerning *yayin* is wrong. The verse reads, "No treader shall tread out *yayin* in the presses." The *yayin* which immediately comes from the winepresses is nonalcoholic grape juice. It cannot be alcoholic since there is no time for fermentation to take place.

Another passage considered concerning the alcohol issue is Song of Solomon 5:1: "Eat, O friends; drink, be drunk, O beloved ones." The Hebrew word *shakar* (*be drunk*) is mistranslated by various English versions. Those who argue for moderation cannot use this verse as a proof text for drinking alcohol, because this verse encourages drunkenness, which moderationists correctly believe to be a sin. This verse is correctly understood as poetically encouraging being drunk on love, not on alcoholic drink.

How is the quote from Sanhedrin 70a significant in understanding *yayin* to not always be an alcoholic drink? (p. 26)

How do the KJV and NIV take away from the meaning of *shakar* in Song of Solomon 5:1? (pp. 27-28)

---

[2] Rev. William Ritchie, *Scripture Testimony Against Intoxicating Wine*, New York, 1866.

THE WORD *Shekar*

The problem of the translation of the Hebrew word *shekar*, translated in older versions *strong drink*, and in the NIV in different places *beer*, *other fermented drink* or *drinks*, is not an easy one. Where it is used in Deuteronomy 14:26 it can be argued from the general consistency of all the Scripture that it was not an intoxicant. Linguistic studies can be used to support this idea.

This passage tells us that under certain conditions a believer could use the money, which he would otherwise give as a tithe for the support of the Levitical priesthood, in giving a feast for his family and for such Levites as might happen to live in his neighborhood (verse 27) and for strangers, fatherless persons, and widows. As the tithe of a wealthy man's income would purchase a great amount of intoxicants, it is inconsistent with the general tenor of the Bible's teaching that, without any mention of moderation, all believers should be told to purchase them to give to people of all ages and both sexes. We know that *yayin* is a word which can mean a non-intoxicant. Is this true of *shekar* also?

The fact that it is to be consumed according to the law of Deuteronomy 14, might lead us to believe that *shekar*, like Hebrew *yayin* and like English *cider* had two meanings, one referring to an alcoholic drink, the other to a nonalcoholic one. But someone may object, is it not certain that alcoholic content is of the essence of the word *shekar*, because the standard word for *to be drunk* in Hebrew is the verb *shakar* which is cognate to *shekar*?

This argument is easily refuted by linguistic study. This shows us that verbs may be derived from nouns in a particular (not necessarily primitive) stage of the noun's development. For example, the Greek word for *to be drunken* is *methuo*. This was derived from a Greek word for wine, *methu*, which was common in the period of Homer, but which had become almost obsolete in the period when the Bible was being put into Greek. It never occurs in the *Septuagint* or the Greek New Testament. One might nevertheless argue, if he had no background in linguistics, that the verb *methuo* is the primitive word, and that the noun *methu* is derivative. Linguistic science removes that possibility, because all scholars trained in this field of learning are agreed that the Greek language got its word *methu* not from the verb *methuo* but from an original Indo-European root "*medhu* (meaning) honey; also mead."[1] The word *medhu* was in use before the Greek language was formed. It is preserved in the word for *honey* in such ancient languages as Old Slavonic (*medu*) and Tocharian B (*mit*).[2] Since the remote original of the word *methu* in Greek meant honey, the idea must be rejected that it can possibly be derived from a verb meaning *to be drunken*. The evidence is compelling. The ancient word *medhu*, passing into archaic Greek shifted in pronunciation to *methu* and in meaning to *wine*. The verb *methuo* was derived from the fact that some (not necessarily all) *methu* was intoxicating.

Similarly, although we are not sure of all of the history of *shekar* and *shakar*, we can postulate that *shekar* is original and *shakar* secondary. *Shekar* may have included both non-intoxicating and intoxicating varieties, and the verb *shakar* may be derived from the intoxicating kind.

The Syriac language has a cognate word which suggests that the primitive meaning of the proto-Semitic root *sh-k-r* may have been a drink made from the date palm or honey.[3] An intoxicating date wine may have, in course of time, come to be the meaning, and the word may have also taken on the meaning of beer.

There is enough evidence to say that it is unjustifiable to claim that *shekar* must essentially be an intoxicating drink, and since the circumstances of its use in Deuteronomy 14:26 are such that an intoxicant is inconsistent with God's commands given in other places, we can be assured that a non-intoxicant is intended here.

---

[1] "Indo-European Roots," in *The American Heritage Dictionary* of English Language, Houghton and Mifflin, 1973, p. 1528.

[2] *Webster's New International Dictionary of the English Language*, Unabridged, G. and C. Merriam Co., Springfield, Mass., 1937, p. 1519.

[3] *A Compendious Syriac Dictionary* Founded Upon the Thesaurus Syriacus of R. Payne Smith, Edited by J. Payne Smith, Oxford: Clarendon Press. Article, "*Shakar*."

Notes and Study Questions

The Hebrew word *shekar* is condemned as an alcoholic drink in almost every passage it is found. Deuteronomy 14:26 is an exception. The Law in this passage lists *shekar* as one of several items which the Old Testament believer could buy with his tithe money, consume and rejoice before the Lord. Since *shekar* is almost always condemned by God, and Deuteronomy 14:26 is favorable to the drinking of *shekar* even in the worship of God, there must be two meanings for the word *shekar*. It must mean both an alcoholic drink and a nonalcoholic drink. It could be argued by those who want to find a case for moderation that the verb shakar always means to be drunken, and therefore the noun *shekar* would always be an alcoholic drink. Dr. Reynolds argues from the Greek parallels of the Hebrew *shakar* and *shekar*, *methuo* and *methu* respectively, that the noun *methu* (wine) does not come from the verb *methuo* (to be drunken) but from the Indo-European root *medhu-*, which means *honey* or *mead*. Then the verb *methuo* arose from the noun *methu*. Therefore, in the Hebrew equivalent, the verb *shakar*, with the specific meaning of *to be drunken*, may have been derived from the noun *shekar*, signifying an alcoholic or nonalcoholic drink possibly made from dates or honey.

What are the various translations for *shekar* cited? (p. 30)

THE WORD *Tirosh*

The meaning of this word is not vital to any interpretation of whether or not alcoholic beverages are forbidden in the Bible. This is because no scholars believe it always refers to an alcoholic drink. Whatever it is, it is usually permitted, sometimes rejoiced in, and only once described as something evil, which either along with wine (*yayin*) or in explanation of what *yayin* is, is said to take away the *leb* (the heart or the mind). This passage is Hosea 4:11.

Earlier lexicographers (e.g. Gesenius, and Brown-Driver-Briggs) said it meant *must, fresh or new wine.* If so its injurious character in Hosea 4:11 must be explained, and references to its being found in the cluster (Isaiah 65:8) and to its suffering in time of drought (Isaiah 24:7) are understood to refer not to *tirosh* itself but to that which is processed into *tirosh*. It is as though we were to say: The whiskey mourns while still in the field when the corn crop fails. This is possible, but a more natural explanation is that *tirosh* may mean both the liquid (grape juice or wine) and the fruit from which the liquid is made.

A more recent dictionary, that of Koehler and Baumgartner[1] says that *tirosh* is an archaic synonym of *yayin*. Evidence that this is true is presented to the scholarly world in a separate article (ZAW, vol. 46, pp. 218 ff.) by Koehler. In this he points out that *tirosh* is used in fossilized expressions along with *yitshar* (oil). So in Deuteronomy 7:13 wine and oil are called *tirosh* and *yitshar* which Koehler believes are archaic synonyms for *yayin* and *shemen*. The retention of archaic words in fixed expressions is a linguistic phenomenon found in other languages, as in German *Kind and Kegel*. In English an example is *kith and kin*, where *kith* is an obsolete word except when used in this combination.

If we accept the idea that *tirosh* is a synonym of *yayin*, it follows, according to the arguments amply provided in this study as well as by other authors, that both words may signify a beverage either nonalcoholic or alcoholic. Yet certain advocates of the teaching that *yayin* may be either alcoholic or nonalcoholic according to its context go to great pains to try to prove that *tirosh* is always nonalcoholic.

Why they do this is not clear, for it strengthens rather than weakens the argument that *yayin* may be either nonalcoholic or alcoholic to demonstrate that *tirosh* may also have both meanings. This is only natural in what is called a prescientific age in which the science of chemistry had not developed. The ancients had no way of analyzing a beverage and of determining that it had within it a substance defined chemically as C_2H_5OH and called in English and other languages by a name derived from the Arabic, namely *alcohol*.

---

[1] *Lexicon in Veteris Testamenti Libros*, ed. Ludwig Koehler and Walter Baumgartner, 1953, vol. 2, p. 1027.

Those who say that *yayin* is always alcoholic (called *One Wine Theorists*[2]) and those who say that *tirosh* is always nonalcoholic fall into the same error. It is the error of expecting chemical scientific accuracy in an age when there was no science of chemistry. The ancients named drinks without regard to their alcoholic or nonalcoholic content. Of course they knew of the intoxicating qualities of certain drinks, but this knowledge did not enter into their language in naming the beverages.

It is for this reason that when God prohibited alcoholic drink in Proverbs 23:31-35, He had to describe its effects on the drinker, and, because He spoke to the people in the language they could understand, He could not prohibit alcohol in one word. Because men did not want to hear and obey they obscured God's meaning by their evasions and traditions.

Dr. Charles Wesley Ewing in his book *The Bible and Its Wines*[3] is very properly concerned to show that *yayin* is not always alcoholic in Old Testament usage. He does this well, citing such passages as Jeremiah 40:10, Jeremiah 40:12, and Jeremiah 48:33 .

But then, without strengthening the argument for total abstinence as a Biblical requirement, he writes: "Tirosh...never carries the sense of anything fermented or intoxicating." He then goes on to suggest that writers who say that *tirosh* may be intoxicating are moved to do so by *zeal to defend fermented wine.*[4]

To quote Dr. Ewing at greater length:

> Some writers in their zeal to defend fermented wine, have written that tirosh is rendered new wine because it gets possession of the brain so quickly. I do not know who was the first to come up with this but I found the statement in Bullinger's Companion Bible, Appendix 29, and other writers have said the same. New wine has no intoxicating effect at all being the freshly expressed grape juice, the reason for the word new.

Taking up the last part of the above quotation, there is nothing

---

[2] *The Bible and Its Wines* by Charles Wesley Ewing, P. 20.

[3] Published by the National Prohibition Foundation, 1985.

[4] Op. Cit., p. 17.

in the etymology or Biblical usage of the word *tirosh* to suggest that the idea of newness is invariably to be associated with it. The *Septuagint* (the earliest translation) never uses the word new in connection with *tirosh*. Almost invariably the simple word *oinos* is used. This, as demonstrated elsewhere, may mean either nonalcoholic or alcoholic grape juice. Once (Hosea 4:11) the word *methusma* is used. This means an intoxicating drink, from *methuo* to be drunken. The reason *methusma* is used appears to be to avoid the repetition, wine and wine. There is a better way of explaining this repetition as will be explained in a following paragraph. But one thing the *Septuagint's* use of *methusma* shows is that in the minds of these translators, who lived much closer to the time the Hebrew Bible was written than did later translators, the word *tirosh* certainly did not mean exclusively something nonalcoholic. They regarded it, at least in this passage, as an intoxicant. Their usual translation of *tirosh* as *oinos* without the word *new* also indicates that they did not exclude the idea that it might be alcoholic.

As to the idea that *tirosh* is so called because it possesses the mind, that is it takes over and perverts the normal mental functions, this ought not to be dismissed as utterly unreasonable. Gesenius-Buhl[5] says under the word *yarash* (to take possession) that *tirosh* may be a derivative. Koehler-Baumgartner says it is without doubt a derivative. If it is, the case for assuming that *tirosh* was primarily an intoxicant is greatly strengthened. It would mean that when this beverage first came on the scene among speakers of proto-Hebrew they observed its mind altering characteristics and called it *the substance which takes possession*. This is as though we were to say, such and such a person is possessed by a demon, the demon rum.

Another argument for the idea that *tirosh* is usually a synonym for *yayin* and that both mean grape juice whether fermented or unfermented is to be found in the way they have been translated. The earlier translators seem to have understood this quite well,

---

[5] Wilhelm Gesenius' *Hebräisches und Aramäishches Handworterbuch über das Alte Testament*...bearbeitet von Dr. Franz Buhl...siehzehnte Auflage. Leipzig, 1921, p. 321.

but in time the synonymous nature of the two words began to be obscured. The general usage of the *Septuagint* has been mentioned. The *Latin Vulgate* likewise translates *tirosh* by the word *vinum* in almost every instance. In Hosea 4:11 the *Vulgate* translates it as *ebrietas* (drunkenness) and in Micah 6:15 as *mustum* (unfermented grape juice), and in Deuteronomy 7:13 as *vindemia* (vintage). But these are special cases and must be discussed in the following paragraphs. They serve to show that the excellent Hebrew scholar Jerome, who translated the *Vulgate,* did not believe that *tirosh* must always be translated *vinum,* but could have other meanings according to the context. Luther's German version usually has *wein* (wine), but in such special cases as Deuteronomy 7:13, Hosea 4:11, 9:2, and Micah 6:15 it has *must* (grape juice). The KJV has *wine* usually, but it has *new wine* in Hosea 4:11, 9:2, and Joel 1:10, and *sweet wine* in Micah 6:15. The NIV usually translates *tirosh* by *new wine* (a conjecture which lacks proof) and in Micah 6:15 by *grapes* (a good choice, as grapes is the only word which fits the context). The *Tanakh* usually translates *tirosh* by *wine,* but in Hosea 4:11 by *new wine* (a choice which does not fit the context) and also in Hosea 9:2 and Joel 1:10 by *new wine* (good choices according to the context). In Micah 6:15 the *Tanakh* (agreeing with the N.I.V.) has *grapes* (the only choice which comes even close to fitting the sense of the passage). It can be seen from the above that translators have very properly not been bound by the idea that *tirosh* must always be translated by the same word. Using the Bible as its own interpreter this word can and ought to be translated *wine* (either fermented or unfermented), specifically *unfermented wine* (i.e. *sweet wine, new wine* or *must*), *intoxicating wine* (Hosea 4:11), or *grapes* (Micah 6:15).

The Talmud gives support to the idea that it was regarded as an intoxicant in post-Biblical (but nevertheless ancient) Hebrew. Thus in Yoma 76 b (p. 372 of the Soncino edition) we read:

> Why is it (wine) called *yayin* and *tirosh*? It is called *yayin* because it brings lamentation into the world, and *tirosh* because he who indulges in it becomes poor.

The editor of the English translation explains: "The first is a play on *ya ya* exclamation of woe, the second on the second syllable of *tirosh* which is connected with *rash*, to become poor."

The Talmud has more on *tirosh*, but much of it is not helpful. For example on Zechariah 9:17 in this section of the Talmud the writer says:

> But is (*tirosh*) not wine? Surely it is written: And *tirosh* makes maids flourish! The thing which is derived from *tirosh* makes maids flourish.

The editor says that according to Rashi the point under consideration is whether *tirosh* is the name for wine (new wine) or for the grapes themselves. If the latter is accepted, wine is "that which is derived from *tirosh* (berries)."

The Talmudist seems to have been laboring under the misconception that what makes maids flourish or be cheerful must be an intoxicant. Simple grapes could not possibly do that! Since the point under discussion is whether *tirosh* here means grapes, they had to extend its meaning to include *that which is derived from grapes*, i.e. (inebriating) wine. The context is strongly against this, for in the same verse young men are said to become cheerful (or flourish) because of grain (an excellent harvest).

The incongruity of the Talmud's reasoning must be considered. Are young men made cheerful when they have a bountiful wheat harvest while girls are only to be made cheerful by an intoxicant? Rather the parallelism requires the meaning here to be: How great is his (God's) goodness, and how great is his beauty! Corn (grain, a nonintoxicating solid) shall make the young men cheerful, and grapes (a nonintoxicating solid) shall make the maids cheerful (in the same way). There is no thought of the young men only being sober, while the maids are boisterous through drink. The maids rejoice at a good harvest of grapes. It is typical Hebrew parallelism. The meaning is that young people of both sexes (and of course this does not exclude people of all ages) are happy when God gives an abundant harvest![6]

---

[6] Cf. Acts 14:17.

Notes and Study Questions

The Hebrew word *tirosh* is not believed to be an alcoholic drink in most of its occurrences. It has a negative connotation in only one passage, Hosea 4:11. Because it is found in a cluster (Isaiah 65:8) and suffering in a drought (Isaiah 24:7), *tirosh* is thought to be a solid as well as a liquid. It is considered by some to be a synonym of *yayin* and *shemen*. This may lend proof for both *tirosh* and *yayin* being alcoholic and nonalcoholic.

When seeking to understand if certain words imply an alcoholic content or no alcoholic content why is it important to remember that the Bible was not written in an age of chemistry and modern scientific accuracy? (p. 34)

Did the translators of the *Septuagint* consider *tirosh* to be only nonalcoholic? (p. 36) What about the Talmud? (p. 36)

What would be the underlying meaning of *tirosh* if it is derived from *yarash* (to take possession)? (pp. 36-37)

Why is *grapes* considered a good translation for *tirosh* in Micah 6:15? (p. 36)

Tirosh IN HOSEA 4:11

The word *tirosh* in this passage has been a cause of great difficulty. Those who believe that *yayin* stands for one substance only (one-wine theorists) and those who believe it has a plurality of meanings have been puzzled. The same is true of those who believe that *tirosh* is never alcoholic. The reason for this puzzle is found in the redundancy of expression if *yayin* and *tirosh* are synonymous, and in the difficulty of explaining why *tirosh* takes away the mind if it is nonalcoholic.

A typical translation is that of the KJV: "Whoredom and wine and new wine take away the heart." Modern translators, e.g. the NIV and the *Tanakh* understand that the last word, *leb*, is better rendered *mind* than *heart*. They do not, however, solve the problem as to why the words *yayin*, translated *wine*, and *tirosh* translated *new wine*, are both used. If *yayin* and *tirosh* are the same thing, why use both? If *tirosh* is the nonalcoholic counterpart of *yayin* how does it *take away*, or *destroy* (so the *Tanakh*) the mind?

The answer is not hard to find if one knows where to look for it. We ought not to try to find the answer as did William Ritchie, who believed that *tirosh* here meant grapes. He thought that men destroy their heart if they overindulge in grapes. He wrote:

> This last (eating grapes) is in itself an innocent medium of pleasurable sensations; but it is liable to abuse according as it is indulged; and when abused, it takes away the heart.[7]

This is a very improbable thing to say, to put innocent grapes without any reference to overindulgence, along with whoredom and alcoholic wine as causes of the destruction of the heart (or mind).

Charles Wesley Ewing has another explanation.

> "Whoredom and wine (*yayin*) and new wine (*tirosh*) take away the heart." By itself new wine (*tirosh*) does not take away the heart, and it is not conducive to evil. But when associated with whoredom it takes away the heart."

This is not convincing. The Bible does not say that unfermented grape juice was used in connection with whoredom or idolatry. Even if it were it would not in itself become sinful, or do damage to heart or mind.

The answer is not hard to find if one is acquainted with Hebrew grammar, but even many who know Hebrew miss the key and thus fail to unlock the door to the solution. What follows is as far as I know an innovation, but not for that reason to be scornfully rejected.

The Hebrew conjunction *waw*, usually translated *and*, has as one of its uses an explaining force. Thus in Koehler-Baumgartner, vol. 1, p. 245, we have the sense given *that is*. A number of examples are given. A good example of *explaining waw* is to be found in I Samuel 17:40 where we read that David put five small stones in a shepherd's bag which he had, even in a scrip (KJV). The word translated *even* is in Hebrew *explaining waw*. If read

[7] William Ritchie, *Scripture Testimony Against Intoxicating Wine*, New York, 1866.

literally with the usual sense of *waw* as *and*, we would understand that David put the stones in two containers, a shepherd's bag and a scrip. No translators have thought that. *Waw* means *that is* or *even*.

The same usage is in Hosea 4:11. The meaning is: "Whoredom and *yayin* that is *tirosh*, destroy the mind." By so understanding it the difficulty is removed. *Yayin* and *tirosh* are the same. *Tirosh* is used to explain *yayin*, and both in this passage stand for a single alcoholic drink, and not two.

If we ask why Hosea felt he had to explain *yayin*, it may be proposed that as Hosea was the only writing prophet whose home was in northern Israel, he may have known that his readers were relatively unfamiliar with the word *yayin* and needed to have it explained by the word *tirosh*. It is as though an usher in the northern part of the United States were to say to a lady from the South entering a church, *I will conduct you to a seat*, and seeing she did not understand he would add: *that is, I will carry you*.[8] In the opposite situation in the South the usher might begin by saying, *I will carry you*, and then seeing the surprise on the face of the northern lady he would say, *that is, I will conduct you*.

Notes and Study Questions

Hosea 4:11 is the one passage which has a negative connotation for the word *tirosh*. It reads, "Whoredom and *yayin* and *tirosh* destroy the mind." The Hebrew conjunction waw (usually translated and) can be explanatory, translated *that is*. The translation would then be "Whoredom and *yayin* that is *tirosh*, destroy the mind." In this understanding, *yayin* and *tirosh* are synonymous.

What is William Ritchie's explanation of *tirosh* in Hosea 4:11? (p. 39)

---

[8] Carry in the sense of *to conduct, escort, lead, 'take' (a person) with one, without reference to the mode of transit* was standard English in the 18th century, but is now archaic and dialectic. The usage is retained in parts of the South.

Why does Dr. Reynolds disagree with Ritchie on this point? (p. 39)

What is Charles Wesley Ewing's explanation of this passage? What is Dr. Reynolds response to this explanation? (pp. 39-40)

THE HEBREW WORD '*Ashishah* AND THE ALCOHOL PROBLEM

An *'Ashishah* is probably a raisin cake. This is generally accepted by modern scholars. Its etymology is supposed to be connected with PostBiblical Hebrew *'sh-sh, to be solid, compact*. The basic idea is that a raisin cake is composed of compacted raisins. It never means anything alcoholic, nor is it ever used in connection with anything alcoholic, and this might at first glance mean that this is all that need be said about the word and the alcohol problem.

The way, however, that it has been mistranslated in some earlier versions, for example in the KJV, has led people to assume that God looks complacently on the idea that a person should be emotionally supported with drinking vessels full of an alcoholic drink. The Song of Solomon 2:5 says *sammekuni bā'ashīshoth* which the KJV renders, *Stay me with flagons.* The correct meaning is probably stay (or support) me with raisin cakes.

This passage ought to be examined as it has been variously translated, to see when and where the idea that alcohol is involved came about.

The *Septuagint,* the earliest translation has *sterisate me en murois,* which can be rendered into English, strengthen me with perfumes. In view of the probable etymology of *'ashishah* and its usage in the other three passages where it occurs, this is improbable. For example, it is hardly likely that David gave perfume to the men as well as to the women when he had the ark of the Lord brought to Jerusalem. See 2 Samuel 6:19. In fact the *Septuagint* translators themselves do not render it perfume in the latter passage.

The *Vulgate* has *floribus,* with flowers; Luther's German has *mit Blumen,* also with flowers, but the KJV, as noted above, has *with flagons.* Later English translations have come to what appears to be a sounder rendering. Thus the NIV has *with raisins* and the *Tanakh* has *with raisin cakes.*

The conclusion is that the KJV stands almost alone in bringing a drinking vessel into this passage. The respect we must all have for this much honored version should not blind us to the fact that it is in error here, and that the error may have contributed to the idea among English speaking people that alcohol is an approved substance in the eyes of God.

The word *'ashishah* in 2 Samuel 6:19 and I Chronicles 16:3.

In these parallel passages we are told of the gifts David distributed among all the people, men and women alike, when he brought the Ark of the Lord to Jerusalem. The last of the gifts named is an *'ashishah.* The *Septuagint,* the earliest translation, calls it *laganon apo teganou,* a cake from the frying pan in Samuel, and an *amoriten,* a sweet cake in Chronicles. It is to be noted that the idea of raisin cakes is lacking from this translation, but this does not prove raisins were not used. It is especially to be observed that there is nothing suggesting alcohol in these renderings.

Luther's German translation suggests that the gift was wine. He calls it *ein Nössel Wein,* a pint of wine. Why Luther chose this translation is not clear. His predecessors had used no word suggesting alcohol, and the proposed etymologies of *'ashishah* do not give support to this idea.

Can it be that Luther, who probably was fond of alcoholic wine in some moderation imagined that David would in all probability have treated his subjects to a little of this popular beverage?

Luther, great Reformer that he was, nevertheless has to be considered as a man of his age. The primitive position of the Christian Church as reflected in the teaching of Jerome had long since disappeared. Jerome advised the Christians of his day *to avoid wine* (meaning alcoholic wine) *as you would a poison.*[1]

Jerome in translating the *Latin Vulgate* saw nothing about wine in either of these passages. Neither did he translate with any word suggesting raisins, but rather flour and oil.

A verse written in the Luther room of the Wartburg has been attributed to Luther, but no proof exists as to its authorship. Translated from German into English, it is:

> Who loves not women, wine, and song
> Remains a fool his whole life long.

We need not believe that Luther wrote this, to observe that nothing exists to prove that it would have been utterly out of character for him to have done so. Luther believed in marriage. He opposed clerical celibacy.

If he did love alcoholic wine, even though in moderation, it is not unreasonable to suppose that his mind-set was such as to lead him to introduce a suggestion that David gave the people an alcoholic drink. Jerome had the opposite mind-set (the correct one as I seek to prove).

The King James translators being partially dependent on Luther, translate *'ashishah* in both passages: *a flagon of wine*. This reference to a large vessel with handle and spout (for so the word flagon is defined) has no adequate support, and, as previously noted, neither does the word wine.

In conclusion: The rendering *raisin cake* or *cake of raisins* (as in modern versions, e.g., *American Revised Version, Revised Standard Version,* NIV and *Tanakh*) is to be preferred. David gave no wine to the people at this celebration.

Notes and Study Questions

The Hebrew word *'ashishah* most likely means a raisin cake. The KJV consistently and incorrectly translates this word as *flagon of wine*. The KJV translators likely followed the lead of Luther

[1] Previously cited, but the citation is repeated here for the convenience of readers. It is to be found in Letters, vol. 6, p. 25, Post Nicene Fathers.

who translated the word *pint of wine*. No implication of alcohol is found in the Hebrew word or in the contexts in which it is used.

What are the various translations of *'ashishah* in the Bible translations cited? (pp. 41-42)

Why is it important to see the error found in the KJV's translation of this Hebrew word? (p. 41)

Did Martin Luther believe in total abstinence from alcoholic beverages? (p. 42) How is this reflected in his translation of 2 Samuel 6:19 and 1 Chronicles 16:3? (p. 42-43)

'Ashishe Kir Hareseth in Isaiah 16:7

In examining this passage one of the first things to note is that there is an irregularity about the gender. This appears to be the construct plural of a masculine noun, yet *'ashishah* (feminine absolute) is usually considered to be the same word.

Thus without comment modern translators (e.g. NIV and *Tanakh*) render it *raisin cakes,* assuming that it is an irregular plural of *'ashishah.* We are at once required to observe that no translators have ever seen it to be an alcoholic drink.

The *Vulgate* renders it *walls of baked brick.* Luther and the KJV have *foundations* as their translation. The *Douay* version, being translated from the *Vulgate,* has *brick walls.*

In this passage Isaiah is speaking of the coming desolation of Moab (the land and the people). It is said that the people will lament (howl with grief) for either the raisin cakes of Kir Hareseth (a city of Moab) or for its walls.

If the meaning is raisin cakes we should understand that it is a figure of speech, a part being taken for the whole. Raisin cakes may have been an important commercial item in Moab and the prophet speaks of the destruction of commerce. If Jerome is right and the meaning is brick walls the passage can be understood literally. The people will howl for grief when their protective walls are battered down.

It is a major thrust of this book that words do not always have the same meaning. Thus *yayin* and *oinos* may be translated either alcoholic wine or nonalcoholic grape juice according to the way they are used, that is according to the context. In the same way *'ashishah* may be raisin cake or fruit cake in some passages, and brick wall in this particular place.

Although the problem of alcohol is not involved, the problem of rendering the Bible in the language of the people is ever with every Bible interpreter. This writer, if he were called again to be a member of a translation committee, would, after his recent studies, feel inclined to give careful attention to the idea that in this particular passage the word might mean something other than raisin cakes, perhaps brick walls.

The reasons are: (1) The etymology, *'-sh-sh, to be solid, compact* could refer to the making of compact bricks of clay as well as to pressing raisins into a compact mass. (2) Jerome, the translator of the *Vulgate,* knew Hebrew well and was in contact with learned rabbis of his day. His rendering *brick walls* should therefore be treated with great respect. (3) Even if *'ashishah* normally means *raisin cakes,* I would be prepared to defend the proposition that Jerome may have been right, on the ground that for people to mourn over the loss of their protective walls is a more natural thing to do than to mourn over the loss of raisin cakes. (4) The NIV and the *Tanakh* translators may have fallen into the error of thinking a word has one meaning and one meaning only, and tend not to notice when the facts suggest that in a particular passage this is not the case. This brings us back to the fallacy of not accepting two meanings for the words *yayin, oinos,* and *wine* in spite of evidence that each of these words, according to its context, may be understood as alcoholic or nonalcoholic.

But the arguments presented above for considering brick walls do not mean that this writer would do more than enter it as a marginal note, indicating that the *Vulgate* has brick walls. The evidence is far too weak to put *walls* in the text and *raisin cakes* in the margin. Raisin cakes should remain as the translation, but a marginal note would be very appropriate to the effect that the word translated raisin cakes may stand here for delicacies, figuratively representing idolatrous worship. Thus readers' minds would be relieved of supposing that raisin cakes to the exclusion of other delicacies held disproportionate place in the Moabites' estimation.

No great matter of modern Christian practice depends on whether people understand raisin cakes (either literally or figuratively) in Isaiah 16:7, or whether they understand brick walls.

On the other hand, there is far greater proof that *yayin* and *oinos* should be translated *grape juice* (or its equivalent) when they are commended for human consumption. To put this into a Bible translation would be proper, and ought not to be considered to be a tampering with the text to serve special interests. No one says the Hebrew word *ro'sh* must always be translated *head*. There is general agreement that it may be rendered *poison* when the context demands it.

So if God both totally condemns and heartily praises *yayin*, the sense of Scripture demands that two different substances are intended. A good translation should be faithful to the rule that every text be made as true as possible to the real meaning and as clear as possible to the people for whom it is intended. When the life-style of people is radically changed by their understanding of *yayin* or *oinos* it is vitally important that these words be correctly translated.

Notes and Study Questions

In Isaiah 16:7, a different form of the word *'ashishah* is used, *'ashishe*. It is significant that even the KJV does not connect this word in this passage with alcoholic beverages. In this passage, the translation *raisin cakes* may be appropriate, though many have understood the word to mean *brick walls*. If *brick walls* is accepted as the translation this evidences yet another word which may have different meanings based on its usage in the various contexts. This would lend further proof to *yayin* and *oinos* representing both alcoholic wine and nonalcoholic grape juice.

What is the meaning of Isaiah 16:7 if *'ashishe* is translated *raisin cakes*? What if it is translated *brick walls*? (p. 44)

What Hebrew word can be translate *head* or *poison* depending on the context in which it is found? (p. 46)

'ashishē 'anabim in Hosea 3:1

In this passage the sinful people of Israel are said to turn to other gods and to love certain things called in Hebrew *'ashishe 'anabim*. These last words have been understood in different ways. The first word has been discussed in the preceding sections but it must be examined once more in this context. The second word means *grapes*, or more properly in this context *raisins*.

The *Septuagint* renders it *cakes with raisins*, a much better translation than that of some who followed after. There is no suggestion of alcohol here.

The *Latin Vulgate* has *vinacia uvarum, husks of grapes*. This avoids any suggestion of alcohol, but is inferior to the translation of the *Septuagint*. There is no support for translating *'ashishe* as husks, and besides, there is no sense in supposing that the sinners literally loved husks (the skin and seeds of grapes left in the vat after the juice had been drained off). Husks would have to be construed as a figure of speech.

Luther's German rendering is *eine Kanne Wein*, a tankard of wine. This cannot be justified in a scholarly way.

The KJV has *flagons of wine*. This is an error, since etymological and historical evidence for it is lacking.

Later translators, by sound scholarly reasoning came to the rendering, *cakes of raisins*. This is the translation of the *Revised Version* 1881-1901, a very good scholarly work. Later translations which are supposed to be better often fall far short of this great work.

The *Revised Standard Version* (1946-1960) also has *cakes of raisins*, but in general it cannot be commended in the high terms to be applied to the *Revised Version* of 1881 .

The NIV (1978) errs by putting the adjective *sacred* before *raisin cakes*. There is no textual support for this. The probable reason it is added will be discussed later.

The *New English Bible* of 1970 is also not a translation at this point, but a paraphrase. It has *the raisin cakes offered to their idols.*

The translators of the NIV and the New English Bible have a right to think that the reason that loving raisin cakes was sinful is that they were considered *sacred* (that is to a false god), but they have no right to put their conjecture into the text as though the inspired and inerrant Hosea actually wrote *sacred* or *offered to their idols.*

The Bible reader to whom the original Hebrew is unavailable also has a right to think the sin of these wicked Israelites included loving raisin cakes offered to idols, but he ought not to be misled into thinking Hosea said that. A commentator may explain the text that way without offense, but a translator ought not to tamper in this way with God's revealed truth.

C. F. Keil in his commentary on Hosea[2] explains that the...

> grape or raisin cakes are delicacies, figuratively representing that idolatrous worship which appeals to the senses, and gratifies the carnal impulses and desires. Compare Job 20:12, where sin is figuratively described as food which is sweet as new honey in the mouth, but turns into the venom of asps in the belly. Loving grape cakes is equivalent to indulging in sensuality.

If Keil is right the raisin cakes were not actually offered to the idols, and translators who put this idea into the text are guilty not only of adding words to Scripture which are not there, but are also untrue to Hosea's meaning.

In conclusion, since this is a study of alcohol and the Bible, it must be said that, in spite of Luther's German translation and the King James English version, Hosea 3:1 has absolutely nothing to do with alcohol. *'Ashishah* in no passage of Scripture where it occurs is a drink or a drinking vessel.

[2] Keil and Delitzsch, *Commentary on the Old Testament.*

Notes and Study Questions

The same Hebrew word *'ashishe* is used in Hosea 3:1. It is used with *'anabim,* and the phrase means *cakes of grapes* or *cakes of raisins.* It has no connection with alcohol.

How does C. F. Keil explain the relationship of these raisin cakes to idolatry in this passage? (p.48)

THE GREEK WORD *Oinos* (Commonly Translated Wine)

Inasmuch as the Greek word *oinos* is the translation in the *Septuagint* of the Hebrew word *yayin* when the latter clearly means the freshly pressed juice of the grapes, this is proof that *oinos* may mean unfermented grape juice. See Isaiah 16:10, "the treaders shall tread out no *yayin* (Hebrew), *oinos* (Greek) in their presses." The meaning of both *yayin* and *oinos* is obviously unfermented grape juice. In Proverbs 3:10 the freshly pressed juice of the grape is also called *oinos* in this same Greek version of the Hebrew Bible, a version which the inspired New Testament writers frequently quoted. In this passage, where the KJV reads "thy presses shall burst out with new wine" (*new wine* translating Hebrew *tirosh*), the *Septuagint* simply uses the word *oinos* without the adjective *new.*[1] What comes from the presses is not alcoholic!

This should be enough to establish the idea that wherever *oinos* appears in the New Testament, we may understand it as unfermented grape juice unless the passage clearly indicates that the inspired writer was speaking of an intoxicating drink. In view of the general rule that, "when there is a question about the true and full sense of Scripture (which is not manifold, but one), it must be searched and known by other places that speak more

[1] On the basis of arguments previously given, we affirm that *tirosh* does mean new (unfermented) wine in this passage, but this is because of the context which demands this meaning. *Yayin* might just as well have been used in the original Hebrew.

clearly,[2]" we must say that we get a clearer understanding of the New Testament if favorable references to *oinos* mean the unfermented kind, and unfavorable ones the fermented.

Notes and Study Questions

The Greek word *oinos* is used by the *Septuagint* to translate the Hebrew word *yayin*. It is used in Isaiah 16:10: "The treaders shall tread out no *oinos* in their presses." As with the Hebrew word *yayin*, this verse is proof that *oinos* is not always an alcoholic beverage, but also is used as nonalcoholic grape juice. Only nonalcoholic grape juice comes out of the winepresses.

What is another passage where *oinos* is used and can only mean nonalcoholic grape juice? (p. 49)

Yayin, *Shekar* AND *Oinos* CONSIDERED TOGETHER

Although in the foregoing brief word studies proof is given concerning the different meanings of the words commonly translated wine and strong drink (or beer), it appears that the tide of usage has caused the meaning of all of these words to drift in popular opinion to the sense of alcoholic drinks exclusively. This is true to the extent that some scholars can assume that the popular opinion is assured, ignore the idea that any other opinion exists or ever has existed, and argue vehemently against required total abstinence on the basis of their assumptions.

Two scholars of a different sort who expressed an opinion on all these words together are quoted below to show that no one ought to assume that of course the words *yayin, shekar* and *oinos* always mean intoxicants.

---

[2] *Westminster Confession of Faith*, Ch. I, Sect. IX.

Lyman Abbott (*in his day no friend of the anti-alcohol movement*[1]) wrote:

> It is tolerably clear that the general words *wine* and *strong drink* do not necessarily imply fermented liquors, the former signifying only a production of the vine, the latter the produce of other fruits than the grape.[2]

Professor Moses Stuart (considered to be not merely unprejudiced and respectable, but *one of the greatest benefactors of the church* by his exegetical method) wrote:

> My final conclusion is this, viz., that when the Scriptures speak of wine as a comfort, a blessing, or a libation to God,...they can mean only such wine as contained no alcohol that could have mischievous tendency; that wherever they denounce it and connect it with drunkenness and revelry, they can mean only alcoholic or intoxicating wine.[3]

Notes and Study Questions

Many regard *yayin, shekar,* and *oinos* as always being alcoholic beverages. Nevertheless, word studies on these words show this understanding is not correct. Those who wish to hold to the one-wine theory do so based on popular opinion, not exegetical facts. The exegetical facts show *yayin, shekar,* and *oinos* to all vary in their meanings from alcoholic and nonalcoholic drinks depending on the context.

What was the understanding of Lyman Abbott and Moses Stuart concerning the meaning of these words? (p. 51)

WHAT IS THE "DOCTRINE OF DEMONS"?

The attempt to get people to assume without adequate proof that *yayin, shekar,* and *oinos* are always intoxicants should be

---

[1] Ernest Gordon, *Christ, the Apostles and Wine*, p. 26.

[2] Lyman Abbott, *Dictionary of Religious Knowledge*, Article *Wine*, p. 973.

[3] Loc. cit.

resisted. A Christian who has written a book on the subject concerning the teaching of the Bible on wine, G. I. Williamson by name, has written:

> Those who desire to impose a law of total abstinence upon Christians are departing from the truth of God and following the doctrine of demons.[1]

He wrote further:

> To treat wine as the cause of sin—in any way shape or form—is to deny the real teaching of Scripture concerning the depravity of man. It is, in effect, to say that there is a fault in the handiwork of God. There is no greater need in the Church today than to reject this doctrine of devils.

The first sentence in the latter paragraph is true, as to the cause of sin. The second sentence implies that anything that can be called the handiwork of God may legitimately be looked at and consumed by man without sin, for pleasure, for sociability, or for escape from minor pain and frustrations. If God likens the effect of alcoholic drinks to adder's poison (Prov. 23:32) ought we to say that there is no greater need in the Church today than to reject the doctrine of anyone who would say never to take the poisonous stuff, save possibly as medicine in the same way we would take opium before a major operation? Adder's poison is a handiwork of God. Fermented beverages would not occur without man's entering into the process.[2] There are a number of greater needs than the one Williamson says is the greatest.

A far greater evil is when what is called *the testimony of the Holy Spirit* is exalted to the detriment of the inerrant Bible.[3] The true Holy Spirit inspired the Holy Bible and the Bible teaches us about His attributes and what He does and what He does not do. If we follow advice to look to some alleged testimony of the Holy Spirit which is not in conformity to the Bible, we will fall into the hands

---

[1] Williamson, *Wine in the Bible and the Church*, p. 14.

[2] Man must press the grapes before the yeast turns the grape sugar into alcohol.

[3] For an explanation of the alleged testimony of the Holy Spirit (*Testimonium Spiritus Sancti*) see *Philosophy and Religion in Old Princeton Westminster Theology* by John C. Van der Stelt. Page 330 of this book is especially revealing.

of religious charlatans, as leaders of the once great *mainstream* churches have done.

Dr. Williamson's starting point for speaking about a *doctrine of devils,* may be taken by some readers to be based on a sound scriptural doctrine, for it appears at first sight to be derived from 1 Timothy 4:1-5. Some people may think it is sound exegesis to enforce from this passage the teaching that total abstinence from intoxicants is a doctrine of devils. It is really intended to enforce an entirely different idea. The *doctrine of devils* was against marriage and foods (*brōmata*). Drinks are not mentioned. Christians who teach abstinence from intoxicants do not oppose marriage or foods. Most sound commentators say the passage is written in opposition to Gnosticism, a doctrinal system which has very little in common with the teaching that the Bible, if properly understood, demands abstinence from alcoholic beverages. The *seducing spirits* referred to by Paul openly and obviously depart from the Bible. The *Christian* teachers of total abstinence seek, by strict conformity to the rules of hermeneutics and with the help of the Holy Spirit, to find what God says to those who have ears to hear. They believe in Bible inerrancy. Many in the other camps do not.

Another scholar in a once conservative denomination ridicules being like the Puritans and attributing our national failures to particular sins such as our national condoning of the abortion evil, and he urges us to cease stressing the doctrine of the inerrancy of the Bible and instead stress the reality of the incarnation.[4] But the inerrant Bible is that which tells us of the incarnation and many other things necessary for our salvation and important for our spiritual development. Without it we would be lost.

Mr. Williamson has got the needs of the church poorly evaluated. Subtle and not so subtle attacks on Bible inerrancy made by professing Christians in what are thought to be conservative churches are injuring Christians and the Church. These attacks are often made in such a way as to cast doubt on the creation account. If believers in total abstinence err by deviating

---

[4] Dr. George W. Marsden in a lecture at Westminster Seminary in October. 1981.

from the inerrant Bible, they should be opposed, but to call wine a (secondary) cause of sin is hardly the great danger that Williamson says it is. Surely no Christian has ever said that wine is *the* cause of sin and is morally evil in itself.

Total abstinence should not be a reason for some Christians calling other Christians followers of a doctrine of demons. Christians who believe in it should base their arguments on the inerrant Bible. They should be willing to have fellowship with those who believe in Bible inerrancy, but who think the Bible teaches moderation in the use of alcohol and who oppose drunkenness as a sin. It is not wrong, however, for them to teach on the basis of the word of God that alcoholic beverages are forbidden, while *yayin, tirosh, shekar* and *oinos*, when they are non-alcoholic, are permitted.

If a person believes in what are known as the five fundamentals of Christianity (which include, of course, Bible inerrancy), other Christians have firm ground on which to continue discussion with him on all matters of faith and practice. If he rejects and ridicules inerrancy, even if subtly, the possibility of meaningful discussion does not exist. Even if he claims to be an excellent Christian because he says he believes in the testimony of the Holy Spirit or because he stresses the doctrine of the incarnation, we cannot have the necessary common ground on which to meet him. Without the inerrant Bible to anchor him, he may in time, if not now, affirm situational ethics, teach that innocent unborn children may lawfully be killed in the womb, and that the homosexual life-style is acceptable to God.

Of course we must reject total abstinence based on non-scriptural commands. Those of the Muslim and Mormons, for example, are improperly based, but whether it is correct to say that Mohammed and the Mormon teacher were at this point teaching a doctrine of demons, or whether God permitted a little common grace to enter into their theology, cannot be determined by our finite minds.

In his book previously cited, G. I. Williamson has a chapter (chapter 6) entitled *The Tyranny of Experts*. In this he urges Christians to be guided by the Bible alone and not by scientists who come to their conclusions by scientific experiments uncontrolled by the Bible. The overwhelming majority of scientists were publishing findings suggesting that total abstinence was healthful and drinking even in moderation was harmful to health. Since Dr. Williamson believed that the Bible commended drinking in moderation, he felt that scientists who suggested that moderate drinking was harmful were tyrants.

Notes and Study Questions

G. I. Williamson considers total abstinence to be a doctrine of demons. (*Wine in the Bible and the Church,* p. 14) Total abstinence is not a doctrine of demons. The passage which mentions doctrines of demons, 1 Timothy 4:1-5, mentions nothing of abstinence from alcoholic beverages. On the other hand, what has been clearly shown from Scripture is that alcoholic drinks are poison which should be rejected by believers. (Proverbs 23:32).

What were the *doctrines of devils* mentioned in 1 Timothy 4:1-5? (p. 53)

Why does Williamson call scientists tyrants? (pp. 54-55)

ALCOHOL AND PHYSICAL HEALTH

In 1982 there was published an account of the findings of a *77 million federally funded Multiple Risk Factor Intervention Trial known as 'Mr. Fit'*. The account says:

> You can *rustproof* your heart and keep it running like a well-maintained machine, says a Philadelphia cardiologist.
>
> "The way to do it," says Dr. Jack Pickering, "is to raise your level of HDL-high-density lipoprotein known as *the good cholesterol.*" It is a 1-2-3-4 process:
>
> • Lose weight, if you are heavy.

- Stop smoking.
- Exercise regularly.
- Drink 1 ½ ounces—not more—of alcohol every day.[1]

Christians who believe the Bible (and there are none others) should turn to the Bible before they submit to these *federally funded* experts. Even if they are right (which is very doubtful), we have a better authority—God's revealed Word, the Bible. It is our duty to search until we find what it really says, and then obey it. If we add years to our life by following Dr. Pickering's program and offend God by doing so, it will profit us nothing.

I hope that Dr. Williamson will agree that the findings of these *federally funded* experts have no bearing on what the Christian should do unless these findings stand the test of sound Bible exegesis. The first three steps of the process probably do, the fourth step does not.

Furthermore, federal funding of projects such as this do not appear to fall under the legitimate rights and duties of civil government as stated in the Bible.

Although a Christian should do nothing sinful to prolong his life, it is right that he should *choose life* (Deut. 30:19) and, other things being equal, live in such a way as to preserve for himself a sound mind in a sound body.

We should so live that we need not fear what will happen to us after our death, but should live in faith in our Lord Jesus Christ and confidence in his promise of eternal life with Him as recorded in John 11:25-26 and 14:1-7. We should also not dread martyrdom or dying in a good cause, but at the same time we should ever live mindful of the fact that it is wrong to risk death or ill health by practices which do no good to ourselves or others.

I believe we should take Proverbs 23:31 as a command of God and not as mere *rhetoric*. I also believe that it is proper to address those who think that those scientists are right who say that alcohol taken in moderation may *rustproof* their hearts and lessen the risk of a coronary attack.

---

[1] *Times-Leader*, Wilkes Barre, Pa., April 3, 1982, p. 12 A.

There is very good reason to reject the findings of the federally funded experts referred to above and to do this on scientific grounds. True science is a handmaid of God and should be gratefully received. The Christian total abstainer may be somewhat surprised to be told by federally funded experts that the daily use of a little alcohol may lessen his risks of a heart attack. If he accepts the idea that they may be right he is not at all persuaded to take his daily alcohol potion. Rather he says, "God forbids it, and if He chooses to call me home by a heart attack, so be it. I will accept whatever He decrees."

Those Christians who believe that drinking in moderation is a Christian liberty, and unbelievers who are of the opinion that drinking in moderation is the course they wish to pursue, should know that further scientific research has proved that even this small *good* that alcohol is alleged to produce is untrue. The findings of disinterested scientists are probably unknown to most people. The reason is not hard to find. Much money may be gained if people can be induced to drink *moderately* for the sake of the *good cholesterol*. Therefore those who are interested in the manufacture and sale of alcoholic beverages will do what they can to have such findings presented to the public.

True scientists, scholars in search of the truth, not paid by either the liquor interests or the total abstinence advocates, have brought to light new evidence that even small amounts of alcohol are harmful to the heart.

It is also true that such small amounts are harmful to the brain and other parts of the human body, and therefore to take them is to kill oneself little by little. This is to sin against the commandment, *Thou shalt not kill*.

Dr. Lawrence E. Lamb has written in 1985:

> It has . . . been shown that *even small amounts of alcohol can damage the diseased heart's ability to function.* Treadmill exercise tests show that these patients have less capacity to exercise after alcohol.[2]

---

[2] *The Health Letter,* San Antonio, Texas. Edited by Lawrence E. Lamb, M.D., F.A.C.P., and F.A.C.C., vol. xxv, no. 4 (Feb. 22, 1985), pp. 2-3. It is to be

So it is with the person having a diseased heart. But what of the healthy? Dr. Lamb continues:

> *But what about the person with a healthy heart who does not drink large amounts of alcohol?* New evidence shows that drinking even small amounts of alcohol can be *more harmful to the heart than was previously thought.* Dr. Robert Lang, cardiologist at the University of Chicago, told the Central Society for Clinical Research meeting that even a few drinks in healthy young people was toxic to the heart. That means the University of Chicago studies show that *social drinking does affect the heart.* You don't have to be a regular drinker, or an alcoholic, or have underlying heart disease to have adverse effects from using alcohol.
>
> Previous studies have shown that the heart still ejected the normal amount of blood after alcohol consumption. This was thought to be a good indication that alcohol had not affected heart function. But Dr. Lang and colleagues showed that alcohol decreases the resistance to blood flow. Alcohol opens your arteries. That is why the face flushes with a cocktail. The low blood pressures, because of the alcohol's effect on the arteries, actually masked the point that *the heart muscle was actually weaker after consuming alcohol.*
>
> Dr. Kenneth Borow of the University of Chicago team of cardiologists pointed out that this was especially important in view of the fact that 450,000 of the nation's alcoholics are between 10 and 19 years of age.

Dr. Lang has excellent credentials as a scientist. He and the other doctors named appear to have approached the problem without any prejudice in favor of total abstinence from alcoholic

---

understood that Dr. Lamb does not appear as a scientist recognized only in circles approving of total abstinence. *The Retired Officer,* a publication of the Retired Officers Association has a regularly appearing health section called, *Ask Dr. Lamb*, which is written by him. The reason for mentioning this is to establish that he is highly respected by a large organization not committed to the cause of total abstinence. Those who have attended social gatherings of T.R.O.A. must surely be convinced that social drinking is approved and practiced, while gross public drunkenness is discountenanced.

beverages. This is true science, and not the *science falsely so-called* condemned in the Bible.

It is certain that God never intended his people to consume this poison, even in small quantities, for pleasure. For religious leaders to teach that because some wine is commended in the Bible, this means that alcoholic wine is approved if taken in moderation is wrong. It puts these teachers in the position of those who become *least in the kingdom of heaven*.

Thus we see that any people who hope to *rustproof* their hearts by taking alcohol daily are doomed to be disappointed. But some who are not yet addicted to this drug may say in their minds, "I don't care if I risk heart disease, if I can be socially acceptable by social drinking it is worth the price."

To such would be social-climbers it is proper to ask this question, "If you are willing to risk your heart, are you also willing to risk your brain? Before saying yes, remember that social acceptance diminishes with reduced ability to think well."

Dr. Galen Bosley has written a well-documented study showing that mental ability decreases when alcoholic consumption is much less than the amount Dr. Pickering recommends to *rustproof* the heart.[3]

Among other very significant things Dr. Bosley has written, is the following:

> Although alcoholics by definition consume more than fifty liters of pure alcohol per year and some as much as 130 liters, findings of decreased performance on mental ability tests are found in light social drinkers consuming as little as four liters per year, a finding also supported by others. This is roughly equivalent to one third of an ounce of alcohol per day (eight ounces of beer, three ounces of wine, or two thirds of a jigger of whiskey). As alcohol consumption increases to the heavy social drinking level, the ability to recall events and information is

[3] "The effects of small quantities of alcohol: Light and moderate drinking is harmful to the brain and the thought processes. The latest research reveals some startling conclusions." *Ministry, International Journal for Clergy*, vol. 59, no. 5, May, 1986, pp. 24-27.

also impaired.

Brain shrinkage? In Australia Dr. L. A. Cala and associates have for many years studied the effects of alcohol and the brain and its ability to function. To determine the point at which alcohol consumption begins brain damage, Cala examined heavy drinkers, using CAT scans, and found brain shrinkage already in progress. Using the same CAT scan procedure, she then examined a group of individuals considered to be moderate to light drinkers. Of thirty-nine drinkers tested, thirty were found to have some brain shrinkage, with frontal lobes bearing the first signs.

The reference to the frontal lobes is significant for it has been proved that decision making and moral value centers of the human character reside in the frontal lobes of the brain.

This confirms what Proverbs 31:4-5 had already told Bible believers, that alcoholic drinks (and as nothing is said of great quantities we may understand small amounts of alcohol) cause forgetfulness of the law and perverse judgments.

No light drinker ought to comfort himself with the thought that he has never become drunk. Brain shrinkage and brain function impairment occur in a social drinker who has never been intoxicated. A brain cell which has been destroyed is never restored.

Notes and Study Questions

Alcohol's effects are detrimental to the physical health of the drinker. Though some medical studies find alcohol in small portions to be helpful to the heart, other medical studies show that alcohol in small portions not only damages the heart, but also shrinks the brain. Even if medical science did consider moderate drinking of alcohol beneficial to the body, God still considers it a poison which He commands us to avoid (Proverbs 23:31-32).

Since drinking alcohol damages one's health, which of the Ten Commandments does it break? (p. 57)

Why are the frontal lobes of the brain important? How does the damage caused to them by drinking alcohol support the teaching of Proverbs 31:4-5? (p. 60)

ALCOHOL AND BRAIN INJURY

There may be some readers who suppose they have acted altogether properly with regard to self-protection and Christian ethics if they drink alcoholic beverages and then let others do the driving.

The Health Letter, edited by Lawrence E. Lamb, M. D., F. A. C. P. and F.A.C.C., Vol. 29, no. 7 (April, 1987), page 4, quoting Dr. Maurice S. Albin and Leonid Bunegin of the University of Texas Health Center in San Antonio (*Critical Care Medicine,* October 6, 1986), indicates that this is not true.

> To the advice, "If you drink, don't drive," you must add, "Don't even ride in a vehicle if there is an increased risk of an accident.

Of course there is always an increased risk of an accident if one is in any moving vehicle. Not only is there the possibility that the driver of the vehicle, even if sober, will have a momentary failure to drive properly, there is also the much greater risk that an intoxicated driver in another vehicle will cause a terrible collision. Mechanical failure is also possible.

It follows that to the ills already established which come from drinking alcohol the danger of any injury to the brain, not merely vehicular, should be added.

Dr. Albin notes that ethyl alcohol is metabolized into acetaldehyde, which in turn produces *free radicals*. "These free radicals combine with fatty acids released from the injured brain tissue to form compounds that literally digest brain tissue."

> To explain how significant the alcohol effect is, Dr. Albin explains, "If brain injury results in a dime-sized lesion in a sober person, the injury expands to the size of a half dollar in

the presence of alcohol in a person with normal blood pressure. In the presence of blood loss with a blood pressure drop, the injury can be extended to the size of a silver dollar or larger.

Since many accidents result not only in brain injury but also in loss of blood, the wisdom of avoiding as far as possible the risk of any violent accident after taking alcohol is evident. A Christian, who must, if he is truly a believer, understand that his body is a temple of God, inevitably sees that he must never risk destroying that temple in whole or in part.

> Don't you know that you yourselves are God's temple and that God's Spirit lives in you? If anyone destroys God's temple, God will destroy him; for God's temple is sacred, and you are that temple. (1 Cor. 3:16-17 NIV).

Notes and Study Questions

Alcohol is even more damaging when someone has an injury to the brain. The alcohol mixes with fatty material from the damaged brain. This mixture then consumes brain tissue.

Is it only brain injuries caused by car accidents or any brain injury which alcohol can affect in this way? (p. 62)

GENESIS 9:18-27 AND THE ALCOHOL PROBLEM

In any discussion of the Bible and alcohol the account of Noah's drunkenness must not be omitted, distasteful though it is to discuss it.

In view of what the idiom *to see the nakedness* of a person means in Leviticus 20:17, the idea that the same expression that Ham *saw the nakedness* of his father means something more than a visual act must at least be considered. It is true that most scholars think Ham saw and told, and nothing more. A minority of scholars, and not necessarily the least worthy of respect, think that Ham did more.[1] They believe that he may have committed an unnatural sexual act on his unconscious father. This is such a horrible idea that a believer's first impulse is to reject it. Alcohol, however, does strange things, and we must therefore study the Hebrew idiom carefully.

To *see the nakedness* and *to uncover the nakedness* of a person are used in the Bible to mean to have illicit sexual intercourse with the one in question. This illicit relationship may be incestuous. See Leviticus 18:6, 7, 8, 9, 11, 12, 13, 15, 16, and 19. Also 20:17, 18, 19, 20, and 21.[2]

To uncover the nakedness of one's father's wife is to uncover the father's nakedness (Lev. 18:8). Committing adultery with the father's wife, here called uncovering her nakedness, is said to be the equivalent of uncovering the father's nakedness.

We cannot, however, see any parallel between the sin of Leviticus 18:8 and the sin of Ham in Genesis 9:22, because Noah's wife was in no way involved.

The evidence is not such as permits the reader to be sure as to what Ham really did. In view of what we know alcohol does to human beings, it is possible to consider that Noah and Ham may have been drinking together. Noah may even have made unseemly jests in the presence of his son, who may have had homosexual tendencies. Noah sank into a drunken stupor. The alcohol may have released the inhibitions which normally would have restrained Ham, and he may have committed a sexual sin on the person of his unconscious father. The seriousness with which Noah regarded the incident may give some support to this interpretation.

On the other hand it is possible to take the words *saw the nakedness* in a literal sense. In this case Ham's sin lay in his not

---

[1] E.g. Hermann Gunkel, *Genesis,* Gottingen, 1910, p. 79.

[2] The verb *ra'ah (to see)* and the noun *'erwath (nakedness)* are used in Genesis 9:22 where scholars are not agreed as to what happened, while in Leviticus 20:17 the same verb and noun are used and in this passage there is general agreement that not merely looking at nakedness, but incestuous sexual intercourse is intended. The identity of the verb and noun points to the act of sodomy which Ham may have practiced on his drunken father.

covering his father and in his telling his brothers of their father's uncovered condition.

In either case Noah, the only righteous man of the generation before the universal flood, was greatly shamed. Every reader must be impressed by what alcoholic wine did to him. Alcoholic wine first appears in the Bible in this very ugly situation. How can anyone believe that the wine which God commends so highly in Psalm 104:15 is the same beverage?

The correct answer to the problem is that what Noah drank was alcoholic wine, once called *yayin ki yith'addam,* and the wine which is a blessing to man is nonalcoholic wine or grape juice, more than once described as what is pressed from grapes (Isaiah 16:10; Jeremiah 48:33).

Notes and Study Questions

This is the first mention of alcohol's effect upon humanity. Noah was greatly shamed by becoming drunk and laying naked. Certainly, this is not a result of the *yayin* which God gives to make man's heart glad in Psalm 104:15.

ALCOHOL AND THE DRIVING OF MOTOR VEHICLES

It is obvious that the Bible says nothing about the sinfulness of driving after drinking alcoholic beverages. But, although motor vehicles did not exist when the Bible was written, the fact that drinking alcohol under any conditions is forbidden, has been demonstrated in this book. Those who are unwilling or unable to accept the evidence that the Bible condemns even the moderate use of alcohol need to have it demonstrated to them that even such moderate use before driving is prohibited.

Every sane person agrees that people far gone in drunkenness should not drive, but the question as to how much alcohol one can take before getting behind the wheel of a car is not generally agreed on. Does the Bible have anything to say to people who are convinced that alcohol may be taken to relax tensions and for the sake of sociability, and that one may drive while mildly relaxed through alcohol?

The answer must be that since the Bible requires that we not even look at the drink which has the ill effects so vividly described in the last part of Proverbs 23, no more need be said by way of prohibiting it before driving.

There is, however, a passage which shows that God puts under greater condemnation a person who has power over the life and property of others and who drinks, even in moderation, than He does a person who has no such power. This passage is Proverbs 31:4 ("It is not for kings . . . to drink wine").

This passage commands total abstinence (not mere moderation) for kings. Kings are specified because in Bible times they had power to make judgments of life and death. Does not the driver of a powerful car have the power of life and death over others? Yes, he has such power far more than the ordinary pedestrian.

A standard book used in driver safety education[1] supports the teaching that alcohol and safe driving do not mix. It says:

> When ingested, alcohol is directly and quickly absorbed into the blood stream through the lining of the digestive tract, carried by the blood to all parts of the body (including the brain) and finally oxidized and eliminated.

Other facts from this book, which the advocates of moderate drinking should consider, follow:

> As the alcohol concentration in the blood stream builds up, body functions are affected.
>
> In spite of deceptive outward signs (flushed face, animated behavior, etc.), alcohol operates as an anesthetic by deadening the nerve centers, and therefore is identified as a *psychological depressant*.

---

[1] *A Resource Curriculum in Driver and Traffic Safety Education,* reprinted 1975 by Michigan State University Press by permission of The American Driver and Traffic Safety Education Association . . . pp. 93-95.

So if a driver says, "I drank a little but I am driving better than ever. I am animated, my perceptions are improved," he is deceiving himself.

The book continues:

> A person may feel gay and pepped up, nevertheless, the nervous system is being depressed, not stimulated.
>
> Alcohol does not *step on the gas* for us (stimulant), it simply paralyzes the brakes (restraints).
>
> Alcohol's paralyzing, numbing effect on the brain begins at the higher center (cerebrum) and moves toward the lower center (medulla) of activity, as the concentration of alcohol in the blood stream increases. (The parts of the brain are affected in reverse order to their development.)
>
> First, the forelobes (cerebrum) of the brain are affected, resulting in decreased ability to reason and make judgments, weakened social inhibitions, and changed attitudes toward others.

No one ought to put himself in a position of power over the life of others with this poison in his body. It decreases his ability to make sound judgments. By so doing he makes himself a potential murderer. This potentially murderous situation can arise in a person who thinks he has drunk only enough to relieve tensions and to become animated.

The *Resource Curriculum* says very truly:

> The driving ability of most persons becomes impaired *before* they display *outward* signs of motor impairment, and other noticeable effects.
>
> The insidious effect of alcohol on judgment and self control, even in the early stages, is particularly serious.
>
> Since self-criticism is affected early the drinker often is unlikely to recognize any change in his behavior.
>
> Even more serious is the likelihood that he feels more perceptive and skillful, and therefore, is likely to take more chances in passing, speeding or negotiating curves (self-confidence increases as skill decreases, the worst possible

combination).[2]

The Bible has a number of commands forbidding any person to endanger others in such a way as in driving unsafely. For example there is the command, commonly known as the Golden Rule: "In everything, do to others what you would have them do to you" (Matt. 7:12; Luke 6:31). This means that if we would have others respect our lives and the lives of our loved ones on the highways, we should respect theirs by never driving when our ability to do so is in any way impaired. As can be readily perceived by any intelligent person whose mind is not clouded by poison, this means that we should drive only when we have absolutely no alcohol in the blood stream.

If we have drunk so much that our judgment and reflexes are permanently impaired, even though we have become total abstainers and have no alcohol in our bodies, this is a serious matter and will be discussed in another chapter, *Permanent Brain Damage and the Moderate Use of Alcohol.*

Notes and Study Questions

Drinking, even in moderation, and driving is very dangerous as alcohol makes a driver a potential murderer. Alcohol is a depressant which slows the driver's ability to make choices. In the split-second situations which sometimes arise in driving, a driver who has consumed alcohol would be unable to make the right choice in time, and it often causes death for someone in his car or whoever was hit by the car.

What verse teaches that one who has the power of life and death should not drink alcohol? (p. 65)

How quickly does alcohol enter the body after it has been drunk? (p. 65)

Why does the drinker of alcohol feel more excited and alert when he is actually less alert? (pp. 65-66)

---

[2] Op. cit., p. 94.

How should the Golden Rule of Matthew 7:12 and Luke 6:31 be applied to drinking and driving? (p. 67)

ISAIAH 25:6 AND THE ALCOHOL PROBLEM

This verse, part of a passage describing in beautiful language a feast to be given by God to all nations, is particularly interesting because of its bearing on the alcohol problem. This is because of two words which may not have been understood or translated correctly.

They are the words *shemarim* which is used twice in this verse. It is the plural of *shemer,* usually interpreted dregs or lees, and the word *mezuqqaqim,* usually interpreted *well refined.*

There are certain striking facts about the way these words are used in this verse which require the serious student to pause and weigh the evidence. He ought to study arguments on all sides and then choose the meaning which fits. After eliminating impossible solutions it is a sound rule in detective work to decide that the only other possibility, no matter if it is improbable, or hitherto unthought of, must be the correct answer.

First, we must take the word *shemer.* From other passages in Scripture and from the lexicographers we understand that this means dregs or lees. But is this possible here? On the principle that *God means what He says,* it is not.

Will God give the people he entertains with loving concern for their welfare a beverage of dregs? The serious reader is invited to note well that the first time *shemarim is* used there is no word *wines* found to justify the KJV's rendering *wines on the lees.* There is no word *aged* found to justify the NIV's rendering *aged wine*. But what must we say of the *Tanakh's* rendering, which is *choice wines*?

Perhaps the *Tanakh's* rendering is correct or closer to the correct meaning than the others. It differs from the *Jewish Publication Society of America's* 1917 translation which agreed with the KJV: *wines on the lees*. Jewish scholarship has changed over the years.

Since God would not offer his chosen guests a drink made up exclusively of dregs, interpreters have made various efforts to avoid the difficulty. Putting the word wines in front of lees does not make the drink sound particularly appetizing, but what is chiefly against it is that there is no Hebrew word known to mean wine in the verse at all. There is only the word known to mean dregs or lees.

Since this is impossible, the improbable must be the correct answer. That is the hypothesis that *shemarim* in Isaiah 25:6 does not mean *lees* at all.

It is true that the lexicographers do not recognize any other meaning for *shemer* than dregs, lees or sediment, but we must face the improbable answer that they are incorrect in this particular verse.

The second time *shemarim is* used in this verse it is used in the expression *shemarim mezuqqaqim.* Here also translators have given their readers renderings which need to be reexamined. The KJV has *wines on the lees well refined.* The NIV has *the finest of wines.* The *Tanakh* has *choice wines well refined* with a note: *Meaning of Heb. uncertain.*

Since we must not be bound by the idea that a word in the Bible has one meaning and one meaning only, and since dregs, lees or sediment do not agree with the context of Isaiah 25:6, some reading similar to the *Tanakh's choice wines* seems indicated as long as we leave open the possibility or probability that God would provide alcohol free wine in this great ecumenical feast. He would want no alcohol induced quarrels or ribaldry, and neither would He be niggardly in restricting the amount each of his guests might drink.

The last word in the verse, if we follow the reading of Luther's German Bible, strengthens the idea that the beverage at this great ecumenical feast will be alcohol free. In his rendering of the passage he translated the last two words of verse 6, *shemarim mezuqqaqim* as the German equivalent of *wine without yeast.* His translation, for one thing, destroys the theory of some *one-wine theorists* that from Bible times to the nineteenth century no one knew of alcohol free wine.

Luther, although not thought to have been the greatest Hebraist of his day, took pains *to engage the collaboration of colleagues better versed than he in Hebrew.*[1] These colleagues may have received their understanding of the word *mezuqqaqim* from the great Christian scholar Johann Reuchlin who spent much time in study with the greatest Jewish scholars of Hebrew of his day. Gesenius-Buhl (Hebrew-German Dictionary) says that the Arabic cognate word *zaqq* in the Oman dialect means *Hefen, Boden-satz* (yeast, dregs). This is supportive of the idea that the words mean choice wines purified of yeast and dregs by heating and straining. Such a drink would be suitable for God to give to all nations. Alcoholic wine would not.

As an additional argument it is to be noted that Luther, according to evidence we have which seems to be accurate, was not an abstainer from alcoholic wine. He would therefore not be predisposed to exclude alcohol from the great ecumenical feast of Isaiah 25:6. The fact that he did so may be significant of his conviction that a proper rendering of the Hebrew required it. The Jewish Hebraists who were the source of his understanding may very possibly have preserved a correct tradition which Judaism subsequently lost.

Etymologically the idea that *shemarim* means choice wines in Isaiah 25:6 can be sustained by noting that *shamar* means to keep. That which is *kept* is probably *choice*. But a warning must be given here. The idea of *choice* because *kept* may make some people think of the aged *vintages* alcoholic wine lovers prize and pay dearly to get. The NIV errs here by translating the first example of *shemarim* in this verse as *aged wine*. This writer is sensitive to the fact that in criticizing the N.I.V. he is criticizing a work in which he had the honor of serving on one of the translation teams, but for the sake of truth he must do so. The term *aged wine* has already been used in published material to help prove the point that God approves of fermented wine. It is probable that the N.I.V. translators of this part of Isaiah were not thinking of the etymology from the verb *keep,* but of the fact that strictly fresh grape juice has not had time to develop lees or dregs. Therefore wine on the lees is *aged* but

---

[1] Roland H. Bainton, *Here Stand I, A Life of Martin Luther*, p. 113.

only to a very slight degree. Wine settled on the lees is spoken of disparagingly in Jeremiah 48:11 and Zephaniah 1:12. Evil men are said to be like wine settled on the lees. Those preparing *choice* alcoholic wine rack off the wine and preserve it for a time until certain subtle, delicate tastes have developed. For this reason we have the expression, *sell no wine before its time*. To rack off means *to draw off* (cider, wine, etc.) *from the dregs*. Wine racked off is considered better than wine still on its dregs. If *shemer* means dregs in Isaiah 25:6, it is not a very choice drink God will offer those who come to his feast, which He will give in a time when death will be destroyed forever (verse 8). It is not even wine on its dregs, but the dregs themselves! This is impossible and the improbable is the only solution: *shemer* in this verse does not mean dregs.

The Christian brother who advances the argument from this verse that God approves of alcoholic wine (in moderation of course) puts himself in an absurd position. His name is not mentioned out of kindness, but it is hoped that he, and all who are influenced by him, will withdraw from this untenable position.

The last phrase of Isaiah 25:6 may properly be translated *of beverages without yeast*. In agreement with the *Tanakh* it would be proper to add a footnote: *Meaning of Hebrew uncertain*. The precise sense of *shemer is* not yet established.

Notes and Study Questions

In this passage the meaning of *shemarim* and *shemarim mezuqqaqim* are significant. God is giving a feast to His people and offering this substance to His people. The Hebrew word *shemarim* is the plural of *shemer* which usually means *dregs*. The word *mezuqqaqim* is a participle of *zeqaq* meaning *to purify* or *refine*. The KJV and NIV find a reference to alcoholic drinks in these words. *Choice wines* is a possible translation. Martin Luther's translation of *wine without yeast* is also a possibility. Whatever the understanding of the words, it is clear from the condemnation of them in other passages that God would not give His people alcoholic drinks.

Can *shemarim* mean something besides *lees* in Isaiah 25:6? (p. 69)

HOSEA 7:5 AND THE QUESTION OF THE POISONOUS NATURE OF WINE WHEN IT IS ALCOHOLIC

The first part of this verse should be translated in agreement with the *Tanakh,* the Jewish translation of the Hebrew text into English recently published (1985). This work has been accomplished by Jewish scholars judged by competent Jewish people to be extremely well qualified to bring the Hebrew Scriptures to the large and generally well-educated world of English speaking adherents of Judaism.

The scholarship of the translators is not the reason for accepting their rendering of Hosea 7:5. The fact is, it stands some of the tests that a Christian scholar may put to it.

The rendering is: "The day they made our king sick (and) officials with the poison of wine..." (The rest of the verse the *Tanakh* translates: "He gave his hand to traitors," but adds in a footnote, *i.e. he trusted traitors; but meaning uncertain*. The translators do not say there is anything uncertain about the words "they made our king sick...with the poison of wine," and as the concern of this study is to prove that the Bible says that alcoholic wine is a poison, we must examine why this translation with the word poison is right and why ones which differ, and leave out the word poison, are wrong.

Readers familiar with the KJV will note that it says: "In the day of our king the princes have made him sick with bottles of wine." The word *bottles,* lovers of the KJV though we may be, we must admit is an error. The word bottles occurs because the translators took *chamath* to be a form of the word *chemeth* which means a small skin bottle. This is a rare word in the Bible, used only in

Genesis 21:14 and 19. Abraham gave Hagar such a skin bottle filled with water. But *chamath* cannot be derived from chemeth. It is the construct form, singular of *chemah,* as modern grammarians, lexicographers and translators are agreed. The question still remains whether *chamath* is properly to be translated heat, anger, or poison. *Chemah* from which it is derived may have any one of these meanings, the context being used to determine which meaning is correct in any particular case.

Here the reader must choose between the heat of wine makes sick, the anger or wrath of wine makes sick, or the poison of wine makes sick. Poison regularly makes the one who takes it sick. Heat and anger may sometimes make the person who is affected by them sick, but not regularly. Therefore poison is to be preferred.

We must notice that the Bible does not say that this poison is something other than alcohol which malicious people have added to the king's wine. It is the poison *of* wine, that is the poison of alcohol, the poison in grape juice which has fermented.

We already have a reference in Proverbs 23:32 to alcoholic wine's being like the bite of a poisonous snake. When adequately translated, Hosea 7:5 is a second reference to the poison of (alcoholic) wine.

The reader is asked to consider. Is the same God, all knowing and loving, to call the same substance a poison, not once but twice, and also a substance which makes glad the heart of man? The answer must be that this is *not* the same substance. The *one-wine theorists* have a lot to answer for. How many people have been misled by their shallow scholarship!

In the first paragraph of this section are the words: "The first part of this verse should be translated in agreement with the *Tanakh...*" This refers to the fact that the good Hebraists who translated the *Tanakh* are correct in taking the word *day* (*yom*) to be absolute and not in construct with *our king.* This they do in opposition to an earlier translation into English by Jewish scholars (that of 1917). They are entirely right in doing so, and in not following the path of least resistance and interpreting as others who have gone before, whether these others were Christians or their coreligionists.

But this writer does not mean to go on record as saying that the *Tanakh* should be followed throughout Hosea 7:5, only in rejecting the much repeated words, *the day of our king*.

If we translate *In the day of our king,* there is no expressed object to the verb *made sick*. Thus, the KJV and the *American Revised Version* of 1901 are in disagreement as to the object. The KJV has it that the king was made sick, the subject being *the princes,* which word can mean high officials. The ARV translated *the princes made themselves sick*. These translators were not sure enough of this rendering to let it stand alone, for they have a marginal note reading "Or, *him.*" Against the idea that the princes made themselves sick are the facts that the verb is not in the reflexive stem (hithpael), and, more significant, this idea does not connect well with the following words: "he stretched out his hand with scorners."

The *Tanakh* should be criticized for having no subject for the verb *made sick* other than the indefinite *they* hidden in the Hebrew verb. The word *princes* the *Tanakh* takes to be a second object of the verb *made sick,* but if it were to be understood in this way, we would expect the Hebrew word for *and* to be before *princes*. These difficulties are obviated if we take *princes* to be the subject of *made sick* and *our king* to be the object. The verb normally goes before its subject in Hebrew as it does here.

This writer proposes that Hosea 7:5 should be translated: "The day princes made our king sick with the poison of wine he gave his hand to mockers."

This is a straightforward sentence every word of which is directly derived from the Hebrew. It means that princes (not necessarily members of the royal family but high officials) made *our king* (the reigning king of Israel) sick (in mind and heart) with the poison of wine (that is, with alcoholic poison), and while he was intoxicated he gave his hand to scorners (in a wicked agreement, cf. Ex 23:1).

A scholar in criticism of the above has said:

> A consideration against *our king* being the object and separated from *sarim* (princes) is that the two are classed

together in verses 3 and 7 where *their judges* replaces *sarim.*

This criticism is answered by following the sensible explanation of C. F. Keil, in the Keil-Delitzsch Commentary, that verse 5 is subordinate to the main thought and is to be taken as a parenthetic remark.

Understood in this way Hosea 5:1-10 is not ambiguous. The general situation in verses 1-4, 6-10 describes the evil condition of the kingdom with a reference to the overthrow of a number of kings. The prophet has Zechariah, Shallum, Menahem, and Pekahiah in mind (2 Kings 15:10, 14, 25).

But in verse 5 he has a particular king and particular princes in view. The king was the king on the throne when Hosea was writing. Understood in this way the princes are not the same as those of verse 3, nor are they the judges of verse 7. The *kings* of verse 7 probably, but not necessarily include the *king* of verse 5.

Finally, what is especially to be noted is that the *poison* of alcohol marred the record of at least one of the kings of Israel in Hosea's time.

Notes and Study Questions

Hosea 7:5 speaks of the *chamath of wine.* The KJV is wrong in translating the phrase *bottles of wine.* The correct translation is *poison of wine.* The whole verse should be translated, "The day princes made our king sick with the poison of wine he gave his hand to mockers." This verse evidences the danger of alcoholic drinks by calling them poison.

Why is poison a better translation than heat or anger? (p. 73)

How does Proverbs 23:32 support the translation poison of wine? (p. 73)

MICAH 2:11 AND SOUND BIBLICAL EXEGESIS

If a man were to go about uttering
Windy, baseless falsehoods:
"I'll preach to you in favor of wine and liquor"
He would be a preacher [acceptable] to that people.

This is the translation of Micah 2:11 according to the version of The Jewish Publication Society of 1985 entitled *Tanakh.* Although it is made by Jews still adhering to Judaism, it is an excellent rendering of the Hebrew, bringing out the proper degree of contempt God has for the opinion of people, specifically in the circumstances in which the prophet spoke, who would be eager to accept the preaching of a man approving the consumption of alcoholic wine or alcoholic liquor (that is, *shekar*).

Other versions, although basically correct, may seem milder in their expression and not necessarily as accurate in translation.

The KJV has, "If a man walking in the spirit and falsehood do lie, saying, I will prophesy unto thee of wine and of strong drink; he shall even be the prophet of this people."

It must be admitted by all students of the KJV that there is no article in the Hebrew before the word *ruach,* which may mean either spirit or wind. Christian interpreters long ago saw that wind, meaning talk without good sense, gives a better meaning. So the *Revised Version* of 1885 has: "If a man in wind and falsehood do lie, saying, I will prophesy unto thee of wine and strong drink..."

The words *of wine* do not say as much about the prophet's meaning as do the words *in favor of* which are in the *Tanakh.* The question must be posed and answered, which is correct, *of wine* or *in favor of wine.*

In this book the point has been made that some modern supporters of the idea that God approves of alcoholic beverages have been guilty of bad exegesis.

For example they have used Colossians 2:16-17 and 1 Timothy 4:1-5 to condemn Christian scholars who say all people should abstain totally on the basis of God's Word from the use of alcohol as a beverage.

These upholders of alcoholic drinks have committed a grave error in exegesis because they have not interpreted according to the context in which these passages are found. Colossians 2:16-17 is written in opposition to Judaizers in the Church who would seek to impose Jewish dietary laws on the early Gentile Christians as well as obsolete Jewish holy days. The passage must be interpreted in the light of what the Apostle Paul was teaching. This is only one of the absurdities that those who interpret out of context fall victim to.

I Timothy 4:1-5 is to be interpreted in the light of God's opposition to heretics of a *gnostic* type, or to heretics connected with the Therapeutae or even the Essenes. They were not Judaizers of any orthodox school of Jewish thought, for these adherents of Judaism never opposed marriage. We know nothing of what the cultists or heretics of I Timothy 4:1-5 taught about beverages; but we can be sure that this passage does not make valid a claim that it should be used to condemn a Christian who teaches that Proverbs 23:31 is a command to total abstinence. If the heretics were Judaizers of the Pharisaic school, we can be sure they did not require total abstinence from alcoholic beverages, since this distinctive does not appear to have been characteristic of any of this religious group.

Having shown the error of those who try to interpret the New Testament without regard to the context, let us return to Micah 2:11. Micah 2 is written in reference to God's irrevocable decision to expel the sinful people from the land. We might say that all the prophet means is that punishment is inevitable and prophecy of prosperity would be wind and deception. Thus, disregarding other considerations, wine and liquor might be morally neutral symbols of prosperity. The false prophet is guilty according to this interpretation of promising prosperity when it is not God's will for it to come.

But this interpretation fails, because the words wine and liquor are not used together in the Bible when God's kindness in granting material blessings is mentioned. *Milk and honey* (Exodus 3:17 and frequently elsewhere), *grain and new wine* (unfermented)

(Genesis 27:28), and *grain, new wine* (unfermented) *and oil* (Joel 2:19) are all used of God's blessing his people, but never the combination *wine and liquor (yayin* and *shekar).* By translating the particle *l* as *in favor of* the *Tanakh* translators have brought out the meaning in a more satisfactory way than earlier translators. The false prophet does not merely speak *of* wine and liquor he speaks *in favor of* these beverages. This shows that God is not merely displeased with deceitful men who give the people false hopes, but He is especially opposed to a false prophet who urges the people to dull their perceptions with the narcotic alcohol. Yet the people are so far gone in depravity that such a preacher is acceptable to them. The inference is inescapable that God holds in contempt preachers who preach in favor of alcoholic beverages even in normal times. To do so in times of immanent peril only makes their sin worse. The people who accept such teaching are also under condemnation.

Those who say the Bible teaches that alcohol may be used as a beverage if used in moderation can find no support in Micah 2:11. The false prophet here condemned may not have encouraged the most disgusting forms of intoxication. It was enough for him to receive God's condemnation as a deceiver that he spoke in favor of alcoholic wine and liquor. Christians and Old Testament believing Jews today should take notice of this.

Notes and Study Questions

Micah 2:11 is a passage which speaks against the people who accepted false prophets. The prophet in this passage speaks in favor of wine and liquor. Those who teach that the Bible allows moderate drinking of alcohol should take note of this verse and realize that they are speaking the same thing the false prophet was speaking.

Why should wine and liquor not be considered *morally neutral symbols of prosperity* in Micah 2:11? (p. 77)

How should the *l* preposition before the Hebrew word for wine be translated, *of wine* or *in favor of wine*? (pp. 77-78)

HABAKKUK CHAPTER 2 AND THE ALCOHOL PROBLEM

This chapter must be looked at on two levels. On one level it deals with the sins of the Chaldeans and the punishment they are to receive. On this level we see the Chaldeans as cruel conquerors who have subjugated and debauched many nations (verse 8) and who will themselves suffer *the violence of Lebanon* (verses 16 and 17).

On another level God calls us to contemplate the evils of drunkenness. These evils are in part veiled from Western eyes by being clothed in Hebrew idiom and only strike us with all their shocking force when, through seeking *the whole counsel of God,* we search the Scriptures and see what the idiom really means.

For example, in verse 15 the evil man is described as giving his neighbor drink in order to make him drunk and to *look on his nakedness.* Read in isolation this may be understood to refer to joy in the shame of the humiliated drunken people. According to this interpretation the conquerors were *voyeurs* meaning they took *an exaggerated interest in viewing sexual objects,* that is, the exposed genitals of their victims.

A Bible passage, however, should not be interpreted without examining other passages of Scripture to see if they throw light on the passage in question. We ought not to avoid taking note of the fact that elsewhere in the Bible the expression to *see the nakedness of a person* means to have illicit sexual intercourse, as scholars are generally agreed. For example, in Leviticus 20:17, 18 there is a consensus among scholars that the sin is illicit sexual intercourse and not *voyeurism.*

If the believer is filled with glowing ideas of the goodness of alcoholic wine derived from a false understanding of Psalm 104:15, he may recoil from even considering what Habakkuk 2:15 may mean.

Of course it is possible to take this verse in a literal sense, meaning that the wicked man after intoxicating his victim takes pleasure in the latter's shame when his nudity is exposed to ridicule.

If, however, in agreement with the idiom of Leviticus 20:17 we understand that the conqueror is a pervert who commits an act of sodomy on his victim, we see the degradation of the poor drunken victim in a more lurid light. The evil that alcohol can do is here exhibited in all its ugliness.

The punishments to come to the conqueror are described in verse 16. He too becomes drunk, his foreskin is uncovered,[1] and his glory is disgraced by shameful vomiting.

The words *shameful vomiting* which Jerome in translating the *Latin Vulgate* saw in verse 16 (*vomitus ignominiae*) need to be explained, because a number of modern translators make no reference to vomiting in this verse. Luther in his German translation found it there, and the KJV gives the same idea with the now little used word *spewing*. The question may be asked, why do certain modern versions omit it? *The New English Bible* in a footnote says the Hebrew is *unintelligible*.

It is not unintelligible, but to understand its full force a play on Hebrew words must be taken into account. Keil and Delitzsch explain it correctly:

> *We qiqalon*, and shameful vomiting, *sc. yihyeh* will be over thine honour, *i.e.* will destroy thee. The *hap. leg. qiqalon* is formed from the pilpal *qlql* from *qll*, and softened down from *qilqalon* and signifies extreme or the greatest contempt. This form of the word, however, is chosen for the sake of the play upon *qi'/qalon*, vomiting of shame...(cf. *qi'/so'ah* in Isa. 28:8) and in order that, when the word was heard, it should call up the subordinate meaning, which suggests itself the more naturally, because excessive drinking is followed by vomiting (cf. Jer. 25:26, 27).

Another problem concerning the inerrant original Hebrew of Habakkuk 2 is the word *chamatheka* in verse 15. Most translators derive it from *chemah* (heat, wrath, poison, venom). Thus the *Vulgate* has *fel* (poison), Luther has *grimm* (anger, fury, rage),

[1] This may mean that alcoholism makes of him an exhibitionist popularly called a *flasher*, defined as *male who briefly exposes genitals in public*.

American Revised Version and the *Jewish Publication Society of America* Version of 1917 have *venom,* and the *Jerusalem Bible* has *poison.*

Others derive it from *chemeth* (a small skin bottle). Thus the KJV has *bottle,* Segond's French version has *outre* (leather bottle), Martin's French version has *bouteille* (bottle) and the NIV has *wineskin.* If *bottle* is taken as the meaning of this word, the word preceding (*mesappeach*) is understood to mean *putting* and the idea of *to him,* that is, to the victim, must be supplied.

Keil and Delitzsch in a careful study of this word and its context explain it as meaning *burning wrath,* and give the sense of the two words *mesappeach chamatheka* as *mixing with thy burning wrath.* In view of the fact that alcoholic wine is called a poison in Deuteronomy 32:33, it is reasonable to agree with Keil and Delitzsch and Luther that *mesappeach* means mixing, and with the *Vulgate,* the *American Revised Version,* and the Jewish Version that *chamatheka* means thy *poison* or *venom.*

The first part of verse 15 therefore means: "Woe unto him who gives his neighbor drink, mixing thy poison and making him drunk..."

In support of this it seems apparent that mixing poison with a drink is a natural act whereas mixing wrath with it is a rather difficult metaphor. Against the translation *bottle* or *wineskin* the argument can be made that *mixing,* which goes with *poison,* is a more satisfactory rendering of *mesappeach* than is *putting,* which meaning is required if the translation *bottle* is used, that is: *putting thy bottle,* and supplying the words *to him* or *to his lips.* The idea of *giving a poison mixture* is a far more striking figure of speech than is *bottle.*

Notes and Study Questions

Habakkuk proclaims a woe against anyone who causes his neighbor to get drunk in order to look upon his nakedness (2:15). *Looking upon one's nakedness* may involve merely looking sexually upon or committing a sexual act upon the naked victim. Those who believe in moderate drinking should be concerned that their belief may lead them to being victimized in this way.

Why do some translations add the idea of vomiting to verse 16? (p. 80)

If the Hebrew word *chamatheka* means *your poison* in verse 15, what other verse can be used as proof that alcoholic drinks are poison? (p. 81)

PSALM 75:8 (Hebrew Verse 9) AND THE ALCOHOL PROBLEM

God speaking through the Psalmist says:

> In the hand of the LORD there is a cup, and the wine (*yayin*) is red (*chamar*); full of mixture, and he poureth out of the same: but the dregs thereof, all the wicked of the earth shall wring them out and drink them. (KJV).

The general meaning of the verse is clear, but some of the details are obscure because the sense of some of the words has become doubtful. This is because of the great amount of time which elapsed from the writing of the Psalm to that of its various translations.

The general meaning is that God is angry with the wicked people of the earth and will punish them. This idea is clothed in a vivid figure of speech about the LORD's hand, a cup, wine (*yayin*), a descriptive verb *chamar*, the mixture of something with the wine in *full* quantity, the pouring out of the wine, and drinking of the dregs by all the wicked of the earth.

Wine (*yayin*) is in the Bible sometimes condemned as evil and sometimes praised as useful to man. When it is a curse it is alcoholic as Proverbs 23 and other passages show. It is here a curse and although the *yayin* is a figure of speech and not a physical cup, we must understand that, to be in conformity with the rest of Scripture, this wine of cursing must be, although only in figurative language, alcoholic wine.

In our search of the deeper, less apparent, meaning of Scripture, we must try to find out if there is anything in the verse to indicate that this wine is alcoholic other than the fact that it is used by God to punish the wicked. The descriptive verb *chamar* is the key which may give the answer.

The problem is complicated by the fact that Biblical Hebrew had two roots, distinct as to meaning but both written *chamar*. One has the meaning, *it is red,* and the other *it foams.*

The Hebrew dictionary Brown-Driver-Briggs cites both meanings, but the writers on this word prefer *it foams* as the correct rendering in this passage, and the dictionary by Koehler and Baumgartner (a more modern work) agrees. The latter dictionary under *chamar it foams* says that the *pealal* stem of this root means *ferment*. The citation of this meaning is *chomarmaru* in Lamentations 1:20; 2:11.

While absolute proof may never be produced, it is not unreasonable to propose that there may be an underlying connection between *chamar* meaning *to be red* and *chomarmar to ferment,* derived from what is supposed to be the distinct root *chamar, to foam*. If so, it is only a step to say that *chamar* in Psalm 75:9 may mean *it is alcoholic,* for a liquid which ferments does in fact become alcoholic.

When the author of Proverbs 23:31 was inspired to put in a single word the idea of the common drink whose effects he vividly described (poisoning, producing hallucinations, confused thinking, nausea, insensitivity to pain and addiction) the word chosen, *yith'addam,* has an underlying connection with the idea of redness.

In the remote period of the history of the Hebrew language when both Psalms and Proverbs were written it may, without violence to any linguistic or logical law, be assumed that alcohol was associated with the idea of redness. The reasons for this have been stated elsewhere as far as *yith'addam* is concerned.

If we examine how translators have rendered the word *chamar* we can see that there has been no certainty. The writers of the *Septuagint,* the most ancient of translations, refuse to take the easy, most obvious rendering and have neither *it is red* nor *it foams*. The rendering they give *full of unmingled wine poured out*, is, however, not acceptable, nor is that of the *Vulgate* which is dependent on the *Septuagint*.

Luther's German and the KJV translate by giving the idea that *chamar* means, *it is red*. Many more recent versions give the idea that the meaning is that this wine foams—so, for example, the *New American Standard*, the *New Catholic Edition*, and the NIV. Bergman's Yiddish version gives the readers a choice in the text, not by way of a footnote, *it is red* (*or foams*).

When we observe that neither a red drink nor a foaming drink is necessarily noxious, a suitable means of punishing the wicked, the idea that *chamar* signifies neither *it is red* nor *it is foaming* but *it is alcoholic* comes to mind. God does not use words that do not press home the point. It is therefore proposed that *chamar* in Psalm 75:9 (8 in English) means *it is alcoholic*.

Furthermore, there is a word in Arabic, *khamr*, cognate to *chamar*, and cited by Koehler and Baumgartner, which means *fermented beverage*. (In determining the meaning of obscure words related meanings in cognate languages are useful aids, but are not usually decisive.)

The words *male mesek*, *full of mixture*, which follows *chamar* have been interpreted in different ways. This wine of wrath has not only been poisoned with alcohol but something has been added to it, a blend of something unnamed or a number of ingredients unnamed. From the general sense of the passage we may assume that this blend adds to the harmful effects of the beverage.

F. Delitzsch in the Keil and Delitzsch Commentary on this Psalm proposes that the blend is of wine mixed with water. Wine may in fact have frequently been mixed with water in antiquity, but this understanding would have the harmful effects of this cup diluted with what is harmless. It is more consistent with the idea of punishment that the blend is with something stronger and more deleterious than water. The *NIV* ventures to put in the text with no real scriptural or linguistic authority the word *spices*, thus *full of foaming wine mixed with spices*.

The same objection can be made to this as to the idea that the blend is with water. Spices do not make the drink more poisonous, but are intended to improve its taste. The NIV translators have not done well in paraphrasing rather than translating, as they add a word to the text which cannot be derived by linguistic laws from the original.

While I do not believe we should add to the text words which are not in the original, I do believe it is right to comment, and it is proper in studying the general force of what God is saying, to assume that the blend is of something very harmful to those who drink (of course we are dealing with figures of speech, but we must try to determine what was the force of the passage on the minds of the ancient people who first read it).

Although I know of no previous writer who has suggested it, I do not think it improper to propose that one of the ingredients may have been an extract of the plant known in the Hebrew Bible as *la'anah,* in English as *wormwood,* and in Latin (the botanical name) as *Artemesia absinthium.* The German word is *wermut.*

The plant was known to the ancient Hebrews of Bible times and is referred to in Jeremiah 23:15 where we read that the LORD in his wrath will make the (false) prophets eat *la'anah* (or wormwood). In modern times oil of wormwood is blended with alcohol in a drink called absinthe which attacks the higher nerve centres and causes excitation, giddiness, hallucinations, terrifying dreams and epilepsy. Those who drink it often become addicts, and the addiction is different from alcoholism.

In this same passage, Jeremiah 23:15, it is said that the LORD will make the false prophets drink what in Hebrew is call *me-ro'sh,* which may be translated *extract of the juice of the opium poppy.* To translate thus would not be a wild guess, but would be an educated deduction from known facts. The facts are that *me* is water in the construct state, and there is credible evidence that *ro'sh* in ancient Hebrew meant *papaver somniferum* or poppy producing opium.

It is true that scholars are not agreed as to this meaning in ancient Hebrew. Koehler-Baumgartner's dictionary is indefinite and says it is (*a not recognized*) *poisonous herb."*

The comprehensive Hebrew dictionary by Avraham Even-Shoshan *haMilon hehadash* does not come to a definite conclusion but does attempt to study the word in more depth than does Koehler-Baumgartner. The suggestions in this all Hebrew dictionary are that it may be the *Papaver* from which opium is taken or that it may be *citrullus colocynthis*.

As for these two possibilities, the general sense of Scripture is that *ro'sh* is a poison. Opium qualifies as a poison while on the other hand colocynths are not really poison, but are very bitter. C. F. Keil in his commentary on 2 Kings 4:39 says, "If eaten in large quantity, colocynths might really produce death."

From Job 20:16 we understand that *ro'sh* is a real poison, not something merely bitter which if taken in great quantity might possibly cause death. Therefore *papaver somniferum* is a more probable rendering of *ro'sh* than is *citrullus colocynthis*.

There is an interesting article by Peter T. White, *The Poppy* in the *National Geographic Magazine*, vol. 167, no. 2 (February, 1985), pp. 143-188. Mr. White after mentioning a possible reference to opium in Homer's Odyssey continues:

> There has even been speculation about the *vinegar mingled with gall* offered to Christ on the Cross (Matthew 27:34); the ancient Hebrew word for gall, *rosh*, means opium (p. 144).

The Reverend James Anderson in his footnotes to the translation of Calvin's Commentary on Psalm 75:8 (9) suggests in one note that the blend might have been with frankincense, and in another note he writes:

> In the East, wines are mixed with drugs of a stimulating[1] and intoxicating kind, so that commonly when drawn from the vessel in which they are preserved, they are strained for use. What remains is the thick sediment of the strong and stimulating ingredients with which they have been mixed.

The conclusion regarding the mixture of Psalm 75:8 (9) is that it may have been with the juice of the wormwood (absinthe) or with the juice of the opium poppy, or with both, or with neither of

---

[1] The word *stimulating* should not have been used.

these drugs. In any case it was a mixture of *yayin* with something harmful, and when the noxious beverage was poured out of the cup the dregs which the wicked must squeeze out and drink is a concentration of a poisonous liquid, a condign punishment for their sins.

We must be open to new suggestions as to the meaning of the whole passage. The ideas of redness or foaming do not add to the dreadful nature of the wine of cursing, but the idea of alcohol does. Therefore it is reasonable to translate *chamar* as *it is alcoholic*.

That Biblical Hebrew should have two words for the formation of alcohol in grape juice and that they should both be derived from words in some way connected with redness is not strange. The redness in the faces, noses and eyes of one who drinks this product is enough to suggest it.

When God wishes in figurative language to describe the punishment of the wicked he has us contemplate them drinking the dregs of a cup containing a concentration of poisons of which alcohol is one.

Notes and Study Questions

In this verse, wine is the symbol of God's punishment on the wicked. The Hebrew word *chamar* indicates that the wine of this passage is fermented. It can be translated *it is alcoholic*.

What are the two meanings usually given to *chamar*? (p. 83)

How can *chamar* in this verse help to explain the idea of redness in *yith-' addam* in Proverbs 23:31? (p. 83)

Why would the phrase *full of mixture* not indicate a mixing of the wine with water? (p. 84)

What substance is mixed with the wine of this passage? (p. 85)

THE HEBREW WORD *Chemer*

In the chapter *Psalm 75:8* (Hebrew verse 9) *and the Alcohol Problem* evidence has been presented that the verb *chamar* means *it is alcoholic.*

It is now the time to give evidence that the noun *chemer,* from the same root as the verb *chamar,* means *alcoholic drink* and in connection with the expression *blood of the grape,* it means *alcoholic wine.*

Many of the arguments previously presented to prove that *chamar* means *it is alcoholic,* may also serve to prove that the noun *chemer* means *alcoholic drink,* but some additional evidence should be presented.

In the first place it should be determined that the word *chemer* is used only once (Deut. 32:14) in the original form or autograph of the Hebrew Bible, according to ancient and modern interpreters. It is true that the Masoretic text has it also in Isaiah 27:2 but this is a scribal error, as the earliest translators read *chemed, pleasantness* here. The *Septuagint,* made before the Masoretic text became established, read *chemed,* and the *Targum,* the *Syriac* and the *Latin Vulgate* translations also show that their underlying text had *chemed* in this passage. Of modern translations the *New English Bible,* the N.I.V., and the *Tanakh* among others may be cited in support of this reading.

It is true that the KJV renders it *red wine,* but in view of the preponderant support of the understanding of *pleasantness* or *delight,* it is safe to say this was original. Thus Deuteronomy 32:14 is the only place *chemer* occurs.

A cognate word *chamar,* an Aramaic noun which occurs in the Aramaic sections of the Old Testament is not proof of what the Hebrew word *chemer* means. Linguistic science would not permit us to say that the same shades of meaning carry over from one language to another. To do so would be as incorrect as to say that because *chemise* in French is used of a man's shirt, the same is true of this word when carried over into English.

The Hebrew expression, where this once occurring noun is

found, Deuteronomy 32:14, has in it the expression *wedam-'enab tishteh chamer*. (*Chamer* is different from *chemer* only because of its position at the end of the expression.) This may be translated according to evidence here presented: And the blood of the grape thou shalt drink—alcoholic wine.

It is true that this translation may appear to be somewhat innovative. It is similar, however, to that of Keil and Delitzsch, a standard commentary. All I ask is that it not be rejected for the sole reason that it may appear innovative. Let all interpretations be examined and weighed in the balance of sound judgment.

Other renderings must be examined. The KJV has it: "And thou didst drink the pure blood of the grape." Comment: There is apparently no philological support for rendering *chemer* as *pure*. The *Septuagint* translates it simply as *oinon* (accusative of *oinos*). The *Vulgate* has *meracissimum* (most pure), but this is without philological evidence in Semitic linguistics to sustain such an understanding.

Keil and Delitzsch in their commentary rightly reject the reading *pure* and *most pure*. Their rendering is translated: "And grape blood thou drankest of fiery wine." Here we have the word *chemer* dealt with in more depth with regard to its philological background than in the earlier versions mentioned above. *Fiery* refers to the heat caused by alcohol as it goes into the mouth and throat.

Mention has been made in the Chapter on Psalm 75:8 of the verb *chomarmaru* in Lamentations 1:20, as meaning *ferment*. The context is that Jeremiah is speaking of his deep grief which was influencing his body (psychosomatic effect) by causing excessive fermentation (production of alcohol) in his intestines. This added physical distress to distress of soul. What is particularly interesting is that centuries before man could scientifically describe alcohol, or know by mere human knowledge that it can be formed in human intestines, God through the prophet Jeremiah spoke of such fermentation.[1]

---

[1] Modern science has determined what could not have been known in antiquity, that alcohol is normally present in all mammals, being produced in the intestinal

Incidentally, this section of Lamentations presents a hard problem to those who say that *yayin* in the Scriptures always means alcoholic wine. We read in verses 11 and 12 of chapter 2 that a baby and a suckling (*'olel* and *yoneq*) say to their mother, *where is corn and wine* (*yayin*). This is surely nonalcoholic wine, as we must not suppose that Israelite mothers had been in the habit of letting very young children have alcoholic wine so frequently that when they were starving one of the two things they asked for was this dangerous substance. What these unweaned children must have meant is what we now call grape juice, then called *yayin*. It may have been grape juice fresh from the press or perhaps it was a drink in which the yeast had been killed by heating. The corn (*dagan*) may have been *pabulum*, a soft cereal made for infants not fully weaned.

It is very significant that the last part of Deuteronomy 32:14, which should be treated as a sentence and not a clause, marks a transition in the section beginning with verse 7. In verses 8-14d Israel is spoken of in the third person and is described as receiving God's gracious blessings and nothing is said or implied about his abusing them. In verse 14e Israel is addressed in the second person and is said to drink what seems to be alcoholic wine. When the verb *chamar* is used of a drink in the Bible, the reference is to a cup of cursing (Psalm 75:9, English verse 8). The noun *chemer*, it is reasonable to infer, is not a drink of blessing. It is significant that in the next verse the reference to Israel (here called Jeshurun) changes. No longer is he treated as a blessed son, but is obese and rebellious, forsaking God and sacrificing to devils. The step by which Israel passed from the good state beginning with verse 7 to being fat and rebellious is, it appears, his drinking the *chemer*, or fiery, that is alcoholic, wine.

It is therefore proposed that the noun *chemer* used only once in the Hebrew Bible, means alcoholic wine, and is not a synonym of

---

tract. The source of this information is a United States Government report which in its totality cannot be recommended by this writer. This particular bit of information has the ring of truth about it. No doubt any scientist can find alcohol in the intestines of men and beasts which can be proved to have been produced in the intestines.

yayin which is neutral, meaning either alcoholic or alcohol free grape juice.

Notes and Study Questions

The Hebrew noun *chemer*, found in Deuteronomy 32:14, has the meaning *alcoholic drink*. The sectional divisions in this passage are important for understanding the statement of verse 14b. God's blessings upon Israel are expressed in the section containing verses 7-14a. Verse 14b, the phrase which reads, *You drank wine* (*chemer*), begins the following section dealing with Israel's rebellion. This can be observed by the change of pronouns. The previous section uses the third personal pronoun to refer to Israel. The latter section uses the second personal pronoun. The statement of verse 14b concerning drinking alcoholic substances is therefore part of Israel's rebellion against God by drinking alcoholic substances. It is not a statement of God's blessing upon Israel.

Why is it significant that a baby and suckling ask for corn and wine in Lamentation 2:11-12? (p. 90)

Is *chemer* a synonym of *yayin*? (pp. 90-91)

"FROM THE EARTH"–WHAT DOES THIS MEAN? (PSALM 104:14)

In the fourteenth and fifteenth verses of Psalm 104 we read of God:

> He makes grass to grow for the cattle, and plants for man to cultivate—bringing forth food from the earth: wine that gladdens the heart of man, oil to make his face shine, and bread that sustains his heart (NIV).

It is meaningful that in this passage the foods mentioned come from the earth. Bread comes from grain, *yayin* (translated wine) comes from grapes and oil in this context comes from olives. All these come from plants rooted in the earth. Yeast does not come from the earth in this sense. It may be air-borne. It lives by devouring substances which do come from the earth.

It is therefore reasonable to say that God is here speaking of bread and wine which have not been worked on by the micro-organisms we call yeast. This is not to say that leavened bread is ever forbidden for human consumption apart from liturgical usages. That alcoholic wine is forbidden is a doctrine derived from other passages of Scripture. From this passage the message is that what God gives with special regard to man's health and welfare comes from the earth, and not from life-forms which are not derived directly from the good earth.

The gladness derived from *yayin* is not such an emotion as is derived from a poison, and alcohol is a poison. This has been proved over and over again in various ways by true scientists.

Some may say that man becomes glad when his taste buds are treated to the most delectable substances. The most expensive wines, for example champagne, are delectable. It may be argued that as God gave us eyes to see with, He also gave us beautiful created works to look at, and it is to honor God to look at beauty and to taste what is delicious.

A delicious poison is one of the things a reasonable man might decide to deny himself, remembering that we are not only commanded to enjoy, but also to deny ourselves.

But perhaps we do not have to deny ourselves any thing that really tastes good.

A recent Associated Press news item (published on October 26, 1986) says:

> A Rhineland vintner says he has produced an alcohol-free wine that retains the bouquet, taste and color of famed Rheingau Riesling.[1]

---

[1] Note that the vintner calls his product wine. It is one of the fixed ideas of the *one-wine theorists* that wine is always alcoholic and that whatever is not alcoholic is not wine. This is false, and the vintner knows it and so ought every person with even a little learning.

Norbert Barth, the vintner, said he will market his alcohol-free 1985 Riesling in half-liter bottles 'with natural corks' starting in late October and November.

To create the white wine, Barth said in an interview, he hired a doctoral student in beverage technology, Monika Christmann.

She said previous brands of alcohol-free wine in West Germany involved a process of cooking the ethanol content out of the wine but that left a flattened, 'somewhat burned' taste.

Her process, she added, preserves the original flavor by straining the liquid through two connected cylinders under gradual, gentle heating to a maximum 104 degrees Fahrenheit.

Ms. Christmann said her procedure from a chemical standpoint resembles dialysis, the mechanical elimination of impurities from human blood in cases of kidney failure.

Barth said it was his personal experience that convinced him of a need for a good alcohol-free wine.

He explained that jaundice forced him to give up wine (i.e. alcoholic wine) and opened his eyes to a market of similar sufferers, as well as motorists worried about driving after drinking, and those who enjoy good wine but not alcohol, juice or mineral water.

Alcohol-free wine, in essence, is grape juice that has been fermented but then purged of the ethanol content accumulated in the fermenting process.

This wine is described as *dry, properly sour, fruity and robust.*

The purpose of putting this quotation and discussion of alcohol-free wine into a book on alcohol and the Bible is to show that those who say it is their good taste as highly civilized people which calls them to glorify God by treating their taste buds to the very best and most expensive of beverages, may, in fact be deceiving themselves.

When controlled testing can be arranged, it would be interesting to test them. Given a choice of this very tasty alcohol-free wine and an alcoholic wine with unsavory pollutions added, would not many Christians who claim they drink good wine to the glory of God, find themselves choosing the alcoholic wine in spite of its inferior taste ?[2]

Alcohol in wine is an additive, and is not a product of the earth. It comes rather from an air-borne microorganism, and is not commended in Psalm 104:14-15.

The alcohol-free wine which Christmann developed and which Barth will market may be similar to the wine without yeast which Luther saw in Isaiah 25:6. This yeastless wine God will give to all people in a great eschatological feast. God certainly would not want the slightest sign of alcohol induced intoxication on such a solemn occasion.

Notes and Study Questions

Psalm 104:15 is used by those who believe in moderate drinking to say that alcoholic wine is given by God to gladden the heart of man. The passage is speaking of food that comes from the earth, specifically *yayin* from grapes, bread from grains, and oil from olives. Since yeast does not come from the earth and yeast is necessary to make grape juice into alcoholic wine, the *yayin* which comes from the earth must be grape juice without yeast. Since the Bible says alcoholic wine is a poison, this verse must not be speaking of God giving a poison to gladden man's heart. Rather, grape juice gladdens the heart of man with its delicious taste.

What is the process used by Monika Christmann to remove alcohol from wine? (p. 93)

---

[2] In *A Severe Mercy* Sheldon Van Auken scorns *grape juice*, comparing it to false religion (p. 126). There are references to his drinking alcoholic beverages with his wife (pp. 48, 129). On one of these occasions they drank together for a considerable period (p. 98). His wife died of a liver ailment. He wrote, "we were only in our thirties and did not drink much" (p. 155). It is apparent that he knew her disease is frequently caused by alcohol, but he does not consider that her liver may have been especially sensitive to the poison of alcohol, and that he may have caused her death by encouraging her to drink this toxic substance.

TRAIN UP A CHILD IN THE WAY HE SHOULD GO... (PROVERBS 22:6)

It is a theory of child training, held by some who believe that it is a Christian liberty to drink alcoholic beverages, that children should be trained by experience in their moderate use under parental supervision. A minister of a well-known religious denomination expounded that theory to a group of his fellow ministers in my hearing. At the time I heard him I too believed that the moderate drinking of alcoholic beverages was a liberty God had graciously granted to mankind. I knew of course that we should train up a child in the way he should go, and if it is our goal to have communities of moderately drinking adults it seemed at first that a good way to begin would be with children. I say *at first*, for the Lord helped me to resist this fallacious argument, and I never accepted it nor practiced it.

I know that alcoholism is a very serious problem in countries where children at an early age are permitted to drink wine. A believer whose only rule of faith and practice is the Bible is not to be persuaded by practical considerations. If anyone speaks of the risk of addiction he will reply,

> I stand on the truth of God's Word, so help me, I can do no other. The Bible says that a man under certain conditions should buy wine and strong drink and should give a feast and invite, among others, the fatherless (presumably fatherless children) to come (Deut. 14:26-29).

Thus a believer will say,

> this establishes a principle. God is not pleased with austere total abstinence even in young people. Furthermore Christ instituted the Lord's Supper with alcoholic wine as one of its elements. Young persons who believe in Christ are commanded to partake in remembrance of Him, for He said, "This do in remembrance of me".

The argument could be advanced that if Christian children old enough to profess faith in Christ must drink a little alcoholic wine, it follows that all children of that age should be initiated into the use of alcohol in moderation. But before discussing children in general, a few words are appropriate to show how deeply the idea of alcohol in communion has become a part of the thinking of some Bible believing Christians.

A Christian minister whose credentials are excellent wrote me recently that a professor of theology *of blessed memory* under whom we both studied, "on being asked if he would go to a certain church to conduct the communion service inquired if fermented wine was the custom there. On learning that it was not, he declined. He would only officiate where fermented wine was in use."

This minister in the same letter reported that one of his predecessors as pastor of the church he is serving,

> was at a Christian Endeavor meeting in the church where a...person questioned the propriety of this church serving fermented wine. He scared the person or persons intimating that *their* idea was virtual blasphemy.

This evangelical professor and this evangelical pastor should have been asked, "On whose authority do you insist that alcoholic wine should be used in the communion service?" If they say that it is on the authority of the Bible, they should be asked to demonstrate it. Alas, too many of those who believe that alcohol is forbidden are unable to refute the shallow thinking of the *one-wine theorists*. In the case of the Lord's Supper there is not even any Biblical reference to wine or to anything suggestive of alcohol.

Christians who use the Bible the way these advocates of alcohol in communion did will find it difficult to say anything against a bill recently passed by the Pennsylvania Senate.[1] This bill would *allow the sale of candy with an alcoholic content of 6 percent...* The bill was opposed by a legislator, George E. Saurman, who said, "Let us not put something as harmful as alcohol potentially is into something that we encourage for our children."

> But supporters of the measure said the arguments against the candy were ridiculous. One of them argued: "This is not a complicated issue. This is a jobs vote. (Candy) is the last place

[1] Don Wolf, *Montgomery County Intelligencer*, May 12, 1986, p. 9.

in the world where a young person would look to find alcohol. I suspect teen-agers will do what they have done in the past and spend $1.50 on a quart of beer long before they will spend $150 on candy."

"He would die of obesity before he would contract alcoholism," agreed one colleague.

Proponents of the bill ridiculed those who did not wish to see children tempted with alcoholic candy, one even going so far as to say he thinks a certain opponent *eats too many Hershey bars.*

So the bill passed. We also now have a major ice cream manufacturer selling alcoholic ice cream.

Of course the answer to this ridicule is that the liquor interests aren't seeking to get young persons drunk, but rather to induce those who won't drink beer or wine to learn not to resist the taste of alcohol when they find it in candy. Once that first barrier has been passed the rest will be easy, or so they hope.

The proper way to bring up a child with regard to the alcohol problem is to tell him the truth, that is, God said not to look at wine when it has made itself alcoholic (Proverbs 23). If we tell him to drink a little alcohol now so he will learn moderation, we can't succeed because we are disobeying God. If we tell him, "abstain now, but when you are of age to drink, then drink in moderation," we are not telling him the truth as God has revealed it. Total abstinence from alcoholic beverages is the true wisdom for young and old. If it is foolish in the eyes of the worldly wise, "hath not God made foolish the wisdom of this world?" (1 Cor. 1:20).

It is probable that many of those who wish to have children drink a little alcohol would agree with those who deplore putting cocaine in small quantities in bubble gum to give or sell to children.[2] The purpose is not to make them *high,* but to familiarize

[2] This is actually practiced according to what appears to be good authority. It has been exposed and commented on by a person shocked by it, who held up a sample of the tainted bubble gum on television.

Similar in evil to bubble gum contaminated with opium are wine coolers intended to trap young people into the alcohol habit. This practice has attracted the attention of a New York state senator who has introduced a bill to limit wine cooler sales in grocery stores after some respondents to a survey in *Weekly*

the children with the use of the drug. It is the same in principle with those who give alcohol to children.

Notes and Study Questions

Those who believe in moderate drinking believe they should train their children in the use of alcohol. They do this by supervising their use. Alcoholism is a major problem in countries that allow the drinking of alcohol at a young age. Rather, parents should teach their children not to even look at the wine according to Proverbs 23.

What is the purpose of those who seek to sell candy and ice cream with alcohol in them? (pp. 97-98)

PROVERBS 31:4-5, REVELATION 1:6, AND MELCHIZEDEK

An advocate of the one-wine theory who writes in favor of the idea that moderate drinking of alcohol is a Christian liberty, has proposed that Proverbs 31:4 is intended to prohibit magistrates

---

Reader, the well known classroom newspaper, said many of their peers had tried some coolers. Those surveyed were in the fourth, fifth and sixth grades.

While people who should know better, or if they know better should react more responsibly, take this lightly, the fact is that it is a deliberate attempt to get the young habituated to alcohol. The editor of the *Montgomery County Record* (a reputable newspaper) in an editorial of May 1, 1988 wrote: "Because some brands could pass for soda pop in taste, they pose a particular hazard for inexperienced drinkers. The manufacturers of these products are merely interested in selling them...Drinking wine coolers is not all fun and games...The dark side can be drunken driving, alcoholism and maybe shattered lives."

The editor writes the truth. For money, sordid people introduce the very young of our country to what may eventually destroy them while the law and public are indifferent.

from drinking alcoholic beverages only *while engaging in affairs of state.*[1]

The passage is:

> It is not for kings, O Lemuel, it is not for kings to drink wine; nor for princes strong drink (*shekar*): Lest they drink and forget the law, and pervert the judgment of any of the afflicted (KJV).

This one-wine theorist seems to suppose that alcohol does not permanently affect the memory and moral judgment of those who use it regularly, even though this use be in what is commonly called moderation.

We have the approval of this interpreter, of kings (and by extension other magistrates) presuming to judge others with brains that have become permanently damaged by alcohol. The damage may come about by drinking this dangerous drug never to the point of drunkenness. With damaged memory of the law and sound legal precedents and with loss of high standards of ethics they issue judgments which are an abomination to God. They may truly say, I have never been drunk in my life, and I have not touched a drop of alcohol while hearing this case, yet they are an offense to public justice and sinners in the eyes of God. But according to this one-wine theorist they have done nothing amiss.

The facts about permanent brain damage in drinkers of alcohol even though they have never been drunk are found elsewhere in this book, *The Biblical Approach to Alcohol*. This information is based on CAT scans in which the gradual and permanent destruction of brain cells in regular but *moderate* drinkers can be observed. Readers are invited and encouraged to study scholarly literature on the subject. A short bibliography is given in this book and is obtainable elsewhere. Of course it is not found in the type of literature favored by *one-wine theorists* who advocate what they call *moderation*. The medical authorities they seem to prefer may be subsidized by the liquor industry. We must always keep in mind that those who make money in selling liquor have vast sums

---

[1] Kenneth L. Gentry, The Christian and Alcoholic Beverages, 24, 58.

at their disposal and can use a small part of it to trap people into drinking without feeling any pinch. Advocates of Biblical prohibition have no such source of funds.

This one-wine theorist goes on to argue that the prohibition of Proverbs 31:4-5 must not be a total prohibition because "wine is not forbidden to kings totally and universally (cf. Gen. 14:18-20)."

The Genesis passage cited tells how "Melchizedek, king of Salem, brought forth bread and wine and he was the priest of the most high God" (KJV).

Of course Proverbs 31:4-5 had not been written in the days of Melchizedek and neither had Leviticus 10:9-10 so he was not bound by these commands for kings and for priests to drink no alcoholic wine, which after they were written were binding on kings at all times and for priests before officiating in their sacred office. Melchizedek might have availed himself of this tacit permission, but there is good reason to believe he did not.

One reason is that this offering of bread and wine is generally believed to be a type of the bread and wine at the Last Supper. The Last Supper is the Christian Lord's Supper and is called by the Apostle Paul our (that is, the Christians') Passover (1 Cor. 5:7-8). Therefore, arguing from the antitype, the Lord's Supper which Paul says is to be kept with unleavened *elements* (*azumois*)—not merely with unleavened bread—back to the type, Melchizedek's offering of bread and wine to Abraham, we may logically conclude that the one as well as the other were free from all kinds of yeast, the Biblical symbol of evil.

Another argument that Melchizedek's wine was alcohol-free is that according to such outstanding scholars as Moses Stuart and Lyman Abbott wine as a beverage and libation is always alcohol-free. Even if Melchizedek, living as he did before Leviticus and Proverbs were written was permitted to use alcoholic wine, God who was overseeing the sacred meeting of Melchizedek with Abraham (then known as Abram) would not have permitted the use of this poisonous drug in a type of the Lord's Supper.

After the book of Proverbs was written the prohibition of drinking *yayin ki yith'addam* became total and universal (Prov.

23:31). Kings were included in this, but as the danger to others if magistrates drink alcohol is very great, the prohibition was made specifically with regard to them.

In this connection it has been argued by one of the one-wine theorists that Christ was not required to obey Leviticus 10:9 because this law belonged to the Old Testament ceremonial code from which Christ freed people of the New Covenant, and from which He himself was free. The answer to this is that while the law against offering sacrifices while drunk may have been ceremonial, it also had its moral aspects and the moral law is not relaxed in the New Testament. Proverbs 23:31 and 31:4-5 are moral laws.

If I, or any advocate of the view that there are two kinds of wine in Scripture, ever said that alcoholic wine is always regarded as bad, the statement should be withdrawn. It may be used medicinally but not as a beverage. One medical use of alcohol is the pouring on of wine (alcoholic as the context shows) by the Samaritan on the wounds of a victim of thieves (Luke 10). This illustrates what some one-wine theorists are loath to admit, that is, that alcohol is a poison. It is a poison to the germs that cause infections in a wound, and therefore it was good that the Samaritan had it to use as an antiseptic. It is a poison to habitual users. This is a fact confirmed by investigators in early times and recently. They show that death may occur suddenly or after many hours of deep coma. If this is not a poison, what is it? The findings of medical science are more and more proving that even moderate use is injurious to health, for example to the heart and to the brain. Those who say otherwise are either working from out of date information or are perhaps prejudiced in favor of liquor and the liquor industry.

If one is a one-wine theorist and believes Christ drank wine with alcoholic content to the quantity required in Talmudic times, he ought to answer the following questions. How long do you think that Old Testament priests were required to abstain from alcohol before going into the tabernacle? Even if you believe Christ was not bound by this prohibition, do you think Jesus had abstained long enough after the Lord's Supper so that all of the toxic effects of the alcohol would have disappeared from his body before He made the great expiatory sacrifice? (Remember that the four cups required in Talmudic and later tradition are not the tiny vessels used in some Protestant churches.) A Jewish rabbi whom I knew told me that Jews of his acquaintance felt that they had not celebrated the Passover correctly unless they got a little drunk.

Although it is assumed that you believe, as I do, that our Lord Jesus Christ was altogether without sin, do you believe that his human body could and did suffer hunger, thirst and other physical pain? Do you believe that a poison if introduced into his body would act on it as it would on other men? Do you think that the toxic effect of the alcohol could have affected Him in any way during his trial?

I and others who believe He drank only unfermented wine are certain there was no alcohol in Him when He offered his sinless body as a sacrifice for our sins, but one-wine theorists should answer these questions frankly. If they propose that He was not at all affected by the alcohol they are saying that his body was not really a human body like ours. If they say He was slightly but not greatly affected, they would be suggesting that his sufferings were at least to some extent diminished by the narcotic in the alcohol. Either of these possible answers would be offensive to Christian doctrine. In Christian orthodoxy his body is altogether human and his sufferings were infinite.

Those who believe that Christ and the Apostles drank alcoholic wine at the Last Supper base their idea on rabbinical tradition as it is known to have existed in later centuries. This tradition required four full cups to be taken by each participant and it also records the ill effects of the substance on one rabbi. Those who think the apostles drank four full cups should answer the question as to whether or not their behavior in the hours following this supper was in any way influenced by this powerful drug. What about the Apostle Peter's behavior? What if a group of secularists were drinking together and one of them a short time later had disobeyed his leader by sleeping when commanded to stay awake, had impetuously cut off a man's ear, and had shortly after denied he knew his leader? If charged with striking a man with a deadly weapon could he not claim in a modern court diminished responsibility as a mitigating circumstance?

Those of us who believe Christ and the Apostles drank no alcohol at the time they celebrated a Seder feast followed by the first Lord's Supper have no problem with regard to the fore-mentioned questions. The human body of Christ was unaffected by any drug. His mind as a human being was clear and his body was capable of the utmost suffering. The apostles, especially Peter, sinned after the Supper, but their sins are to be attributed to their fallen human nature and not to alcohol. Those who think they did drink an alcoholic substance ought to search their hearts deeply to see if their reasons for thinking they drank alcohol are arrived at by sound reasoning, or on the other hand are the result of what is called wishful thinking.

Notes and Study Questions

Proverbs 31:4-5 teaches kings not to drink alcohol. Some would understand this command to apply only when the king was doing his duties of government, but since alcohol has permanent effects on memory and moral judgment, the time when the king might drink alcohol is not the issue. He must not drink it at all.

Melchizedek is used by one-wine theorists as an example of a king who drank wine, because he brought it to Abram. His offering of bread and wine are a type of the elements of the Lord's Supper. According to 1 Corinthians 5:7-8, these elements are to be without leaven, and the wine, therefore, could not be alcoholic.

Christ's duties as priest and His sacrifice of Himself demonstrate that the wine of the Lord's Supper must not be alcoholic. Leviticus 10:9 commands priests not to drink any alcohol when they go to the Tabernacle. In obedience to this, Christ, the High Priest, would not have prepared to offer His sacrifice to God having drunk alcoholic wine at the supper with His disciples. The alcohol would have also numbed His body to the pains of the cross. Since Christ had to experience the full agony of the cross as the perfect sacrifice, it is unacceptable to think that He drank alcohol at this meal.

According to rabbinic tradition, how many cups were to be drunk at the Passover meal? (p. 102) Why is this significant for Christ's priestly duty and the sacrifice He offered? (p. 102)

PROVERBS 31:4-5 AND THE DOCTRINE THAT CHRISTIAN BELIEVERS ARE KINGS AND PRIESTS

In this passage we read:

> It is not for kings, O Lemuel, it is not for kings to drink wine; nor for princes strong drink: Lest they drink and forget the law, and pervert the judgment of any of the afflicted (KJV).

The wine (*yayin*) and *shekar* (for these are two words in the original) are here obviously alcoholic. Those who take them are troubled with bad memories and low ethical standards. Many suppose that memory and judgment are not affected until a user of alcoholic beverages becomes *drunk* according to whatever standards the judicial system of a particular jurisdiction says is the definition of drunkenness. In lectures to military personnel those persons (usually chaplains) who are assigned this task of instruction are required to tell their hearers that slower physical reflexes result from the intake of an astonishingly small amount of alcohol. This means that people drive with impaired capacity to react quickly to an emergency long before they could be convicted of drunkenness in any court.

It is reasonable to suppose that a king (or judge) who is not drunk, but has retarded reflexes due to drinking would not be as adequate a dispenser of justice as one who is totally sober. Therefore kings should not drink alcoholic beverages even in moderation.

When we turn to Revelation 1:6 in the *Textus Receptus* and the early translations we learn that we (that is ordinary Christian believers) are *kings and priests*. It follows, if we accept this reading, that all Bible believers must be abstainers, since what was required of kings in the Old Testament is required of kings under the New.

It may be argued, in opposition to this interpretation, that the *Textus Receptus* and the KJV are wrong and that we are a *kingdom* and not *kings*. We must evaluate this argument according to the way we consider God preserved the Bible as He wanted the people to have it over the centuries. If we decide that we are not called *kings* in Revelation 1:6, we nevertheless know that citizens today, by the power of voting, have some of the authority of kings. If ancient kings were warned not to drink intoxicants lest they forget the law, modern believers who wish to keep God's law in their heart, should accept this prohibition as binding on themselves.

Notes and Study Questions

Proverbs 31:4-5 instructs kings not to drink *yayin* or *shekar*. These two drinks are evidently alcoholic drinks as they impair the memory and judgment of the king. Because all believers are declared to be kings and priests according to Revelation 1:6, this prohibition in Proverbs 31 applies to all believers.

PROVERBS 31:6-7 AND THE ALCOHOL PROBLEM

We read in this passage:

> Give *shekar* unto him that is ready to perish, and *yayin* unto those who are bitter of soul. Let him drink and forget his poverty, and remember his misery no more.

The words *shekar* and *yayin* may be narcotics, that is alcoholic drugs. They may also be nonalcoholic, as has been demonstrated in this paper. When these drinks are commended as beverages we have sought to demonstrate that they are nonalcoholic.

Here, however, they appear to be alcoholic and are commended, but not as a beverage which one takes for pleasure. Many readers may understand it so, but incorrectly. According to one interpretation, the word *'obed* (perishing). should be taken literally and in its grimmest sense. It is not as when a person says lightly, "I am dying of thirst. I must have a beer." No. We are here dealing with the case of one dying in agony, as by crucifixion. This fact is noted in the Talmud, Sanhedrin 43a where it is said:

> Rab Chisda has said, "To him who went forth to be executed there was given a little frankincense mixed with wine to deprive him of consciousness."

Heinrich Seesemann relates this passage to Mark 15:23 and Matthew 27:34.[1] Charitable persons, knowing the agony of death by crucifixion customarily gave this narcotic to those being crucified, and Christ was offered this means of forgetting His misery. He refused it, because it was necessary that He suffer the utmost agony in atonement for the sins of the redeemed. Had He not been the redeeming Savior He could have taken it. This may be what Proverbs 31:6-7 means. One about to die in extreme agony may take a narcotic. These verses do not say that one whose pains are not agonizing may drown his sorrows in drink. The passage says for others to give the sufferer his narcotic, not that he is to get it himself. This suggests that in modern times such drugs should only be given to a sufferer on the orders of a qualified physician.

It is to be noted that Christ refused the *oinos* mingled with myrrh (a narcotic) as we are told in these passages, but when He was offered vinegar (*oxos*), a non-intoxicant, He received it. This was almost immediately before His sacrificial death (John 19:29).

There is another explanation of Proverbs 31:6-7 which is a possible alternative to the one given above. It is that the words *shekar* and *oinos* are used in these verses as the nonalcoholic variety of these beverages. If *bitter of soul* and *poverty* are to be understood as something less severe than the extreme agony and loss of normal support systems associated with crucifixion or

---

[1] Friedrich's *Theological Dictionary of the New Testament*, vol. 5, article *Oinos*.

equally painful deaths, it must be that these words do *not* designate a narcotic.

We know that if we see a person suffering from what we (or our social planners) ordinarily call poverty (is it one having less than $15,000, or $30,000 a year with a family?) the worst thing we can do for him is to ply him with liquor that he may *forget his poverty*.

If anyone says that God would not put an enigma before us by using *shekar* and *oinos* in two different senses so close together as verses 4 and 5 (where they are alcoholic) and 6 and 7 (where they are just possibly nonalcoholic), the answer is found in Proverbs 26:4-5, where *kesil* is used in two different senses of a person who lacks wisdom. We are supposed to get the idea that we ought not to jump to any conclusions as to what a word means in a particular passage. Search the whole Bible to find the whole counsel of God. God may place these enigmas in the Bible here and there to make believers search diligently. The Bible is inerrant, but it may have little pitfalls for the people who are trying to justify their own self-indulgence—also for the people who take the first meaning that occurs to them or is suggested to them, and who will not consider any others.

God does not tempt to evil, but He does test people as to the strength of their faith. He tested (tempted in the KJV) Abraham as we read in Genesis 22:1-19. Job was severely tested with God's permission.

These heroes of the faith passed their tests, but others failed. The leaders of first century Judaism failed because they had not searched the Scriptures enough with minds attuned to the Holy Spirit, and did not recognize the fact that Jesus of Nazareth fulfilled the prophecies concerning the long promised Messiah. God could have made the test easier for them by giving His Son signs of His being the Messiah that even those most blinded by man-made traditions could easily have recognized. But He did not.

In the same way He may have left the teaching concerning the command to total abstinence somewhat obscure as a test to determine who among those who profess to believe in Him would discern His true meaning. Some, understanding that alcoholic beverages are a Christian liberty, overindulge themselves to the point of total ruin; others become soft and flabby in their Christian warfare; others who are teachers of religion mar their record by giving the people who follow them bad instruction. In the end God accomplishes His purpose of sorting wheat from chaff, and in grading how much each servant has made from his *talent*, or *talents*.

Christ spoke of His parables (which were enigmas to many) when He answered the question of His disciples why He spoke in parables.

> And he answered and said unto them, Unto you (his immediate disciples) it is given to know the mysteries of the kingdom of heaven, but to them it is not given, For whosoever hath, to him shall be given, and he shall have abundance; but whosoever hath not, from him shall be taken away even that which he hath. Therefore I speak to them in parables: because seeing they see not, and hearing they hear not, neither do they understand (Matt. 13:10-14, ARV).

Notes and Study Questions

This passage teaches that *yayin* and *shekar* should be given to those who are ready to die. This passage may be teaching compassion to those who are in a situation where death is inevitable, and the alcoholic drink will numb them to the pain. An example of this is Jesus Christ being offered a narcotic to diminish His pain while He hung on the cross. He refused the drink because He needed to suffer the full agony of the cross on His people's behalf. Another explanation of Proverbs 31:6-7 is that *yayin* and *shekar* are nonalcoholic drinks. In this explanation, the king gives financial support to those who are about to die in their poverty, or, if taken more literally, he gives these drinks intended to give one final joy to the dying, poor man.

Does it make sense to understand Proverbs 31:6-7 as instructing kings to give alcoholic drinks to those who are financially poor so that they can forget their poverty? (p. 107)

THE WEDDING AT CANA

As for the wedding feast at Cana described in John 2:1-11, it is clear that Christ was righteously indignant at His mother for her suggestion in verse 3 that He do something about the wedding party's running out of wine. He said to her, "Woman, what have I to do with thee?" An expression which is only used elsewhere in the Bible in cases of very severe reproof and rejection. (See 2 Sam. 19:22; Judges 11:12; Matt. 8:29; Luke 4:34; 8:28.) Scholars who try to make it seem mild have no support from Biblical usage.[1] Why did He use such strong language? He would not have been indignant at a kindly intended but sinless error of His mother because she requested a miracle which He knew would have been untimely. Rather we must understand that the stern words were brought forth by the circumstances which our Lord observed. People at the wedding party were already intoxicated. The governor of the feast so indicated when, in expressing astonishment at the offering of the good wine last, he indicated that this was after *they* (the wedding party) had become drunk (*methusthosin*). There is little to support the idea that this is not said in reference to the wedding party, or that it does not mean that they were intoxicated.

The situation appears to have been as follows: The wedding party had been indulging in wine which may have been cheap and of inferior taste made perhaps partly from diseased grapes, and having a high alcoholic content. The people were to some extent drunk and were behaving in a manner which moved to righteous indignation our Lord who was and is absolutely and totally pure of mind and body. His mother's sorrow that the party had run out of that sort of wine and her implied suggestion that He provide more of the same caused Him in righteous sorrow to speak stern words to her which have much puzzled Bible commentators.

---

[1] The Hebrew original, as in Judges 11:12, means, "What do you have against us?" (So NIV). In Luke 4:34 the same expression is used by demons in addressing Christ. They feared He would destroy them.

He would not have blamed her for not knowing that His hour had not yet come if by this expression He meant the time for performing His first miracle. The reason for His indignation must be sought elsewhere. His time had not yet come (and never would come) to create an intoxicant, but the time *had* come, as He immediately demonstrated, to perform His first miracle. With this event, as Ernest Gordon wrote: "The new era had now come with its New Covenant, the good wine."[2]

The nonintoxicating drink which our Lord created was recognized by the governor of the feast, who because of his responsibilities had surely not become drunk, as the best wine (grape juice), seeming to have come from the very best grapes. He therefore said to the bridegroom, "you have kept the good wine until now." This he said as a connoisseur of choice vintage without regard to alcoholic content. It may be true that the drunken members of the wedding party would miss the alcoholic beverage which their depraved tastes probably craved, but it was nevertheless the best wine they had tasted that day. It may be that Christ miraculously healed their bodies of a craving for alcohol.

The foregoing explanation makes understandable Christ's indignation at His own mother, who, as we know, although blessed among women, could sin, and make poor judgments on moral matters. It also explains how He could make a great quantity of *oinos* for people who were described as already intoxicated, and how He could say, "My hour is not yet come," and proceed to act immediately in what has commonly been supposed to be the fulfillment of Mary's wish.

It is to be observed that some, even of those who believe Christ did not create an intoxicant, resist the idea that there was drunkenness at the wedding. From the expressions used in modern English translations it might be understood that the wedding party had drunk enough to remove some of their thirst, but were still sober and were behaving decorously. The Greek word *methuo* does not allow such an interpretation. Liddel and Scott's highly respected Greek English Lexicon says it means *to be*

---

[2] Gordon, *Christ, the Apostles, and Wine*, p. 14.

drunken, and when used metaphorically of persons it means *to be intoxicated with passion,* or *to be stupefied, stunned.*

In Matthew 24:49 it is used literally, *to be drunken;* in Revelation 17:6 it is used metaphorically. In no passage in the Bible or out of it does it mean to have quenched the thirst while remaining sober.[3]

We need not assume that Christ lingered for a while at the party after observing the condition of those present. He had probably arrived late and a quick glance was enough for Him to make the decision to reject His mother's request. We need not assume that Mary was really complacent at drunkenness. She too probably had arrived late. Nevertheless, Christ's words to her are sharply critical. He seems to have felt that she had made a serious error when she spoke to Him as she did.

Notes and Study Questions

At the wedding feast at Cana, Jesus Christ scolded His mother because she wanted Him to make alcoholic wine. Instead of wine, He made nonalcoholic grape juice. This drink was praised by the governor of the feast, not for being a better quality wine, but a better quality drink and tastier than the previous beverage.

What did Christ mean that His hour had not yet come? (p. 110)

Can *methuo* in this passage mean *to drink fully* rather than *to be drunk*? (p. 110-111)

---

[3] Only wishful thinking, a strong desire to preserve the reputation of Joseph and his brothers, would have led people to try to give the impression they were sober in Gen 43:34, where in the Hebrew a form of *shakar* is used, and in the Septuagint a form of *methuo*. These words are the standard words for *to be drunk*, not for *to be merry*.

Of course we cannot tell how far their intoxication went, but there is a great probability they could not have passed a modern breathalyzer test. Yet many translators in most recent times conceal the force of the word in the original. Not so the great scholar Jerome—*inebriati sunt*, he wrote. The forthright truth teller Luther translated *sie wurden trunken*. Modern translators tend to cast a veil over the state of the celebrants at this family reunion. It should be kept in mind that there was no Biblical rule against inebriation at the time Joseph revealed himself to his brothers.

A GLUTTONOUS MAN AND A WINE BIBBER!

Some see in the words of Jesus Christ as recorded in Matthew 11:19 and Luke 7:34 where He says of Himself, "The Son of man came eating and drinking," an assertion that He drank alcoholic beverages. He did in fact assert that He ate and drank, but of course He intended all His hearers to understand that He was not a glutton or a drunkard. By saying He came drinking it is not necessary to understand that He was asserting that He drank alcoholic beverages even in moderation. He was pointing out the difference between John the Baptist and Himself. John was a Nazarite from his mother's womb. This is the way we must understand Luke 1:15 where we are told that he should neither drink *oinos* or *sikera*. (*Sikera* is the Greek representation of the Hebrew *shekar*.) The Nazarite was prohibited from drinking *yayin* or *shekar*, or *chomets yayin* (*vinegar of yayin*), or *chomets shekar* (*vinegar of shekar*), "nor shall he drink any beverage of grapes, nor eat moist grapes, or dried" (Numbers 6:1-4).

In view of these restriction under which John lived, Christ might have intended to set Himself apart from John in that He drank and ate nonalcoholic products of the grape, whereas John, who did not, was considered by the enemies of both John and Christ to be demon possessed. Christ ate grapes and raisins while John did not. There is no reason to infer from these passages that Christ drank intoxicants. The point Christ was making was that the enemies used whatever occurred to them to slander the great forerunner of the Messiah and the Messiah Himself.

Notes and Study Questions

Jesus Christ was accused of being a glutton and a drunkard because He ate and drank. Such drinking does not imply the drinking of alcohol. Jesus compares his slandered reputation to John's who neither ate nor drank, but was considered demon-possessed. John obviously ate and drank some food and drink to sustain his life, but He was a Nazarite, restricted from all products of the grape. He did not enjoy the fine foods and drinks of society, such as grapes and grape juice. He maintained a diet of eating locusts and honey which is the intended meaning of John's not eating or drinking. In comparison to John, Jesus did not restrict Himself from the fine foods and drinks of society, but neither did He partake of alcoholic drinks in obedience to God's law (Proverbs 23:31).

What New Testament passage teaches that John the Baptist was a Nazarite? (p. 112)

NEW WINE IN NEW BOTTLES

Jesus said,

> and no one puts new wine into old wine skins; else the new wine will burst the wine skins and be spilled, and the bottles shall perish. But new wine must be put into new wine skins; and both preserved (Luke 5:37-38; cf. Mark 2:22).

The passage can best be explained if it is understood that the new wine (*neos oinos*) is grape juice specially prepared not to ferment before being poured into the skins. Wine skins, either new or old, were not suitable for the fermentation process for, as Alexander Balmain Bruce pertinently asks, *could even new, tough skins stand the process of fermentation?* He suggests that Jesus was not thinking at all of fermented intoxicating wine, but of *must*, a nonintoxicating beverage, which could be kept safely in new leather bottles, but not in old skins, which had previously contained ordinary wine,[1] because particles of albuminoidal

[1] Concerning the making of wine, a modern authority (*Nelson...Encyclopedia*, New York 1905, vol. 12, p. 605) says: "The wine is not 'bottle ripe' till after about two years or more..." Certainly the ancients did not put any grape juice they intended to have ferment into such a fragile container as an animal skin. Grape juice which they intended to keep unfermented as *neos oinos* they heated to kill the yeast, after which it could be poured into new skins without danger of fermentation and consequent breaking of the skins.

matter adhering to the skin would set up fermentation and develop gas with an enormous pressure.[2]

Notes and Study Questions

The new wine which is put in wine skins is a nonalcoholic drink. If this drink were put into old wineskins, fermentation would begin and cause both the wineskin and the drink to be wasted. Unfermented wine must be put into new wineskins so that the fermentation process will not begin and both will be preserved.

Can either old or new wineskins endure the fermentation process? (p. 113)

WHO SAID, "THE OLD (WINE) IS BETTER" AND WHY?

Luke 5:39 is a passage which some say teaches that Christ accepted as correct the idea that old wine (that in which the fermentation process had been allowed to run its course) was better than new (*neos*—that which is fresh from the press). This is not true, but before dealing with the correct exegesis, we must examine a question of textual criticism. The verse reads in the *Textus Receptus* followed by the KJV and others: "No man also having drunk old wine straightway desireth new; for he saith, The old is better." Textual critics, having examined ancient manuscripts thought to be of the best quality have for the most part agreed that the word *eutheōs* (immediately or straightway) was not in the original or autograph manuscript. This reading without *immediately* is strongly attested. So the NIV reads: "And no one after drinking old wine wants the new, for he says, 'The

---

[2] Exposition of Luke 5:37-8 in *The Expositor's Greek Testament*, New York, 1897, p. 500.

old is better.'"

Read out of context the passage seems to put Christ's stamp of approval on this preference for old wine, but if studied in its context it is seen in an entirely different light.

Christ is thinking of those who cling to the old misleading traditions of the Pharisees. No one who has drunk deeply of these wishes to drink of the pure Gospel of Jesus Christ, here called, by a figure of speech, *neos* (*oinos*) or new (wine). If the word *immediately* was in the original manuscript, the sense would be to emphasize that the initial impact of the Gospel on those deeply committed to Pharisaism is negative. If *immediately* was not in the original it would still remain true that some such word as *immediately* would have to be understood with regard to Pharisaism and Gospel truth, for a genuine convert, such as the Apostle Paul, has no longing for his old religion, but says the new is better. But with regard to old and new wine, the omission of *immediately* suggests the fact that no one who has drunk repeatedly of alcoholic beverages probably ever has as great delight in pure unfermented grape juice as does a man who has always been a total abstainer. This teaches us that we should not risk corrupting our bodies so that their cells cry out for an addictive poison. Regeneration does great things, but what we do to our bodies probably remains with them until the resurrection. If by reason of sinful drunken driving we lose an arm, regeneration does not give it back.

As noted above some writers have understood that Christ was speaking in support of the idea that old wine is better than new. This is inconsistent with the fact that just previously He had used the same word (*palaios*) of old garments, which He obviously did not mean were better than new ones. These writers are at a loss to understand the connection of this saying, which they are forced to understand has something to do with a comparison of the teaching of the Pharisees, or perhaps of that of John the Baptist, with that of Christ. None seem bold enough to suggest that Christ was calling His teaching *old*, and that of the Pharisees *new*.

Dr. Seesemann, in *The Theological Dictionary of the New*

Testament,[1] gives a proper view of the passage when he writes: "Luke 5:39 seems to contradict what goes before, since it favors the retention of the old. In the context of Luke, however, it is regarded as a warning against over-estimation of the old."

This is true. Christ warns against over-estimation of Pharisaism (old wine), but the figure of speech carries with it more than the thought that the Gospel should be regarded more highly than Pharisaism. It also strongly suggests that to those who are perceptive of truth, new wine (unfermented grape juice) is preferable to old (intoxicating) wine. Only the natural man with corrupted taste thinks otherwise.

On the textual critical problem of whether we should read *the old is good* or *the old is better,* it appears that on the basis of what are called the *best* manuscripts the word *good* has better attestation than the word *better*. The Bible Society Greek text of 1966[2] had *good,* but the NIV, which usually tends to follow this Greek text and others like it, here has *better*. The NIV translators may have felt that, although *good* has better ancient support, they ought to paraphrase with *better* to have a more natural meaning. But Christ was speaking of people so devoted to an old and false religion that they would not even taste the new. "They found it good (*chrēstos*), so good that they did not even wish to taste any other, and could therefore make no comparisons. (Hence *chrēstos* is preferable to *chrēstoteros*...)"[3] Alcohol lovers in the same way do not even taste grape juice in an unfermented state. They say what they like is *good,* and ignore what they don't like.

Notes and Study Questions

Luke 5:39 is used by some who believe in moderate drinking to argue that Christ considered old, fermented wine to be better than

---

[1] Heinrich Seesemann in the Article *Oinos*. vol. 5, p. 163. Gerhard Friedrich, Editor.

[2] *The Greek Testament*, Edited by Kurt Aland, Matthew Black, Bruce M. Metzger, Allen Wikgran, American Bible Society, 1966.

[3] Alexander Balmain Bruce in *The Expositor's Greek Testament*, vol. 1, p. 500.

new, unfermented grape juice. In the context of Luke 5, that which is old refers to the teaching of the Pharisees. So Christ's statement in verse 39 does not reflect His preference for the old, fermented wine of the Pharisees. This is the preference of the people who rejected Christ. It is the new, unfermented grape juice of Christ's teaching which should be preferred.

Would those who drink alcohol prefer wine or grape juice? Is this a good preference? (p. 116)

DRUNKENNESS, INTOXICATION AND "FEELING NO PAIN"

The Bible does not define drunkenness, intoxication, or that condition sometimes called *feeling no pain*. The last named condition is a kind of euphoria that comes from having inhibitions released and physical aches and pains relieved by the narcotic effects of alcohol. This condition is believed by a certain *one-wine theorist* to be a blessing God graciously gives to humanity plagued by inhibitions which keep them from enjoying themselves exuberantly. This he thinks is the state of the virgins of Zechariah 9:17. They were euphoric because of the alcohol supposedly in the *tirosh*.

If we grant the thesis that *yayin* and *tirosh* are always intoxicants when mentioned in the Bible it is hard to refute the idea that a so called euphoria or *feeling no pain* induced by alcohol is not sinful. If any say that *yayin* is always alcoholic but *tirosh* may not be, it would still be hard to refute it.

When alcoholic wine first appears in the Bible there is no doubt that it caused drunkenness. No one doubts that Noah was drunk. Yet God did not choose to legislate against alcoholic wine at this time. He did, in the days of Moses, legislate against priests taking alcohol before ministering at the altar, and He also legislated about a Nazirite total abstinence vow which He did not, however, require everyone to take.

When centuries later He caused Proverbs 23:31 and 31:4-5 to be written in the Bible, He spoke clearly, but the *one-wine theorists* explain away the unambiguous words of God.

If we accept for the sake of the argument that euphoria induced by taking alcohol is pleasing to God, but that drunkenness (loss of self-control) is not, the *one-wine theorists* ought to tell us precisely from Biblical texts where the line should be drawn.

The need is so great that the lack of such a line of distinction has led one holder of the one-wine theory to slander me. In fact the slander is so serious that it and other things he wrote about me and published in a book leave me no choice but to approach him according to Matthew 18:15-17.

The occasion for this particular slander is the wedding at Cana (John 2:1-11). I had written that I understand the passage to mean that Jesus spoke severely to his mother because she suggested that He make more of the same kind of wine which had made the wedding party drunk. From this the theorist sees me as doing damage to the honor of the mother of our Lord. He writes: "Reynolds's interpretation implicates Mary in a grossly sinful tolerance of radically evil conduct."

If anyone believes that, my reputation as a Christian scholar is utterly destroyed in his eyes. Therefore, not only to save what I can of my reputation, but also to gain my brother, I must, as far as God enables me, do all I can to fulfill Matthew 18:15-17.

The slander arises because he assumes that the manner in which the people were behaving as seen by me was what a normal person, Christian or non-Christian, would call *radically evil conduct.* I never said or implied that.

The master of the feast, according to the most natural reading of the text, said that those for whom the miraculous wine was created were drunk (*methusthōsin*). We do not know what his test was for determining when people passed from being euphoric to being drunk. Of course, he was not inspired. Mary may have come late (as I suggested) and may only have seen part of what was going on. What she saw may have led her to suppose that the people were only being happy in an innocent way. Christ had a better judgment. There were other occasions in which He did not agree with her, but never did He or any right thinking Christian implicate Mary in grossly sinful tolerance of radically evil conduct.

This theorist goes on to suggest that my interpretation puts Christ in a bad light. He writes:

> Why is there no rebuke for those who were drunk? Or for the governor of the feast? Why did Jesus do any thing at all to assist them at their riotous party? Why did he stay around until the wine ran out!

I believe it was because Mary was closer to Jesus than were the others that He rebuked her and not them. She ought to have learned from his teachings more of the difference between right and wrong. The master of the feast, the wedding party, Mary and Jesus may all have had different ideas as to when a party ceases to be an innocently happy one and becomes something else. I do not say nor did I imply that any but our sinless Lord has any judgment of ultimate value. Perhaps if we had been there the one-wine theorist and I would have had differences of opinion as to the signs of sinful drunkenness which I believe our Lord saw and Mary did not. I believe Jesus arrived late and did not stay around while the people were passing the line from sobriety to the beginnings of drunkenness. The nonalcoholic wine Jesus made did not contribute to any intoxication they may have had, and the party, I believe, never reached a stage of being *riotous*.

Since we can never be sure that what we think of as a Christian liberty may not be regarded as sinful in the judgment of Christ, we ought not to take any intoxicating drug—alcohol, cocaine, opium, marijuana, or whatever, for pleasure, relaxation or sociability. We know God condemns drunkenness, which is intoxication. How can we be sure when the amount of any toxic substance we may take into our bodies may become sinful in his holy eyes? At least one of them, alcohol, is, I have attempted to prove, to be avoided to the extent of not being looked at lustfully.

In a well developed discussion of intoxication more needs to be said about intoxication by other drugs besides alcohol. This is particularly important because a remark by G. I. Williamson may open to the naïve a path to what they may assume to be a moderate use of these drugs.

Williamson wrote (and this has been quoted before but should be repeated in this context):

> To treat wine as the cause of sin—in any way shape or form—is to deny the real teaching of Scripture concerning the depravity of man. It is, in effect, to say that there is a fault in the handiwork of God.

In answer to this we should take notice of the fact that the Bible is not specific about forbidding the use of opium (perhaps it is *ro'sh* in Hebrew) or absinthe (Hebrew *la'anah*). It is presumed that cocaine was unknown to the people to whom the Bible was revealed as it comes from a handiwork of God found in the New World. Coca leaves are chewed to their hurt by the Indians of South America. The coca leaves are more directly a handiwork of God than are alcoholic beverages which would not exist without human hands. What would a missionary of Mr. Williamson's school of thought say to an Indian who wished to receive permission to continue chewing coca leaves? He would be required to say that this is a Christian liberty if used in moderation. I submit that this would not be a good answer and for the reason set forth below.

If a Christian goes to a party where marijuana is being smoked (let us say for the sake of the argument that it is legal to smoke it) what should his attitude be? Should he continue in happy attendance until he sees an act or hears a remark which his own conscience tells him is sinful? Maybe his conscience is not sensitive enough to please God. When the Scriptures are not explicit about a particular substance that intoxicates we should apply *the light of nature and Christian prudence.* We should apply *thou shalt not kill,* because all of these drugs, including alcohol, tend to kill their users and others.

It is a quibble unworthy of being advanced as a serious argument to point out that alcohol occurs in nature without human hands. An opponent has written:

> Reynolds is a case in point: "Fermented beverages would

not occur without man's entering into the process. (Man must press the grapes before the yeast turns the grape sugar into alcohol.)" Again there arises the uneasy feeling that evidence is being virtually created ex nihilo in order to *prove* a point.

In the first place it is not scientifically accurate. The authoritative Encyclopedia of Alcohol notes that "fermentation can occur naturally, with airborne yeasts converting any sugary mash into ethyl alcohol and carbon dioxide."

It is to be hoped that every candid reader will observe that I am falsely accused of having been scientifically inaccurate. I said fermented *beverages* would not occur in nature, not that alcohol itself would not occur in sugary substances left lying around. These are not beverages. Grape juice in an unfermented state is a human product. It is a beverage and if it ferments without the intention of its owners it becomes an alcoholic beverage, but it cannot be said that the end product comes into being without human hands.

Alcohol is even made by fermentation in the human intestines. This has no bearing on the question of alcohol drinking, but it does contribute support to the idea that alcohol may have been called *red* or associated with redness in Biblical Hebrew. This is because of Lamentations 1:20 and 2:11 where a literally sound translation of *chomarmeru me'ai* is *my bowels ferment*. This term for *to ferment* is related to a word for *red*. Along with other evidence this is presented to show that *yayin ki yith'addam* in Proverbs 23:31 does not mean *wine when it is red,* but rather *wine when it is alcoholic*. God of course knew all the time what modern science has at last discovered, that human bowels do ferment and produce alcohol, but not in sufficient quantity to intoxicate.

However, it cannot be too strongly emphasized that this fermentation has nothing to do with alcoholic beverages.

Notes and Study Questions

The *one-wine theorists* believe a distinction needs to be made between drunkenness and euphoria. Euphoria is the effect of alcohol on the body to remove inhibitions and pain. Drunkenness is the loss of self-control which drinking too much alcohol brings to the body. According to such theorists, euphoria is a gift of God and is not sinful. Drunkenness is an abuse of God's gift and sinful. The Bible does not make such a fine distinction. Rather, Proverbs 23:31 and 31:4-5 restrict all drinking of alcohol, whether to the degree of euphoria or drunkenness.

When the Bible does not speak specifically against a harmful drug, which of the Ten Commandments can be cited as a basis for not using that drug? (p. 120)

THE LORD'S SUPPER

It is frequently argued that Christ commanded alcoholic wine to be used at the Last Supper. An editor of the *Church Times* (Anglican) is quoted as saying: "Communions with unfermented liquor may be deeply edifying feasts of fellowship, but they are not Christian Eucharists."[1]

On the contrary, the Gospels and other New Testament references to the Communion (or Eucharist) carefully avoid all use of the word *oinos* (commonly thought to denote an alcoholic beverage) when speaking of the liquid element used at the Communion service. The words used are the *cup* (Matt. 26:27 et al.) and the *fruit of the vine* (Matt. 26:29). Presumably because the word *oinos* might suggest to some an intoxicant, Christ preferred to use other terms less suggestive of alcohol. In fact, the words *fruit of the vine* really exclude alcohol, as the latter substance is but the excrement of yeast and is therefore not the fruit of the vine. The excrement of no living organism is *fruit*.

Although the question of alcohol is not involved, by using the words *fruit of the vine*, Christ excluded from valid communion all but the fruit of the grape. Any fruit growing on bushes or trees does not qualify, as also does not water, which the Mormons use. Distressing as it is to report, this writer knows of one congregation

[1] Quoted by Ernest Gordon in *Christ, the Apostles and Wine*, p. 28.

of Protestant believers where a drink containing only ten per cent grape juice was used in a communion service.[2]

Christ did not say that He would drink no more of the fruit of the vine until He would drink it *again* (*palin*) with his disciples in the Kingdom of His Father. He was not implying that in the Kingdom to come He would once more drink precisely the same liquid as He had just drunk with them. No, He will drink something new (*kainos*) which will nevertheless still be called properly *the fruit of the vine*. We must notice that He did not use the word *neos*, normally used for new in the sense of fresh, as *neos oinos*, new wine, a term used repeatedly in the Bible. Rather He used the word *kainos*, which means *new* in the sense of something not previously present. This is the word for new used in the expression *a new heaven and a new earth* (2 Peter 3:13; Rev. 21:1). Christ is here indicating that the fruit of the vine from which He will drink in the eternal kingdom of His Father will be from a new kind of fruit entirely. This suggests that as all nature became corrupted by the Fall of Adam, and therefore subject to decay, the fruit of the kingdom yet to be inaugurated will have fruit of a new kind, not ever subject to fermentation. The liquid beverage prepared in this new earth will not merely be *neos* (new in the

---

[2] This was a commercially prepared drink going by the name of *Hi-C*. When the product of the vine properly advertised as being grape juice is available, the use of this greatly diluted substitute is cause for concern. Commercially available grape juice, advertised and sold as such, admittedly has a small amount of additives *to maintain flavor and freshness*. If any Christians are concerned that these additives make the product no longer essentially *the fruit of the vine*, they may of course make their own. What they make can be preserved without additives for a considerable period of time.

As a Naval Chaplain in a course of special training at what was called *Chaplains School*, I was advised to use alcoholic wine in Communion on the ground that it was easier to keep during long voyages than it was to keep unfermented grape juice. I now perceive that this instruction was intended to persuade those who formerly used grape juice to use alcoholic wine, rather than because of any genuine concern about the difficulty of keeping nonalcoholic grape juice. I now believe it to have been the result of false ecumenism, designed to lead all who profess Christianity to the same ill-advised practices. This, I believe, was a step toward the one great ecumenical unorthodox church which some see predicted in Matthew 24:24, and elsewhere in the Bible. To preserve nonalcoholic grape juice for long periods of time is not particularly difficult if there is a will to do it.

sense of fresh, unfermented) but *kainos* (new in the sense of a kind of grape juice previously unknown, and unfermentable).

Readers who accept this exegesis may say: "Yes, but this does not tell us that the drink at the Last Supper was *neos oinos;* Christ merely said that the beverage He will drink with His disciples in the coming kingdom will be a new (*kainos*) kind of beverage." True, but in the following paragraphs we shall attempt to prove that the drink at the Last Supper was *neos oinos* (unfermented grape juice) and not *palaios oinos* (old, or fermented grape juice).

It is sometimes argued that as Christ had been participating in the Feast of the Passover at the time He instituted the Lord's Supper, the beverage He used must have been an intoxicant. This is not at all convincing, for there is reason to believe that the produce of the micro-organisms collectively known as yeast was removed from the homes of all truly perceptive observers of God's revealed truth when they prepared to celebrate this divinely established feast. It is proper to assume that these, unless they were influenced by man-made tradition, understood what the inerrant Bible was saying when it commended the removal of all *se'or* (leaven or yeast) and also the product of yeast after it had been allowed to work for a time on another substance.

Modern Jews understand that the product of leaven working on dough or on liquors made from grain (e.g. whiskey) is *hames* (more commonly transliterated *chamets*). All *se'or* and *chamets* was to be removed from the homes of all those obedient to God's law (Ex. 12:15-19). A modern Jewish Rabbi[3] had advised me that modern Jews make a distinction between ferment, which is permitted at Passover, and leaven, which is not. By this distinction he says that alcoholic beverages made from grain are prohibited and those made from substances other than grain are permitted. Thus alcoholic wine is permitted and also vodka when made from potatoes. Rum which is made from molasses would also be allowed. In the *Encyclopedia Judaica* in the article *Passover*, we read:

---

[3] Rabbi Aaron Landes of Congregation Beth Sholom in Elkins Park, Pa., a scholar whose learning and character are to be respected highly by people of all faiths. Before giving his final answer he consulted an authority on Judaism whom he considered even more learned.

"Lithuanian Jews, even the ultra-orthodox, eat a fermented beet soup, called *risel borsht*."

The distinction between *leaven*, said to exist only in products made from grains (bread or liquor) and *ferment* said to exist in other substances (wine, soup, vodka when made from potatoes and rum} is a distinction which appears to be difficult to sustain from the Hebrew of the Old Testament. The alcohol, the end result of this leavening or fermentation (whichever we call it), is the same in either case, and has the same effects on the human body and mind.

As modern Jews consider alcoholic drinks made from grain to be *chamets*, their rule is that it be kept out of sight during the Passover season. *Chamets*, however, need not be removed from the homes of Jews according to current rules, but must be locked up and the key given to a non-Jew. This non-Jew is stated in a written contract to be the owner of the *chamets* (grain liquor, breakfast cereal, etc.) and he must sell it back to the Jews at the end of the Passover season. As can be seen by anyone trained in the ethics and method of Bible interpretation taught by Christ, this scarcely conforms to the Old Testament requirement that there should be no *leaven* or *thing leavened found in your houses*. Since what is really a fictitious avoidance of the rule concerning what is *in your houses* has been resorted to, it is not at all unreasonable for Christians to consider this a man-made tradition similar to the ones Jesus condemned (Mark 7:1-13). Since over the centuries Jews have developed traditions to make it possible for them to keep the letter of the Law and avoid what the Holy Spirit teaches, we do not wrong them if we propose that they have erred in permitting the alcoholic drink made from grapes, commonly known as wine, to be used at Passover. Christians should avoid traditions of men and seek to penetrate the deep meaning of God's truth. What was He really telling ancient Israel and what does He mean the new Israel to understand?

It is important to point out that although modern Jews do not consider alcoholic wine to be *chamets* as intended in Exodus 12:15-19, their scholars do not agree with the Anglicans previously mentioned, or with certain Reformed scholars whose ideas will be discussed later, that alcohol is of the essence of sacramental wine. For example, the *Encyclopedia Judaica*[4] says that a *responsum* by the Talmudic scholar Louis Ginzburg permitted *grape juice* to be used for religious purposes *instead of wine*.[5]

An important Bible allusion to the Passover is found in 1 Corinthians 5:7-8 where we read:

> Purge out therefore the old leaven, that ye may be a new lump, as ye are unleavened. For even Christ our Passover is sacrificed for us: therefore let us keep the feast, not with the old leaven, neither with the leaven of malice and wickedness; but with the unleavened (plural, i.e. unleavened elements) of sincerity and truth.

The shift from the old leaven (singular) to unleavened (plural) denotes the plurality of the elements used at the Passover which figuratively speaking represent sincerity and truth. The old leaven (not used in the Passover) represents malice and wickedness.

The English versions have for the most part ignored the fact that the word unleavened (*azumois*) is plural, and have translated it *unleavened bread*. Some do so without any indication that the

---

[4] Article, *Wine and the Liquor Trade*, vol. 16, p. 546, column 2. This responsum was made because in the period when the United States Constitution prohibited the manufacture and sale of alcoholic beverages, an exception was made of such beverages when needed for religious purposes. "Abuses of this privilege by some Jews to supply the illegal liquor market disturbed U.S. Jewry." This is the reason for the responsum, but, although the article does not say so, it would seem that alcoholic Jews may take advantage of this permission. Jews who wish to take no alcohol for any reason should do so also.

[5] A brief statement concerning the ancient Jewish community of Cochin in India may be significant concerning the use of wine in the time of Christ. This is to be found in *Apostle of Sight* by Dorothy Clarke Wilson, a biography of the distinguished medical missionary Dr. Victor Rambo. On page 196 we are told that the official of a synagogue at Cochin gave Dr. Rambo two bottles of sacramental wine, saying they were *absolutely without alcohol*. Dr. Rambo tasted the wine and was convinced.

The community is known to date from no later than A.D. 1020 (see *Encyclopedia Judaica*, article Cochin). Some think it may be much older. It is possible that the origin of their tradition goes back to Judea in the first century, and may be a purer tradition than the one which favors the use of alcoholic wine. Further study is needed.

word *bread* is not in the original, e.g. Tyndale, the Great Bible, the Geneva Bible, the *American Standard Version*, and the NIV. The Bishop's Bible and the KJV put bread in italics (thereby indicating that it is not in the original, but there is in them no indication that *azumois* is plural. The *Latin Vulgate* speaks of *fermento malitiae et nequitiae*, the fermented *substance* of malice and wickedness. It also speaks of the *azymis sinceritatis et veritatis*, the unleavened (or unfermented) elements (dative plural) of sincerity and truth. The *Vulgate* is here closer to the original Greek, not only in putting the word *unleavened* in the plural, but in indicating that unleavened is the opposite of fermented. Nevertheless not many, if any, modern users of the *Vulgate* or the original Greek came to the conclusion (which seems rather obvious) that all ferment should be excluded from the Christian sacrament which replaces the Jewish Passover.[6] It seems clear that Paul is saying that we Christians should keep our Christian Passover (the Lord's Supper) with unleavened (unfermented things, that is, elements), representing sincerity and truth. They also, of course, represent the body and blood of the Lord Jesus Christ. The blood of the Lord certainly had no poison in it.

Christ who instituted the Lord's Supper was the great High Priest soon to offer the one great sacrifice for human sin upon the cross. Old Testament priests were forbidden to drink alcoholic beverages before sacrificing at the altar (Lev. 10:8-11). In view of this fact, and for other reasons as well it is impossible to believe that our Lord would go to the most holy and solemn sacrifice of which the Old Testament sacrifices were merely a prefiguration with the effects of what is popularly called an alcoholic *hang-over*

[6] Jerome, who called alcoholic wine a poison and taught that Christians should avoid it (that is, abstain from it), must have realized that there was a great inconsistency in permitting it to be used in the Lord's Supper. We may reasonably assume that in early times when Christ's practice and unrecorded sayings were known, the early Church celebrated the Lord's Supper with unfermented wine. In later times the Roman Catholic Church permitted alcoholic wine, then considered it the general practice, but never absolutely prohibited the use of unfermented grape juice. Those who believe alcohol is essential to communion can appeal neither to valid tradition over the centuries, nor to valid Bible exegesis.

still lingering in His body. For if alcoholic wine were used and if the Jewish extra-Biblical requirement of four cups were consumed, the effects would not have been negligible even on the God-man, whose human body was subject to human weakness.

Among such Jews (poorly taught we believe) who in ancient times took alcoholic wine at Passover, the problem of the ill effects of the four cups on some who participated in the feast did not go unobserved. It was noted in the Talmud that a certain Rabbi Judah had great difficulty with the four cups of alcoholic wine which he felt obligated to drink. In Nedarim 49b we read,

> ...a certain matron said to R. Judah, 'a teacher and a drunkard!' He replied, 'you may well believe me that I taste (no wine) but that of Kiddush and Habdalah and the four cups of Passover, on account of which I have to bind my temples from Passover until Pentecost'.

Rabbi Judah lived after the time of Christ, and his belief that he had to drink four cups of alcoholic wine at Passover is not proof of what Christ believed and practiced. Nor is it proof of what the majority of religious Jews of Christ's time did.

Incidentally, one might get the impression from the *Encyclopedia Judaica* that R. Judah's only problem was tipsy behavior, for it says that *his capacity was severely tested by the four seder cups.*[7] Although the matron's words seem to suggest unedifying conduct, it appears from what Judah replied that he was especially allergic to the toxic effects of alcohol, and suffered cruelly and for a long time from alcohol induced headaches. He was the victim of being a disciple of Jewish tradition, but another (and better) interpretation is that alcohol is *chamets*, and not only might, but should be avoided at Passover. This interpretation is based on the nature of alcohol as the product of yeast, and on the severe denunciation of alcoholic beverages found in different places in the Bible.

Dr. Johannes Vos and Dr. G. I. Williamson, two Reformed (Calvinistic) scholars, say Christians who are especially weak in their capacity to take alcohol should nevertheless drink it at

---

[7] Article "*Wine*," Vol. 16, p. 539, Col. 1.

communion, since it is a command of God to do so. Dr. Vos says they should depend on divine grace to help them resist the ill effects of the drug. He says of Christians who use nonalcoholic fruit of the vine at the Lord's Supper and cite the danger of even a little alcohol on alcoholics:

> They fail to take the power of the Holy Spirit into their reckoning. What the Church should do, in dealing with such persons, is not to educate them in falsehood—by making them think there is more power in a little wine than there is in the Third Person of the God-head. No, it should teach them the truth. The truth is that there is not—and never was—any destructive power inherent in wine...So, radical though it may seem to many in the Christian Church today, the best interests of the converted alcoholic are served by having wine in the communion service.[8]

Dr. Vos is misled by the fact that material things do not have the capacity to sin and hence are not in themselves morally evil. Yet the Scripture has many passages proving without a doubt that alcoholic beverages are conducive to evil. This being the case, and since no Biblical passage says that Christians are to drink alcoholic wine at communion, there is no reason why he should tell modern Christians to do so.

Roman Catholics, whose teachings may sometimes possibly be useful to Protestants in understanding genuine apostolic tradition, may have something to teach in rebuttal to the opinions of Drs. Vos and Williamson. It is significant that the Roman Catholics, who ordinarily use alcoholic wine in their mass, nevertheless do not consider alcohol to be essential to sacramental wine. They relish it for its taste, but do not go as far as those Anglicans and Calvinists who say it is a requirement. Unfermented grape juice may, they say, be used when fermented wine is not available, or when priests who have become alcoholics celebrate the mass and fear that the altar wine, if alcoholic, will create havoc in their lives.

The *New Catholic Encyclopedia*, article, *Wine*, in the Section,

---

[8] Vos, *The Separated Life*, pp. 25-27. Quoted by Williamson, *Wine in the Bible and the Church*, p. 25.

Requirements,[9] says:

> For Mass, Canon Law (CIC c 815 2) requires that "the wine must be natural wine of the grape and not corrupted." Where fresh grapes are unobtainable, altar wine may be made from dried grapes or raisins, but not from any other fruit. The wine may be either red or white. Since the 16th century, when the use of the purificator became common, white wine has been more often used because it leaves fewer traces on the linen.
>
> Altar wine is not valid material for Mass if a notable part (more than a third) has become vinegar, or if added substances make up a notable part of it; such wine would be corrupted or not natural. Altar wine which has begun to turn to vinegar or to which significant additions have been made is illicit; it may be used only in an emergency.
>
> However, in the production of altar wine, especially sweet altar wine, the Holy Office (Act S sed 29 (1896-97) 317-319) has permitted the addition of alcohol distilled from grape wine if this is done before the completion of fermentation. The maximum alcoholic content for licit sweet altar wine is 18 per cent; for licit dry altar wine to which alcohol has been added, 12 percent; for valid altar wine 21 per cent. The alcohol added should be of a high concentration so that the addition does not approach one-third of the final mixture.
>
> For grape juice low in sugar, raisins or grape brandy should be used to make the wine stable and palatable. High acidity in grape juice should be reduced by a very small amount of basic salts or ions rather than by dilution with considerable water. The very small amounts of water or chemicals picked up by the wine during normal wine processing do not prevent the wine from being both licit and valid.

Readers of the above quotation are requested to notice that, while Roman Catholic authority is precise as to the upper limit of alcohol permitted in valid sacramental wine, no minimum is set. It follows, therefore, that totally nonalcoholic grape juice is valid and permitted (licit).

[9] Vol. 14, p. 959, column 1. The article is by M.R.P. McGuire and T. D. Terry.

The statement about alcoholic priests is based on a printed response by higher Roman Catholic authority to one such priest who requested information as to whether he could use unfermented grape juice. He was told that he could, but that he should prepare it himself. This requirement is somewhat difficult, and is therefore a deterrent to the use of unfermented grape juice by priests, but at least the permission was granted.

Whether all alcoholic priests take advantage of this permission is not the point in referring to it here. The point is that authorities in this religious body granted a permission concerning the beverage to be used in the sacrament which Drs. Vos and Williamson would not allow to Reformed Christians. These Calvinists scholars are, of course, under no obligation to follow Roman Catholic (or Jewish) examples, but should people who feel the way they do not examine themselves to see if their views are really Biblical? They should search their hearts to see if they have not overreacted to the total abstinence movement by rejecting the idea that it is a Christian liberty to use unfermented grape juice in communion.

Since Drs. Johannes Vos and G. I. Williamson say that it is gravely wrong to use other than fermented wine in the Lord's Supper, and since they do not say in their books that *fortified* or *brandied* wines are to be excluded, or that there is any limit to the percentage of alcohol in a valid mixture, we must suppose that some followers of Vos and Williamson may use a brandied wine. They may even use a mixture with a higher percentage of alcoholic content than the 21 percent which the Roman Catholics set as the upper limit. It is even possible that these highly regarded Calvinistic scholars are themselves of the opinion that no limit should be placed on the amount of this toxic substance which may be put in communion wine, since it is, according to some Reformed teaching, a *good thing*, given to make *glad the heart of man*, which God has given us *richly to enjoy*.

This conclusion would be a reasonable one if we beg a number of questions and assume without proof that the *cup*, also called *the fruit of the vine*, referred to as the liquid element of the first Lord's Supper was essentially an alcoholic drink. Then, if we assume without proof that what makes glad the heart of man in Psalm 104:15 is the alcoholic content supposed to be in the *yayin*, we can argue that the more alcohol in communion wine the better, as long as it is derived from grape brandy.

Logically, in accepting this position, it would be perfectly reasonable to use *only* grape brandy in the Lord's Supper, and not to use ordinary, naturally fermented, wine at all. Men may argue with consistency that brandywine (brandy) is in fact wine, and that this settles the question.

Some people may be led to assume that in communion and in secular social occasions, or even in solitude, alcoholic beverages make men's hearts glad. This assumption does not agree with facts; so it must be rejected. It is well known that alcohol releases inhibitions; so that people behave in unusual manners when restraints which normally control their behavior are removed. Some people who are naturally morose reveal their real temperament with only a little intake of alcohol. They do not go through a phase of being *merry*. Even those who are boisterous and ribald have no genuine gladness.

Unfermented grape juice, on the other hand, puts pure grape sugar into the blood stream and makes people glad in a healthy way. The yeast which produces alcohol in grape juice destroys the healthful grape sugar. Alcohol does *not* make glad the heart of man; it only makes him foolish, perhaps foolishly rowdy or foolishly angry, but never full of genuine, sensible joy. Since *yayin* is not necessarily an alcoholic drink, we should reject the idea that it is so in Psalm 104:15, and even more firmly should we resist the idea that the *cup*, also called *the fruit of the vine* referred to in connection with the Lord's Supper, is alcoholic.

The Christians whom the inspired Apostle Paul criticized so sharply in 1 Corinthians 11:20-22 did not become drunk at church gatherings from the communion cup, but from drinks they consumed as part of their own individual suppers, which they brought with them to the meeting place (verse 21). Paul distinguishes this private feasting from the Lord's Supper. This scandal, which was increased by the lack of concern the wealthy Christians had for the poor, seems to have been limited to the church at Corinth.

Scholars have called attention to a passage in Herodotus where the fruit of the vine is referred to as an intoxicant.[10] From this some people have derived the idea that in the Greek language in New Testament times the words translated *the fruit of the vine* was used to describe an intoxicant and that this intoxicant was used by Christ at the time He instituted the Lord's Supper.

To refute this idea it is only necessary to point out that the expression did not originate in Greek and never became naturalized in that language in the sense of an intoxicant. Even if Herodotus, who quotes the expression from the mouth of a queen of a tribe in central Asia, accepted it as a proper term for alcoholic wine (which is very doubtful), the language of Herodotus is quite different from the Greek of the New Testament. There is no reason to think that Christ was going back centuries to a rare expression of Herodotus when He spoke of the fruit of the vine.

The context of the Herodotus passage is that Tomyris, Queen of the Massagetae, whose son had been tricked into drunkenness by Cyrus and taken prisoner, sent a herald to Cyrus with this message:

> Blood thirsty Cyrus, be not uplifted by this that thou hast done; it is no matter of pride if the fruit of the vine (*ampelino karpo*)—that fruit whereof the Persians drink even unto madness, so that the wine passing into your bodies makes evil words to arise in a flood to your lips—has served you as a drug (*pharmako*) to master my son withal, by guile and not in fair fight.

This queen, who lived in what is now a part of the USSR, and was neither Greek nor Persian, used an expression which Herodotus quoted not necessarily because he thought it was good Greek. Perhaps he quoted it for its quaintness. The queen hated the drink which brought captivity to her son and ultimately led to his death by suicide. In revenge, her army defeated that of Cyrus in a battle in which that great conqueror of much of the known world lost his life.

---

[10] Herodotus, *History* I, pp. 211-212 (Clio).

Since the expression *fruit of the vine* for intoxicating wine seems not to have been taken up by other writers of classical Greek, and since Christ would not have taken it from this historical event into the *koine* Greek, any attempt to prove that Christ was referring to an intoxicant fails utterly. Christ meant to exclude alcohol, the excrement of yeast which is not the fruit of the vine.

Furthermore, to derive Christ's words *tou gennēmatos tēs ampelou* (Matt. 26:29) from Queen Tomyris's words *ampelino karpo* is linguistically impossible. There is an apparent (but not real) similarity of ideas, but the expressions are grammatically different. Christ used a word which is derived from the idea of begetting. His meaning could be taken literally as that which is begotten of the vine. Herodotus, translating Tomyris, used the more common word for fruit, and he has the word for vine as an adjective and not a noun. The chief reason for mentioning this dissimilarity is that fixed expressions usually come from century to century unchanged. Therefore to say that Christ's words are in any way derived from this unique expression in Herodotus is not sustained.

All references used to support the idea that Christ used an intoxicant at the Last Supper fail. They are, like this reference to Herodotus's story of Tomyris, proving nothing about what Christ used. Some references are late, derived from the Talmud composed by Jews who lived after the time of Christ and who were strongly antagonistic to Him and to his followers. They can prove nothing about the beverage at the Last Supper. Some references used are ancient, but they refer to the nonalcoholic wine which was permitted to all but Nazirites and Rechabites. These are on the side of an alcohol-free sacrament.

One other thing, and this is a question, do the one-wine theorists wish to follow Queen Tomyris and call communion wine a drug (*pharmakon*)? We should all remember how this word is used in the New Testament (Rev. 9:21 in the American Bible Society Edition of 1966). It is thought to mean *poison* or *witchcraft* in this passage.

There are words of Dunlop Moore which should be challenged and shown to be misleading. He wrote that "the fruit of the vine is literally the grape. But the Jews from time immemorial have used the phrase to designate the wine partaken of on sacred occasions."[11] We must ask, what does this mean *from time immemorial*? It is used by Moore to attempt to prove that Christ used alcoholic wine at the Holy Supper. But *from time immemorial* is an unscholarly way of implying that this use of alcoholic wine antedates the time of Christ. But this cannot be proved and attempts to prove it are examples of reasoning in circles. Where is it said in the Bible that wine, either alcoholic or alcohol-free was to be used at the Passover?

Mr. Dunlop Moore is dead, but I challenge any who accept his statement that wine (meaning alcoholic wine) was used from time immemorial on sacred occasions to demonstrate from the Bible where wine of any sort was authorized to be used at the Passover service. The original Biblical requirements are a lamb roasted whole, unleavened bread, and bitter herbs (Ex. 12:8-10), but nothing is said of wine or the fruit of the vine, or in fact of any beverage. We know that Christ had a beverage at the Passover feast at which He instituted the Lord's Supper, but as He certainly would not go to his trial and crucifixion with a mind-numbing poison in his body, we can assume that it was nonalcoholic. Furthermore, the apostle Paul says the elements at the Christian Passover (the Lord's Supper) should be without leaven (*azumois*). Leaven is yeast.

There may be no memory of the time a beverage was introduced into the Passover service, but it is unscholarly to suggest that this lack of memory is any way proof that Christ drank alcohol. Christ used the words *gennēmatos tēs ampelou* (begotten of the vine) to exclude alcohol, the excrement of an entirely different organism. If Jews and Church fathers later assumed that the expression meant alcoholic wine, that was their error.

---

[11] Moore, "*Wine*," in Schaff, *Encyclopedia*, pp. 2537-2538.

Notes and Study Questions

The drink of the Lord's Supper is nonalcoholic grape juice. The New Testament uses the terms cup and fruit of the vine when speaking of the drink. These terms do not imply an alcoholic beverage. It does not use *oinos,* which can mean either nonalcoholic grape juice or alcoholic wine.

Jesus Christ instituted the Lord's Supper on the night of the Passover. Some believe that this would require the grape juice to be fermented because of the time lapse from the grape harvest to the Passover. Actually, during the Passover, which occurred during the Feast of Unleavened Bread, there was not to be any leaven or yeast in the house. Yeast is the organism which produces the alcohol in grape juice, so if all yeast was to be removed from the house, all alcoholic drinks were to be removed, as well. Christ would have violated the Law if He drank alcoholic wine on the Passover.

A significant passage in determining the beverage of the Lord's Supper to be nonalcoholic is 1 Corinthians 5:7-8. In this passage, unleavened elements (the plural form of the adjective *azumos,* unleavened) indicates that both Passover elements were to be without leaven. Therefore the Passover drink could not be alcoholic.

It is also significant to recognize Christ's priestly work by sacrificing Himself to God on behalf of His people. According to Leviticus 10:8-11, priests were not allowed to drink alcohol before they did the work of the priesthood. The Lord's Supper took place only hours before His sacrifice. Christ, according to the Law, would not have been allowed to do the work of a priest if the beverage used during the Lord's Supper was alcoholic.

Why does the term *fruit of the vine* not indicate an alcoholic drink? (p. 122)

What did Christ mean when He spoke of drinking with His disciple the new (*kainos*) fruit of the vine? (p. 123)

How do modern Jews justify their use of alcoholic wine in their Passover celebrations? (p. 125)

How does Dr. Reynolds respond to Dr. Vos' comment that there is no inherent evil in wine? (p. 129)

What is the Roman Catholic position on the use of grape juice during the Mass? (pp. 129-130)

How does Dr. Reynolds answer the observation that Herodotus used *fruit of the vine* as an intoxicant? (p. 134) Did Christ and Herodotus use the same phrase? (p. 134)

THE MEANING OF THE MOCKERY "THESE MEN ARE FULL OF NEW WINE." (ACTS 2:13)

Incredible as it may seem, this text has been used to support the idea that the members of the apostolic church normally, and with apostolic approval, drank an intoxicating beverage. One who believes this is himself a Bible believer, accepts the idea that the Christians were not really drunk, but under the influence of the Holy Spirit. Nevertheless the taunt is accepted to the extent that the charge is thought to have been a reasonable one, and on occasions other than that described in Acts the Christians might have been observed in a state of being drunk with new wine. Therefore, it is assumed that intoxicating beverages were permitted to believers in the apostolic church and, by extension, they are permitted to Christians today.

In opposition to this strange interpretation it should be enough to point out that the word the mockers used would only have been used if they knew the Christians abstained from alcoholic beverages. The word they used, *gleukos,* refers to the sweetness of unfermented grape juice before the yeast has destroyed the natural sugar.[1] Wine with alcoholic content can be sweetened by mixing in sugar before or after the microorganisms which produce

[1] Galen uses this word in the sense of *grape juice*. Vol. 6, p. 575, ed. C. G. Kuhn.

the alcohol have died, but scholars do not accept the idea that such artificially sweetened wine was the meaning of *gleukos*. If the mockers had not known the Christians were abstainers from alcoholic beverages they would have said, *these men are drunk*, or words to that effect.

There is no reason, other than that the enemies were ridiculing the total abstinence of the Christians, for using the word *gleukos*. The occasion for the insult happened at Pentecost, a Spring-time festival, and *gleukos* could only have been preserved from the previous grape harvest by a special process. Incidentally, some people, ignorant of the facts, think that men in the first century knew no way to keep grape juice from fermenting or turning into vinegar, but this is not true. For ancient authorities who disprove this idea, see:

- Vergil, *Georgics*, 1:295
- Pliny, *Natural History*, 14:11, 19;
- Columella, *De Re Rustica*, Book 12, chapter 29.

Vergil lived in the first century before Christ, Pliny and Columella lived in the first century A.D., and were therefore men of the same century as Jesus Christ and the Apostles. All three wrote of methods for preserving grape juice from fermentation. Pliny was particularly severe in his condemnation of alcoholic wine. He wrote:

> There is no department of man's life on which more labour is spent—as if nature had not given us the most healthy of beverages to drink, water, which all animals make use of, whereas we compel even our beasts of burden to drink wine! And so much toil and labour and outlay is paid as the price of a thing that perverts men's minds and produces madness, having caused the commission of thousands of crimes, and being so attractive that a large part of mankind knows of nothing else worth living for![2]

Pliny mentions in this section some deplorable results of drinking wine:

---

[2] *Natural History*, Book XIV, Section XXVIII. Found in *Loeb Classical Library*, Book IV, p. 277.

> Think of the drinking matches! Think of the vessels engraved with scenes of adultery, as though tippling were not enough by itself to give lessons in licentiousness! Thus wine-bibbing is caused by license, and actually a prize is offered to promote drunkenness—heaven help us, it is actually purchased...
>
> Then it is that greedy eyes bid a price for a married woman, and their heavy glances betray it to her husband; then it is that the secrets of the heart are published abroad: some men specify the provisions of their wills, others let out facts of fatal import, and do not keep to themselves words that will come back to them through a slit in their throat—how many men having lost their lives in that way.

Pliny's words associating wine tippling with adultery are similar to God's revealed truth in Ephesians 5:18: "Be not drunk with wine in which is debauchery." Some commentators say that the words *in which* refer to the whole phrase, *Be not drunk with wine,* and not just to *wine*. The wish not to accept the idea that debauchery is *in* wine makes them reject this obvious sense, and choose instead the idea that it lies in being drunk. But end results are sometimes attributed to the substance which causes the result. Thus when Elisha was warned, *there is death in the pot* (2 Kings 4:40), we do not say that the speakers should have exclaimed that there was death in eating the contents of the pot. No, death by poison was *in* the pot; debauchery is *in* wine.

Notes and Study Questions

On the day of Pentecost, the disciples of Christ received the Holy Spirit and began to speak in tongues. Some mockers in the audience accused them of drinking new wine (*gleukos*). This Greek word signifies sweetness. It was a sweet drink, not an alcoholic drink.

What three sources were written around the time of Christ and explained methods used during that time to preserve grape juice from fermentation? (p. 138)

In Ephesians 5:18, does the phrase *in which is debauchery* refer to the whole clause *Be not drunk with wine* or just the word *wine*? (p. 139)

COLOSSIANS 2:16 AND ALCOHOLIC BEVERAGES

> Let no man judge you in food or drink, or in respect of a religious festival, a new moon celebration or a Sabbath day (verse 16). These are a shadow of things which were to come; the reality, however, is found in Christ (verse 17).

Verse 16 above has been proposed as the ground for an argument that drinking alcoholic beverages is a liberty given to mankind by God. But in examining the passage we should note its context, especially verse 17. We should also be aware that the Gospel of Jesus Christ *does* set believers free from bondage to sin, and that man-made rules which destroy genuine Christian liberty should be resisted.

The question must be answered. Does Colossians 2:16 set Christians free from the command in Proverbs 23:31 not to look at the substance the effects of which on the human mind and body are described in verses 29-35?

The first thing to observe in answering this question is that there are no textual critical problems in verse 16, and that all versions give the readers about the same meaning, although in different words. The KJV and some others by translating *en brōsei* as *in meat* are using an obsolete sense of the word *meat*. The seventeenth century readers correctly understood *food* when they read *meat*, but modern readers, unless they are informed, think of the word *meat* as *flesh to be eaten* in particular, and not as *food* in general. There is, however, no difficulty in the Greek expression *en posei*, which refers to drink in any form, nonalcoholic or alcoholic.

If God permits alcoholic drinks to mankind, every human being is told by God to refuse to be judged by man on this matter. But it is another question as to whether or not God, in the Bible, does grant such permission.

Verses 16 and 17 are shown to refer to Judaizers. The reference to sabbaths shows this, for none but Jews and Judaizing Christians would be critical of the Colossian Christians on the matter of sabbaths. The pagans, the other part of the population with whom the Christians had to deal, are not in view here. They cared not at all for sabbaths.

Those who believed that Old Testament laws on diet, or Jewish traditions supposed to be implied in the Old Testament, were to be enforced on Christians, would be harshly critical of Christians if they saw them eating what they considered unclean food (the flesh of animals prohibited for human consumption in the Old Testament), or if they saw them drinking milk at the same time they were eating flesh. This last prohibition, supposed to be derived from Deuteronomy 14:21, is carefully observed by Orthodox Jews today, and is apparently ancient.

It appears therefore that Colossians 2:16 is not intended to free the Christian from the prohibition of Proverbs 23:31, which is not to look at the drink so vividly described in the verses immediately before and after verse 31. God's prohibition still remains. It is of only minor importance whether men judge us, but we should beware of God's judgment. If, however, a Jew or Judaizing Christian should attempt to judge us on food (e. g. pork) or on drink (e. g. milk when taken with flesh), we should not be dismayed by his judgment. We should try to show him that we love him as Christ commanded. We may say we disagree and show him why. We may (perhaps should?) follow the example of the Apostle Paul as recorded in 1 Corinthians 8:13 and abstain totally and forever from what is causing our brother to stumble. This is not because pork, oysters, or milk with meat are forbidden by the dietary laws (which are abrogated), but because of a higher law, the law of love, which may lead us to deny ourselves something innocent in order that our brother may not stumble and turn away from Christ.

The expression *these things are the shadow of things to come* (verse 17) makes the meaning of verse 16 very clear. The dietary laws are but a shadow of Christ, and when Christ is come Christians have no need of the *shadow*; they have the reality. The dietary laws are abolished for Christians, but the moral law is still in full force. Proverbs 23:31, the prohibition of a certain sort of *yayin*, of which there can be no doubt that it is alcoholic *yayin*, is a moral law. It is not a ceremonial law foreshadowing Christ. Therefore Colossians 2:16[1] has nothing to do with Proverbs 23:31. Other prohibitions in Proverbs 23 also are commands not to break the moral law, not the ceremonial or dietary laws. Thus verse 10 forbids stealing, verse 13 forbids withholding correction from the child, etc. In fact Proverbs in general deals with the moral law.

Notes and Study Questions

Some Christians use Colossians 2:16 as argument that Christians have a liberty to drink whatever they want, including alcoholic beverages. This understanding fails to recognize that this verse speaks of the foods and drinks which were ceremonially prohibited by the dietary law. They were shadows of things which were to come [things pertaining to Christ] (verse 17). Verse 16 does not negate the moral prohibition on alcohol found in Proverbs 23:31.

Is the moral law abolished by Christ's coming? (pp. 141-142)

WHAT WAS TIMOTHY DIRECTED TO TAKE, AND WHY?

In 1 Tim. 5:23 the Apostle Paul wrote to Timothy, "Drink no longer water, but use a little wine for thy stomach's sake and thine often infirmities" (KJV). There are no textual critical problems

---

[1] Matthew Henry in his commentary on this passage says, with excellent exegetical skill: "Here is a caution to take heed to Judaizing teachers, or those who would impose upon Christians the yoke of the ceremonial law; Let no man therefore judge you in meat or in drink, &c., v. 16."

about this verse, but there are problems of interpretation. The passage has been used to condemn the teaching of those who say that total abstinence from alcohol is a Bible requirement.

On the face of the passage it could be interpreted to mean that since Timothy was a man given to frequent infirmities of the stomach, he is directed to abstain totally from water and substitute for it a *little oinos*. It cannot mean this, because if Timothy were to drink no water and substitute *oinos* he would not be consuming a *little,* but much. He would need more than a little liquid to support life.

The doctrine of inerrancy means that the words were entirely without error, and could be understood by the people to whom they were first addressed. These people had the advantage of knowing the frame of reference in which the inspired writers expressed themselves.

If Paul meant that Timothy should drink exclusively alcoholic *oinos* he would have been contradicting what he had previously said in this same epistle, 1 Timothy 3:2-3, where he said a bishop (and Timothy was a bishop) should be sober (*nephalios*) and not given to wine (*paroinos*).

One possible interpretation is that Paul had previously shown to Timothy in general what he meant and was now giving in shortened form the gist of his teaching on this subject. He may have meant, and on this there is general agreement, drink no longer water *exclusively*. As for the next words, he is understood by many, including some total abstainers, to have meant, take a little alcoholic *oinos* for your stomach's sake. This medicinal use of a *little oinos* would not be a breaking of a rule against the use of alcoholic beverages for pleasure.

Jerome, the great translator of the Bible into Latin in the fifth century, wrote of the difficulties he had experienced and then advised his young correspondent Eustochium as follows:

> Now, if such are the temptations of men who, since their bodies are emaciated with fasting, have only evil thoughts to face, how must it fare with a girl whose surroundings are those of luxury and ease? Sure, to use the apostle's words, "She is

> dead while she lives."[1] Therefore, if experience gives me a right to advise, or clothe my words with credit, I would begin by urging you as Christ's spouse to avoid wine as you would a poison. For wine is the final weapon used by demons against the young. Greed does not shake, nor pride puff up, nor ambition infatuate so much as this. Other vices we easily escape, but this enemy is shut up within us, and wherever we go we carry him with us. Wine and youth between them kindle the fire of sensual pleasure. Why do we throw oil on the flame—why do we add fresh fuel to a miserable body which is already ablaze?

Thus we see that Jerome urged total avoidance of alcoholic wine as of any other poison. How then did he interpret 1 Timothy 5:23? He wrote in the letter quoted in the previous paragraph that Paul "was advising rather as a physician than as an apostle (though indeed, an apostle is a spiritual physician)."[2]

A physician prescribes for his particular patient. Thus Jerome sought to avoid the conclusion that all persons with unhealthy stomachs should prescribe for themselves *a little wine,* citing Holy Writ as their authority.

A fatal flaw, however, in the idea that Paul directed Timothy to take alcoholic wine, even in moderation, can be seen when we consider that Timothy is advised to use this medicine for his *stomach's sake*. Alcoholic *oinos* might have been indicated in antiquity if Timothy's problem were that he had difficulty in falling to sleep at night. There are far better soporifics available today, but when Paul wrote, it is at least conceivable that he would have prescribed this narcotic for the tension ravaged body of his friend Timothy. But for Timothy's *stomach* he could never have recommended alcohol. It is known now, and was probably known then, that alcohol does nothing good to the stomach. If it was not generally known, the Holy Spirit would nevertheless not have let Paul fall into an error in writing under inspiration. What Paul may have thought and expressed privately could have been erroneous, but what God inspired him to put into the Bible is

[1] 1 Tim. 5:6.

[2] *Post Nicene Fathers*, vol. 6, p. 25.

entirely without error. It may, however, not be hedged against misunderstanding by modern readers.

If *oinos* has as part of its essence alcohol we would have to conclude that medical science is wrong in taking people with serious digestive problems off of alcohol, but since there is nonalcoholic *oinos*, we are led to the conclusion that this is what Paul intended, and that medical science is right.

There is literature on the medicinal value of grape sugar. Ernest Gordon wrote: "No better medicine for Timothy's stomach and chronic infirmities could have been recommended by Paul than the juice of the grape."[3]

He added in a footnote:

> The body maintains the concentration of grape sugar in the blood at a constant low level (from .98 to 1.45). Beyond this point there is no increase even if 50 to 100 grams is taken in through the mouth. For the liver absorbs any excess from the blood and stores it as glycogen, to be released as required by the body.
>
> Against alcohol no such protective mechanism exists. If one continues to drink, the blood will attain a fatal concentration. Grape sugar is meant for the body, alcohol is not. This is why the words preceding (1 Timothy 4:4), 'Every creature of God is good and nothing to be refused' cannot be applied to alcoholic drink. Nor could it 'be sanctified by the word of God and prayer'. For alcohol, as we have seen, is the excrement of the yeast. It can, therefore, hardly be described as 'a created thing' or 'a creature of God' any more than a dungheap in a barnyard.

Notes and Study Questions

Paul directed Timothy to drink a little wine (*oinos*) for his stomach's sake. The Greek word *oinos* can be understood as either alcoholic or nonalcoholic. Since Paul says that bishops should not be given to wine (1 Timothy 3:2-3), it would be contradictory for

[3] Gordon, *Christ, the Apostles and Wine*, pp. 27-28.

Paul to then instruct Timothy to take a little wine in 1 Timothy 5:23. Medically speaking, grape juice would have helped Timothy's stomach, but an alcoholic wine would not.

THE QUESTION OF ABSTINENCE OR MODERATION IN THE PASTORAL EPISTLES OF PAUL

Paul the Apostle in his epistles to Timothy and Titus refers to wine in a negative way, but not always by what appears to be an absolute prohibition. In 1 Timothy 3:3 and Titus 1:7 the bishop is commanded to be not given to wine (*mē paroinon*) which could be interpreted to mean to be a total abstainer, or possibly it could be understood to mean to be very moderate in the use of alcoholic wine. Since Proverbs 23:31 forbids looking at a substance which from the way it is described must be alcoholic wine, it is legitimate to say that Paul is not abrogating Proverbs in this passage. *Not given to wine* means totally abstain from alcoholic wine, if the Bible is consistent—and it is.

There are passages in 1 Timothy and Titus where the word *much* is used in connection with prohibition. In 1 Timothy 3:8 in stating the qualifications of deacons Paul says they should be not given to much wine, and in Titus 2:3 he says that aged women should not be enslaved (*dedoulōmenas*) to much wine. The use of the word *much* in the prohibitions suggests that alcoholic wine in moderation is not forbidden, only its use in great quantities.

Can a total prohibition such as Proverbs 23:31 be changed to a command to moderation, and may this be called an explanation and application?

To answer this question we must examine where Old Testament laws were changed in the New Testament.

When Old Testament commands on moral matters are changed in the New Testament, they are changed to make them more difficult for human beings to obey, they are not relaxed as concessions to the weakness of fallen humanity.

Thus Christ teaches that commandments of the Old Testament moral law are not to be broken and that whoever shall break one of these least commandments, and shall teach men so, he shall be called least in the Kingdom of Heaven (Matthew 5:19).

It is to be noted very strictly that Paul did not teach anyone to break the law of Proverbs 23. He did not permit any drinking of wine. What he did was forbid being given to much wine. To forbid much does not permit a little. Such a prohibition merely fails to speak of moderation and there is no reason the apostle should be charged with permitting a little merely because he prohibited much.

If an authority says, do not kill your father or your mother, and then much later, under other circumstances says, don't kill your mother, what should the hearer understand? Should he say the less inclusive prohibition now abrogates the more inclusive one, and I am now permitted to kill my father? No. Unless the more inclusive prohibition is abrogated in plain language, it still stands and will be enforced.

Let us return to how Christ treated Old Testament moral law. He came to fulfill (*plērōsai*) it. This means to make it fuller of meaning.

Thus with regard to the law against murder Christ filled it with greater meaning by including unjust anger and contempt under the heading of murder. They are emotions which often lead to the actual wrongful taking of the life of another human being (Matt. 5:21-26).

Where the Old Testament forbids adultery, Christ fulfilled this law by forbidding lustful ogling (Matt. 5:27-30).

The Old Testament forbids a man to divorce his wife without giving her a bill of divorcement. Christ forbids divorce for minor causes, allowing only the cause of fornication (*porneia*) (Matt. 5:31-32).

Other examples can be given, but this is enough to show that Christ does not relax Old Testament moral laws, but fills them with a greater, more inclusive and stricter meaning, harder for frail humanity to obey.

Where in the New Testament strict laws of the Old Testament are abrogated, these are fulfilled in another sense. These are ceremonial laws whose reason for being are done away with by the work of Christ in establishing the Christian dispensation. The Old Testament laws about unclean foods have nothing to do with the eternal, unchanging moral law. They were evidently intended to help in keeping God's ancient people separated from the gentile nations. After Christ's redemptive work was accomplished and it was time to admit masses of gentiles into the Church, the dietary laws were abrogated (Acts 10:9-16).

Thus since moral laws are only changed in the direction of greater strictness and ceremonial laws are abrogated, we can examine correctly the problem of what we should consume. We may eat the flesh of swine, crows or even snakes (ceremonially unclean animals). The laws which formerly prohibited them are abrogated. On the other hand, what Proverbs 23:31 prohibits is part of the moral law and is placed along side of adultery and stealing. These prohibitions are eternal.

Following the analogy of how Christ dealt with the moral matters of murder, adultery and divorce, we would expect the moral matter of the prohibition of delighting in alcohol to be more strictly interpreted in the New Testament and not relaxed.

Christ said,

> Whosoever therefore shall break one of these least commandments, and shall teach men so, he shall be called least in the kingdom of heaven: but whosoever shall do and teach them, the same shall be called great in the kingdom of heaven (Matt. 5:19).

It is proper to understand this reference to commandments to include every moral law in the Old Testament. If the prohibition against looking at the beverage of Proverbs 23 is one of the *least,* it is nevertheless a commandment. Persons in the kingdom of heaven (saved persons) are told they will lose status (will become least) if they break such a *least* commandment, or even if they personally keep it they will become *least* if they teach others to break it.

In view of this stern statement of Christ, we should look very closely at what Paul in the Pastoral Epistles is teaching. If we do so, we can become sure that there is nothing in the New Testament, not even in these epistles, to lead us to say that the prohibition of Proverbs 23:29-34 is now repealed and that Christian bishops, deacons, and elderly women may drink some of the poison, but not *much*.

Of course *much* is forbidden, but the total prohibition remains in force.

If some alcohol for pleasure or relief from tensions or for sociability is permitted and *much* is prohibited, the question must arise, how much is *much*? What is much for one person can be tolerated by another. It is impossible to believe that God would expect *aged women*, who are often frail physically, to follow the example of a robust man weighing two hundred pounds in determining how much is *much*. If not by example, how should they know? They might try only a little and find that they are prone to alcohol addiction. Many have done so. It is inconsistent with the consensus of Scripture to suppose that Paul changed the rule of Proverbs 23 which demands total abstinence from the drink described there.

Children have been known to drink hard liquor they found available and die as a result. They had no doubt been told it is a pleasure to drink it. Some say to avoid this, introduce them to light wine a little at a time. If Christians studied the Bible well they would avoid both of these courses. Do not let children have liquor of any percentage of alcohol. If a number of children are given a small amount of wine, some of them will become victims of a habit they cannot control.

1 Timothy 4:4 is sometimes cited to prove that Paul approved of alcohol as a beverage because it is a created thing. Those who use this verse admit that Paul is not speaking of alcohol, or opposing people who prohibited its use, but they grasp blindly at the idea that alcohol is a *creature* of God, and therefore *not to be refused, if it be received with thanksgiving*. But alcohol is not a thing directly created by God. It is an excrement of a microorganism

which *is* created by God, but what a creature excretes as waste matter is not created by God. If anyone wishes to eat or drink the excretions of living organisms he is free to do so if they are not poisonous and if they are not specifically forbidden. He may thank God for them, but he should not call them creatures of God. But alcohol is specifically prohibited in Proverbs 23, and even if it were not, it kills those who use it in many ways. It is a poison, and to take it is to threaten one's own life. It is prohibited, although not specifically, in the commandment, "Thou shalt not kill."

Medical science brings to light new evidence that even small amounts of alcohol are harmful to the human body, and therefore to take them is to sin against the commandment, *Thou shalt not kill.*

If anyone should ask, why did God not make the total prohibition of alcoholic beverages for pleasure so clear in all parts of the Bible, that everyone, no matter what his stage of spiritual development, can understand, the answer is, He is under no obligation to do that. In fact God has never promised that He will make it so easy to understand the Bible that people can approach it with proud self-confidence. He has tested and promises to continue to test those who profess to serve Him.

God tests people directly (Gen. 22:1), or permits them to be tested in various ways (Heb. 11:37; 1 Tim. 6:9; James 1:2,12). He does not entrap into evil (James 1:13), but He *tests* and we should all expect our own individual tests.

The Christians of Berea, because they expected themselves to be held accountable, knew that they must examine even the teaching of Paul and Silas by searching the Scriptures daily (Acts 17:11). Paul did not resent having his teaching examined in the light of the Old Testament by new Christians. Rather we are given to understand that he rejoiced in it, and Luke his companion and author of the Acts of the Apostles says they were *more noble* than certain others who failed to search.

Even today it will not do for us to say such-and-such a Christian (great, or near great, or not so great) said drinking alcohol is a liberty permitted Christians, and therefore we can rest assured that it is so. We love all men (or should), and we respect as well as love all Christians. We must highly revere great

Christians of the past who were greatly used of God, but we know they had their tests and we have ours. I think that few modern Christians think that Luther passed very well a test of loving moderation in what he said about the peasants of the Peasants' War, or about the Jews. Would we want to take precisely the same stand Calvin did in the matter of the punishment of Servetus and expect to present ourselves before God as guiltless because of the example of Calvin? I do not think so. We must examine what Paul said in the light of the Scriptures of the Old Testament. He would wish us to do so. See Acts 17:11. Paul considered them *noble* who tested his teachings with Scripture. Remember that he did not say that a Christian is permitted to drink alcoholic wine in moderation—that would have been an abrogation of Proverbs 23:31. He said Christians of certain classes should not be given to or enslaved by much wine. In logic this permits nothing.[1] It cannot be said to abrogate Proverbs 23.

It may be that this is a test for Christians today. With how much humility, denial of the desires of the flesh, and earnest searching of the Old Testament and New Testament with constant prayer for guidance of the Holy Spirit, do we approach the alcohol problem? Or any problem?

God may be smiling when he sees how we Christians attempt to run around hurdles in the race of life. This is not in hatred, but in loving kindness, as a kind father may smile a little when his small child does something foolish. The Christian himself will be saved, but perhaps some of what he considered his good work will be destroyed (1 Cor. 3:11-17).

Notes and Study Questions

In 1 Timothy 3:8 and Titus 2:3, Paul explains that deacons and aged women should not be given to much wine. Some have taken occasion in interpreting these verses to understand Paul to allow some alcoholic drinking, just so it did not become too much.

[1] God created logic and no doubt expects those with the capacity to use it to act and think accordingly. God's gifts are not to be abused.

Proverbs 23:31 still contradicts this understanding telling the believer not to even look at wine, let alone take a small amount of it. So Paul in these passages must not be understood as giving liberty to believers to break God's prohibition of Proverbs 23:31. Because he tells believers not to drink much, this statement does not imply *drink a little.* Rather, Paul's *do not drink much* is completely consistent with Proverbs 23 which implies *do not drink alcohol at all.*

How much alcohol is needed to make it harmful for the body? (p. 150)

PROHIBITED ONLY ONCE!

That the beverage described as to its effects on the human body in Proverbs 23 is prohibited only once in the Bible has been used by some to say the prohibition may be ignored. But those who use this argument against the prohibition of looking at the drink that is called a poison in Proverbs 23 must admit that the prohibition against eating the forbidden fruit in the Garden of Eden was given only once, and disobedience was punished. The prohibition of looking back at Sodom was given only once, but Lot's wife was punished severely for disobeying.

Are there prohibitions in the Bible given only once which are still in force? Yes, and one example is the prohibition against cursing or insulting the deaf. Leviticus 19:14 says: *Lo'theqallel cheresh,* which may be translated: *thou shalt not* (or *you shall not*) *curse* (or *make contemptible,* or *revile* or *insult*) *a deaf person* (or *the deaf* in general). The exact shade of meaning which we ought to attach to *theqallel* may never be agreed upon by all, but what can be agreed upon is that this commandment against taking advantage of the deafness of another person by saying things against him, knowing that he cannot understand and defend his honor, is said only once in Scripture. We will probably not find the people who reject the prohibition of Proverbs 23:31 on the ground that it is found only once in the Bible saying we are free to curse the deaf knowing he will not hear us. But both prohibitions are eternally binding, even though they are not repeated in the Bible. Alcoholic wine is shown elsewhere in the Bible to be deceitful; so that even without Proverbs 23:31 a careful student of God's revealed truth would be wise to be a total abstainer. See Proverbs 20:1.

Christians also would have reason not to say insulting things about the deaf. To do so would be taking cowardly refuge in knowing that they cannot hear. The words of Christ which have been called *The Golden Rule* are enough, or should be enough, to warn us against such an act. The Golden Rule itself, however, might be disregarded as not necessary to be observed by such as wish to brush aside Proverbs 23:31, on the ground that the prohibition is found only once in the Bible. The reason? The Golden Rule itself ("Whatever you wish that men would do to you, do so to them, for this is the law and the prophets.") was apparently only uttered once by divine authority. It occurs in two different Gospels (Matt. 7:12; Luke 6:31) as having been spoken by Christ, but these are parallel records of what seems to have been a single utterance. Yet all Christians and most non-Christians admit that it is valid as a rule of ethics.

In short, a single utterance with divine authority is eternally binding. The prohibition of Proverbs 23:31 is not to be denied because it occurs only once in the Bible.

Notes and Study Questions

Proverbs 23:31 is a strong prohibition against drinking alcohol. Some would seek to ignore Proverbs 23:31 because there are no other prohibitions against alcohol in the Bible. Though it is not true that this is the only prohibition against alcohol in the Bible, this verse could stand alone and be just as binding upon believers. There are other prohibitions given just once in the Bible which are still binding upon believers because it is God who has given these commands for all time.

What are some examples cited of commands given by God one time which are binding for all believers all the time? (pp. 152-153)

THE FALLACY OF THE ARGUMENT THAT TO BE STRICTLY BIBLICAL CHURCHES MUST NOT REQUIRE THEIR MEMBERS TO ABSTAIN FROM ALCOHOLIC BEVERAGES

It is hoped that this study will be useful to Christians of all denominations, and even to some extent to non-Christians, but, inasmuch as the author has been a member of the Orthodox Presbyterian Church (hereafter designated the OPC), a denomination which dealt with the problem in the early years of its existence, the following section is presented in the hope that it may be especially useful to members of that body of Christians. Countless Christians in other denominations have been taught to think along the same lines as the OPC and perhaps some of them may rethink their position.

It is a very sound Protestant position, upheld vigorously in the Reformed Churches, that to make rules not commanded in the Bible leads to the abandonment of rules the Bible gives us explicitly. This is because God does not burden us with unnecessary rules, and even though some man-made rules may be good, if they are presented as though they were from God, the heavy burden of them and the falsity of the way they are presented leads to disobedience of what God actually does command. The depravity of fallen human nature makes this inevitable.

But it has also been argued that to make rules which are believed to be derived from the Bible according to the principles of exegesis of the whole counsel of God, when the Bible may not give explicit commands, is not in agreement with Reformed principles and may even be *unBiblica*l. This is incorrect.

For example, the Bible does not explicitly forbid gambling, yet the Westminster divines in Standards accepted by the OPC , included a rule against *wasteful gaming*, that is, gambling, in the Larger Catechism, 142. No proof text against this particular vice is given, yet Orthodox Presbyterians who complain against other churches who have legislated against the use of alcohol as a beverage, seem to live comfortably with the Larger Catechism's rule against gambling, even though a specific proof text is lacking. They evidently believe that the whole Bible, studied as a unity, *by good and necessary consequence...deduced from Scripture* permits a church to legislate against gambling. They are right in this.

Similarly, the whole Bible, studied as a unity, enjoins total abstinence from intoxicants except possibly as a narcotic medicine under special controlled conditions.

The Orthodox Presbyterians who are convinced that rules commanding total abstinence are dead wrong may not know all that happened at the Third General Assembly of the Presbyterian Church of America (the original name of the Orthodox Presbyterian Church), which met in Philadelphia in 1937. At this General Assembly the Presbytery of Chicago presented a long, carefully written overture on the matter of total abstinence. In this we read:

> ...for more than a hundred years before the lamentable apostasy of the body now bearing the name of the Presbyterian Church in the U.S.A., the testimony of that body in opposition to intemperance was clear. The Assembly of 1818 declared: "We earnestly recommend to the officers and members of our church to abstain from the common use of ardent spirits".

The reunited Assemblies of 1877 recommended avoiding even the appearance of evil and disentangling (all members) from all implication with the traffic and manufacture of alcoholic drinks and *especially presenting in their whole lives a standing and unvarying exemplification of the only true principle of temperance – total abstinence from everything that will intoxicate.*

The Chicago Presbytery of the OPC overtured the General Assembly of 1937 recommending total abstinence, but an overture of the Presbytery of Philadelphia was approved. The Philadelphia overture had no arguments except to say that the Larger Catechism 91 to 148 and a corresponding part of the Shorter Catechism are enough guidance as to alcoholic beverages.

But it is apparent that these sections of the Catechisms do not resolve the problem as to how much of any substance, once it is known to be a poison, may be taken by a Christian for pleasure or escape. Christians ought to have this guidance. This must be determined by studies in great depth as to what the inerrant (not self-contradictory) Word of God really says. Paradoxes must be resolved if possible. The poisonous effects of nicotine, for example, are far better known now than they were in the seventeenth century when the Westminster Standards were written, and this is true to a considerable extent with regard to alcohol. But nicotine is not forbidden by name, whereas we believe that alcohol actually is forbidden in the Holy Bible.

If anyone says that the Orthodox Presbyterians have a firm principle that nothing by way of clarification to the teaching of the Bible *and* the Westminster Standards on matters of faith and practice may be added, the answer must be that this is untrue. An overture was carried in the General Assembly of 1937 warning the people against Communism. The vote was 42 to 30, not a large majority to be sure, but it *was* carried. Here the Assembly gave moral guidance to the people on an issue to which the Bible and the Westminster Standards did not speak so clearly that all could understand. (The political theory known as Communism had not been developed when the Bible and the Standards were written.)

Although these devout, Bible believing Christians added clarification by condemning Communism by name (which was right) and did not forbid the drinking of alcoholic beverages by name, I do not intend to bring anger on myself by opposing in anything but the most gentle manner what they did. It is important to turn aside the wrath of the OP's who may be inclined to think that this study is harmful to the memory of such men as Dr. J. Gresham Machen, who was in favor of the overture of the Presbytery of Philadelphia. Dr. Machen and those who stood with him were right in rejecting arguments based on precedents of the parent denomination as long as they were not convinced these precedents were Biblical. I stand firmly with the position of Dr. Machen, Dr. Cornelius Van Til, and the theologians of Princeton Seminary of the nineteenth and early twentieth centuries. The position I refer to is that Christian apologetics should be based on the doctrine of the inerrant Bible. This doctrine was not only believed in, but vigorously proclaimed in the early days of Westminster Seminary.

The people who opposed the majority of the General Assembly of 1937 used arguments concerning the need for Christians to set good examples and to avoid the appearance of evil, but they did *not* advance the argument that references to *yayin, oinos* and *shekar* in the Bible *need* not refer to intoxicants. The arguments they used were not judged to be adequate. They were rejected on the ground that *moderate* drinking is in fact a good example. Thus the men of the majority of the Assembly of 1937 were able to say that if drinking alcoholic beverages is setting a bad example, Christ set a bad example. Since all Christians are agreed that Christ did not and could not set a bad example moderate drinking of intoxicants today, for pleasure, escape from tensions, sociability and like reasons, cannot be wrong. This deduction is correct as a rebuttal to the arguments set forth in the overture of the Presbytery of Chicago. It does not, however, rebut arguments based on the idea that no word known always to signify an intoxicant is ever recommended or even permitted as a beverage in holy writ. I believe that if Dr. Machen and the Majority of the General Assembly of 1937 had faced these arguments they would have been convinced of their soundness. They would then have examined the passages which condemn what, from the way the word is used, must mean alcoholic wine, and would have accepted a properly worded, Biblically based overture on abstinence. It is even conceivable that in course of time, and after much searching of the Scripture, the doctrinal Standards might have been expanded to give the people adequate guidance against destroying their physical lives by beginning a habit of consuming toxic substances for pleasure. If the Westminster divines were right in legislating to protect the believers against wasting their property in *gaming*, would not modern Christian churches, with more precise Bible teaching on the subject, be justified in legislating to protect them from ravaging their bodies with intoxicants?

Rules made by human authority should be obeyed if the *authority* is duly constituted by God and if the rules themselves do not conflict with the law of God. Proverbs 23:31 is God's authority, not man's, and it forbids looking at (and therefore it forbids drinking) some sort of *yayin*. This must be obeyed. As an exegetical principle we must understand that *yayin* from which we must abstain totally is that which has the ill effects described in the passage in which this verse is found. It poisons (verse 32)—many die of alcoholic poisoning. It affects heart (mind), eyes, and speech in a bad way (verse 33). It has an effect on the body like seasickness (verse 34). It is a narcotic, taking away the pain of beatings, and it is habit forming (verse 35). All of these ills are caused by alcohol, not unfermented grape juice. Therefore God's authority forbids *yayin* that is alcoholic (*yith'addam*), and other sections of the Bible commend *yayin* that has not been corrupted by fermentation.

Notes and Study Questions

The Word of God prohibits all drinking of alcohol, with the sole exception of its use for one who is about to die (Proverbs 31:6-7). The Word of God has not been correctly used in the past to defend total abstinence. This has left many Christians to believe that total abstinence cannot be defended from the Bible, but the studies performed in *The Biblical Approach to Alcohol* demonstrate that total abstinence can be defended from the Bible. Total abstinence is what God requires of His people in His Word.

Does the Larger Catechism questions 91 to 148 adequately explain the Biblical teaching concerning alcohol? (pp. 155-156)

What were the arguments presented in 1937 by those who argued for total abstinence? What is one key argument they did not present which should have been presented? (p. 157)

THE ENGLISH WORD *Wine*

The definition of the word *wine* has shifted in meaning from grape juice either unfermented or fermented to the sense of fermented only.

We ought therefore not to blame the translators of the King James Bible or other early versions for using the word *wine* when the context shows that the liquid is certainly nonalcoholic. Why? Because *wine* was a perfectly correct word to use at that period of time if the meaning was the unfermented juice of the grape.

If our minds are locked into the idea that *wine* is always alcoholic we have to conclude that the translators were wrong when they rendered Isaiah 16:10e as *the treaders shall tread out no wine in their presses*. They were not wrong, because *wine* in their day was a perfectly proper word to use for the liquid pressed out of the grapes, grape juice being the common word for this substance in our late twentieth century day. The treaders expected to press out what speakers of twentieth century English call grape juice, but because of adverse conditions they were unable to do so. But if they had expected to press out fermented grape juice their expectation would have been absurd. Yet modern translators, even those who claim to write in modern colloquial English, continue to use the word *wine* modified by the adjective *new* when they obviously mean freshly pressed grape juice. Of course if a substance can be called new wine it may also be called wine.

Joel 2:24 is rendered in modern translations either *the presses* (or vats) *shall overflow with wine and oil* (New Catholic Version, Revised Standard Version) or *...with new wine and oil* (New International Version). Every reader will at once understand that the meaning is that the presses will overflow with what standard English dictionaries inform us must never be called *wine*, but grape juice or *must*. The point of this paragraph is that we must not rely even on generally accepted English dictionaries in determining what a word may or may not mean when used by educated speakers of the English language. Dictionary writers are bound up in their prejudices, a common human failing. The words wine and new wine (or even fresh wine) are perfectly acceptable ways of speaking of unfermented wine commonly called grape juice.

If anyone should say that if one puts the adjectives new or fresh before the word wine it ceases to be essentially wine, that is as senseless as it would be to say that if we put the words black or white or yellow before the word man the being described ceases to be a man—according to whatever may be our particular prejudices.

Why do people not accept the idea that this English word *wine* is not limited in meaning to alcoholic wine? Why do some Christians insist that the liquid element of the communion service (the Lord's Supper) be limited to alcoholic wine even though the Bible refers to it merely as *the cup* and *the fruit of the vine*? No matter how much we search for the reason the only one that seems to help in solving the problem is that it is prejudice. This prejudice was a long time in building up. Dr. Charles Wesley Ewing in his book, *The Bible and Its Wines,*[1] shows with a number of excellent examples how the definition of *wine* has changed over the centuries. Thus Thomas Bailey in *The New Universal Dictionary of Words and of Arts and Sciences*...(published in 1759) gives us the first definition of Wine: "Natural WINE, is such as comes from the grape, without any mixture or sophistication." Ewing observes: "This of course is unfermented, nonintoxicating grape juice." Later dictionaries drop from their definitions anything which suggests that wine can be nonalcoholic. See, for example, *Webster's New World Dictionary of the American Language,* Second College Edition, David B. Guralink, Editor, copyright 1984.

In view of the citations from translations of the Bible where wine is used of a nonalcoholic drink the above noted failure to refer to this sense of the word wine can only be attributed to ignorance or prejudice, and the more likely assumption is that the cause is prejudice.

That prejudice prevails in different strata of society should not surprise us. William Makepeace Thackeray, a keen observer of humanity wrote:

> Such is the constitution of mankind, that men have, as it were, entered into a conspiracy among themselves to pursue the fig leaf system 'a l'outrance and to cry down all who oppose it. Humbug they will have. Humbugs themselves, they

---

[1] Denver, Colorado, 1985, pp. 1-6.

> will respect humbugs. Their daily victuals of life must be seasoned with humbug. Certain things are there in the world that they will not allow to be called by their right names, and will insist on our admiring, whether we will or no. Woe to the man who would enter too far into the recesses of that magnificent temple where our Goddess is enshrined, peep through the vast embroidered curtains indiscreetly, penetrate the secret of secrets, and expose the Gammon of Gammons! And as you must not peer too curiously within, so neither must you remain scornfully without .[2]

Thackeray had his own idea of who or what this great humbug is, but in view of the great deception leaders of the liquor industry and others have imposed on mankind, it is proper that we study Thackeray's passage, substituting the words alcohol and alcohol lovers for the word humbug.

Clear thinking requires accurate definition of terms. Humbug thrives when wrong definitions of words prevail. In no area of human life is it more deplorable to resort to false definitions than it is in explaining the Holy Bible.

Translation may be called a science and an art at the same time. Bible translation should not be undertaken by one who does not only have some human science and some human literary art, but he ought also to be a devout believer in God and in the Holy Spirit's inerrant inspiration of the Bible in its original form (the autographa). Two things about translation must always be kept in mind. One is that words in the original sometimes have more than one meaning and it may not always be easy to find and choose the right one. The other is that words in the language to which the text is to be translated (for example English) also may have more than one meaning and the right one should be chosen. This is further complicated by the fact that words in English (or any other language) change their meanings in time.

An example of the first is that the Hebrew word *ro'sh* means

---

[2] Thackeray's essay, *The Second Funeral of Napoleon.* Thackeray considered Napoleon I the great humbug. Although he might not have agreed that alcohol is a great humbug, his writings show a keen appreciation of the evil it causes.

head and also means *poison*. These meanings are unrelated except that the same Hebrew word represents both. The translator must use judgment. In Job 20:16 ("He shall suck the poison of asps") readers would have been badly misled if translators had chosen the more common usage, and given us: "He shall suck the head of asps."

It is sad indeed to know that although translators have known for years that *yayin* had two meanings (alcoholic and nonalcoholic grape juice) and that wine in the eighteenth century (and presumably in the seventeenth century as well) had the same two meanings, yet they have persisted in translating unscientifically and inartistically as though English *wine* were in the twentieth century the proper rendering of Hebrew *yayin* in all cases.

The modern English speaking person is taught by dictionaries and contemporary usage that *wine* is always alcoholic and he therefore, if he is a Christian, has to cope with the harshly conflicting ideas that wine is first mentioned as having made Noah shamefully drunk (Gen. 9:21) and is later said to be like the bite of a poisonous serpent (Prov. 23:32), and on the other hand it is said to make glad the heart of man (Ps. 104:15). Did our infallible God speak such conflicting things about precisely the same substance?

Did Christ tell his followers to deny themselves and did He also make a great quantity of wine (assumed to have been alcoholic) for people who were said by the master of the banquet to have been drunk (cf. Matt. 16:24 and parallel passages with John 2:1-10 in the original)? So firmly is the idea that Christ created an alcoholic beverage implanted in the mind of Christians that a devout, educated, Bible believing Christian expressed outrage at anyone who would profess that he believed that Christ abstained from alcohol. Yet there is nothing in the Bible to prove He ever touched a single drop of this poison.

The conclusion of this discussion is that in general wherever the Hebrew words *yayin, tirosh,* or *'asis* or the Greek word *oinos* are regarded as noxious they should be translated *wine*. Wherever they are regarded as beneficial they should be translated *grape juice*. It is true that if any translator or board of translators should present to the public a translation using this guide line, the work would be regarded with scorn and derision. It is too bad that there is no commonly understood single word in English meaning unfermented wine or unfermented grape juice, but such being the present state of the English language some translators capable of doing so in a scholarly manner should present to the Christian public a Bible in modern English not loaded with the *humbug* of the alcohol lovers and the liquor industry.

There is a word *must* which could be used. It is defined in Webster's dictionary of 1984 as *the juice pressed from grapes or other fruit before it has fermented; new wine*. This by its definition would be a good word to substitute for wine when the sense of Scripture demands it, but it appears not to be known by the general populace. If put in the Bible as *must that makes glad the heart of man* it would probably meet with great resistance. Besides its being a relatively unknown word, it suggests the idea of musty, *having a stale, moldy smell or taste*. There is no connection between the two words, but the similarity of sounds is suggestive. Manufacturers of grape juice for the table avoid it.

Whether *grape juice* or *alcohol free wine* is to be introduced into the Bible put out by people sensitive to the demand of God to make His Word understandable to the people of every language in every period of time, should be carefully considered. Scholars competent to undertake the task will no doubt be helped, after prayer, to choose the right words.

Translators should not heed voices of popular disapproval. When Jerome in the fifth century presented his version of the Bible to be read in churches some of the hearers made a public disturbance because of their intense disapproval. These hearers preferred the *Old Latin* version, a faulty rendering in many particulars. The *Vulgate,* however, continued to be read and ultimately the Old Latin version gave place to Jerome's translation which came to be known as the *Vulgate,* that is, the common or usual version. Persistent use rendered it popular.

The *one-wine theorists* have been unwaveringly firm in their insistence that wine is always alcoholic. It is to be hoped that sound arguments will prevail against this false theory.

As bad money drives out good (a generally recognized law of economics), the bad sense of a word tends to drive out the good. So it is with the English word wine. An analogy may be seen in the word *gay*. This used to mean joyous and lively, happy and lighthearted. More recently this word has been used in the sense of homosexual. It has now entered the latest edition of Webster's Dictionary in this sense. As a result a speaker is already inhibited against saying to a group of hearers, "I want you all to be gay." If he wishes to be understood to mean happy, he must avoid the double meaning of the word gay.

So the bad meaning is driving out the good. We can imagine a time when people, particularly homosexuals, will reject the idea that gay ever has meant anything but homosexual. Thus they may explain that the Christmas carol words about donning gay apparel have always meant transvestite clothing such as is favored by some (but not all) homosexuals. They may resist, as *one-wine theorists* do now, the idea that the word in question has ever meant anything other than the debased sense of the word.

What we need is better linguistic scholarship. The *One-Wine Theory* must go. It begins with the lazy man's idea that we do not have to work hard on the matter of multiple and shifting meanings of words, and is sustained by the self-indulgent man's desire to retain the use and the pleasure of a habit forming drug.

Notes and Study Questions

The English word *wine* has changed its meaning over the centuries. In times past, the word *wine* was considered both alcoholic and nonalcoholic grape juice. Modern English makes a distinction between alcoholic grape juice, wine, and nonalcoholic grape juice, simply grape juice. It is understandable for older translations of the Bible to use *wine* for both wine and grape juice, but it is neglectful for modern translations, seeking to present the Bible in modern English, to show no distinction by using the words wine and grape juice. This neglect on the part of modern translations has led many modern English speaking Christians to accept alcoholic wine as a blessing from God, when the Bible says it is poison.

How did Thomas Bailey define *wine* in *The New Universal Dictionary of Words and of Arts and Sciences* (1759)? (p. 160)

How should *yayin, tirosh,* and *'asis* be translated when they have either a detrimental or beneficial meaning? (p. 162)

Why would *must* not be a good English word to use in a translation for nonalcoholic grape juice? (p. 163)

"RULY ENGLISH" AND THE ALCOHOL PROBLEM

Ruly English is defined as "English language adapted so that each word has a single meaning and each meaning a single word, utilized with a set of ambiguity-avoiding rules, esp. for patents, computer commands."[1]

Readers of this book will readily see that if there had been such things as ruly-Hebrew,[2] ruly-Greek, or if ruly English had been used in translating God's truth as revealed in the Holy Scriptures, much confusion would have been avoided. God, however, in his wisdom chose to inspire his prophets to speak and write in the language of the day. He left it to his people in later generations to *search the Scripture* and reverently to bring out the meaning of difficult passages.

Sometimes the fact that natural (as opposed to *ruly*) Hebrew, Greek, or English gives a wrong impression is not serious as to any point of faith or practice. An example of this is Ezekiel 16:26 where the KJV says that certain Egyptian neighbors were *great of*

---

[1] N. H. and S. K. Mager: *The Morrow Book of New Words, 8500 Terms Not Yet in Standard Dictionaries*, New York, Quill, 1982, p. 226.

[2] The terms *ruly-Hebrew* and *ruly-Greek* are coined on the analogy of *ruly-English*. They are not in any dictionary, but they are useful terms to distinguish what we would have if the inspired books were written after the manner of *ruly-English*, from what we actually have—the vivid every day language of the people.

flesh. Young and uninstructed readers may at first understand this to mean that they were corpulent or obese, as we might say in exaggeration that a fat man is a mountain of flesh. A knowledge of Hebrew would inform such a reader that Ezekiel was referring, by a figure of speech, to the *membrum virile*, and by so doing suggested that their sexual appetites were powerful and unrestrained. The point of mentioning this is to show that it is important to know that the Hebrew word *basar*, usually translated flesh, has other meanings, one of which is the male sexual organ.

Bible readers usually accept the fact that *basar* has more than one meaning, but most refuse to admit that *yayin* has any other meaning than the fermented juice of the grape—and this they do in spite of Isaiah 16:10, where it would be absurd to translate *yayin* as *fermented grape juice*.

New Testament Greek as well as Old Testament Hebrew are not written in such a way that every word has a single meaning and every meaning a single word.

Even such important theological words as *pistis* (commonly translated *faith*) and *ergon* (commonly translated *work*) have different meanings. The word *faith* in Romans 3:28 and the word *works* in James 2:24 seem to make Paul and James in contradiction on the means of salvation. This has led to various false ideas and bad practices. A great New Testament scholar, Dr. J. Gresham Machen wrote: "The difference...between Paul and James is difference in terminology, not in meaning."[3] If the meaning is precisely the same this must mean that by *works* James means what Paul means by *faith* and *vice versa*. This is hard for many to accept, but other interpretations fail to conform to sound rules of Bible exegesis.

---

[3] *What Is Faith?*, p. 204. If what Machen says is true, *pistis* in Rom. 3:28 must mean not bare assent, but a God-given quality in which works of obedience to God are of the essence. On occasion, where the intent is to distinguish it from bare assent it may be designated by a word commonly translated *works*.

Ergon in James 2:24 are not mere deeds, even deeds conforming to God's law, but they are works of which *pistis* is of the essence. On occasion, where the intent is to distinguish them from mere deeds, they may be called *pistis*, a word commonly translated faith.

Another case where scholarship shows that the New Testament was not written in *ruly-Greek,* but in a vivid *koine* form of the language which freely admitted Semitisms when the inspired author felt that such usages helped to express the meaning, has to do with *holy children*. It is probable that many people think that the children of a Christian and a non-Christian are *holy* according to 1 Corinthians 7:14 in the usual sense of the word *hagios.* Most commentators and theologians have done little to help the common people to understand. But John Gill long ago solved the problem[4] and Paul K. Jewett has added supporting evidence.[5] They show that Paul must have used *hagios* in a different sense, show what that sense was, and demonstrate the probability of their conclusion.

The usual interpretation is very confusing, because it teaches that children and spouses of Christians have holiness before they have faith, which is contrary to the consensus of Scripture.

The conclusion is that since the Bible was not written in *ruly Hebrew* or *ruly Greek* we must be open to the idea that we not be locked into the idea that *yayin, shekar, tirosh, 'asis, oinos* or *sikera* are always alcoholic. Neither should we be locked into the idea that they are always nonalcoholic.

If we are so locked in we are in the absurd position of teaching that God in the Bible condemns and praises the same substance. When He condemns it He calls it a poison and totally prohibits it, even to the extent of looking at it lustfully, and when He praises it He does so totally with no reference to moderation in its use.

The conclusion is that *ruly Hebrew* and *ruly Greek* would have removed a number of problems, but believers guided by the Spirit, ought to solve these problems without such languages designed for mindless computers and for patent law.

---

[4] John Gill, *An Exposition of the Christian Faith*, vol. 2, pp. 668-669.
[5] Paul K. Jewett, *Infant Baptism* (c. 1960), pp. 114-122.

Notes and Study Questions

Ruly English seeks to apply one meaning to one word. Such a language greatly helps to remove ambiguity from the message being conveyed by the language. If Hebrew and Greek were *ruly,* in this sense, one could argue that *yayin* and *oinos* always indicate alcoholic drinks, as the one-wine theorists do, but Hebrew and Greek are not *ruly* in this sense. Both *yayin* and *oinos* can mean alcoholic or nonalcoholic drinks depending on their contexts.

Can *yayin* mean fermented grape juice in Isaiah 16:10? (p. 166)

WHAT IS TO BE DONE?

The question naturally arises, how much alcohol in a drink incurs divine displeasure according to the Bible. Every right-minded Christian rejects the idea that any genuine Christian liberty should be withdrawn from believers. It has been demonstrated that alcoholic beverages are not permitted to Bible believers, although nonalcoholic beverages bearing the same names are not only permitted, but, in the case of *yayin,* highly approved.

Since nonalcoholic grape juice turns into alcoholic grape juice, commonly called wine, because of microorganisms called saccharomycetes (sugar-eating fungi) or yeast which are on the skin of the grapes before they are pressed, people considering themselves total abstainers may drink a little alcohol without intending to do so.

Others may drink a little alcohol at social functions because they wish to ask *no question for conscience sake* (1 Cor. 10:27).

What should be the attitude of one who believes that abstinence is required in these situations, and what should his attitude be toward those who do not agree that total abstinence is required, and who drink only moderately, never to drunkenness and never at all before driving a motor vehicle?

In each of these cases a Christian believer in total abstinence should not make the occasion a reason for harsh judgments in his own mind, much less should he seek to make a case in church courts about it. On the other hand he should not be cowed into accepting the idea of the opposition that the teaching of total abstinence for Christians is *a doctrine of demons*. He should attempt gentle persuasion and not render *railing for railing* (1 Pet. 3:9).

The first occasions of minor types of drinking, like the first occasions of minor gambling, while not necessarily a Christian liberty, should be handled gently. The person involved should probably not be brought before a Church Court, but the fathers and brethren should be prayerfully concerned. If he begins to injure himself or his family by his drinking or gambling, the steps leading up to discipline in his church court will be necessary.

It is the intent of this book to prove that Proverbs teaches an absolute prohibition against the beverage use of alcohol, and that as soon as a Christian becomes convinced of this meaning he should abstain and not seek excuses for indulging his unnatural taste. He should not conceal the true reason for abstaining, as some are tempted to do in order to escape the scorn of drinkers, or to seek to win their favor.

In Chaplains School during World War II the class this writer attended was advised by a Roman Catholic Chaplain instructor not to say bluntly, *I do not drink* (alcohol), or *I never touch the stuff,* as such refusals would destroy respect for one who would be so tactless. Instead the instructor suggested that the non-drinker say, *I never drink on Friday* (or whatever day of the week it might happen to be).

In retrospect, I see that this evasion of the real reason for not drinking in companionship with others, whose respect one would like to have, might be proper if one does not believe that total abstinence is a command of God. For example, if we have decided not to eat cake for fear of obesity, but for no other reason, we might use such an excuse when offered it by people who are in no danger of such a condition. If, however, the temptation is to something we know to be a sin in God's law, we should never evade telling the reason why we should not participate.

I believe that the hurt feelings of friendly wine drinkers, even though they be bound to us by affinity, should not be a reason to drink *a little* with them. Actually they may not be as friendly as we suppose, and may be hoping we will drink to the point of drunkenness, in which case these habitual drinkers will have reason to make sport of us. William Golding's book, *Rites of Passage*, gives a horrifying example of this.

Christians are to honor marriage and be absolute in their condemnation of extra-marital sexual practices. In like manner they should honor nonalcoholic drinks made from the pure fruit of the vine and should be total abstainers from the alcoholic drink which God absolutely forbids us even to look at. We should also give a reason based on the inerrant Bible, our understanding guided by the light of the Holy Spirit.

Notes and Study Questions

When a believer understands the truth that God considers drinking alcohol to be a sin, he should not continue to partake of it. When he is offered an alcoholic drink by others, he should lovingly refuse and take the opportunity to explain why he believes the Bible opposes the drinking of alcohol.

APPENDICES

SOME IMPORTANT HERMENEUTICAL PRINCIPLES AND THE ALCOHOL PROBLEM

In this section two terms used in hermeneutics will be discussed. They are *prolepsis* and *usus loquendi*. All who enter into the discussion of alcohol in the Bible should learn to apply the rules governing these terms as well as other figures of speech. To the shame of writers on both sides of the controversy (the one-wine theorists and those who believe that there are at least two major distinctions in wine) the proper rules have not always been observed.

As examples of two men eminent in their day who were on opposite sides, there are Dr. Charles Hodge, Professor of Theology at Princeton Theological Seminary and his older contemporary, Dr. Moses Stuart, Professor at Andover Theological Seminary. Both were active in the early and mid-nineteenth century. Dr. Hodge held to the one wine theory which he seemed to have believed was so self-evident as to need no defense. He felt so strongly about it that he wrote concerning a resolution denouncing the manufacture, sale and use of intoxicating drinks that it was *infidel in its spirit and tendency,* however many good men had been cajoled or driven into the sin of giving it their sanction.[1]

Dr. Moses Stuart was a distinguished theologian and also a student of the Biblical languages in depth. Dr. Hodge devoted much of his writing to the defense of five points of Calvinist theology and seems not to have concerned himself with different meanings of words which may have sometimes signified an intoxicant and sometimes a non-intoxicant. It was enough for him that Christ created a drink called *oinos,* translated wine, and as wine to him meant and always had meant an intoxicant, anyone who said Christians should not drink intoxicants had been moved by an idea infidel in its spirit and tendency.

[1] Cited by G. 1. Williamson, *Wine in the Bible*...p. 7. See also: *Presbyterian Church in America, The Presbyterian Guardian*, vol. IV, no. 6 (June 26, 1937), p. 87.

The point to be made is that Dr. Hodge, who was eminently fair in his judgments when he took time to examine the facts, spoke highly of Dr. Stuart. Dr. Hodge's son, A. A. Hodge, wrote in his biography of his father: "For Professor Stuart, Professor Hodge felt and expressed the strongest admiration and gratitude." He quotes his father's words:

> We have, therefore, long been in the habit of regarding Prof. Stuart as one of the greatest benefactors of the Church in our century, because he has been the principal means of turning the attention of the rising generation of ministers to this method (philological and exegetical) of studying the Bible. This we doubt not is the great service of his life: a service for which the whole church owes him gratitude and honor, and which will be remembered when present differences and difficulties are forgotten. We do him therefore unfeigned homage as the great American reformer of Biblical study; as the introducer of a new era, and the most efficient opponent of metaphysical theology...[2]

One point to be remembered in this quotation is that Dr. Hodge praised Dr. Stuart for his philological and exegetical method. In the same connection Dr. Hodge criticized Dr. Stuart for failure to deal with the doctrine of imputation in his interpretation of the Epistle to the Romans, but adds the idea that his greatness was such that he could bear the burden of one sad failure.[3]

As we see, Dr. Hodge looked up to Dr. Stuart for his philological and exegetical method. It is precisely his great philological and exegetical skills that Dr. Stuart used in dealing with the question of alcoholic and nonalcoholic wine. Dr. Stuart, after much deep study, wrote:

> Wherever the Scriptures speak of wine as a comfort, a blessing or a libation to God, and rank it with such articles as corn and oil, they mean—they can mean only—such wine as contained no alcohol that could have a mischievous tendency;

---

[2] A. A. Hodge, *The Life of Charles Hodge*, p. 269.

[3] Op. cit. p. 270.

> that wherever they denounce it, prohibit it and connect it with drunkenness and reveling, they can mean only alcoholic or intoxicating wines.[4]

Dr. Hodge was a great man in defense of Calvinistic theology against such opponents, for example, as those who would deny the imputation of Adam's sin to all who descend from him by natural generation. As a theologian in the major doctrines, such as the five points of Calvinism he was outstanding. Alas the modern professors of Princeton Theological Seminary have fallen away. This writer asked the current President of the Seminary what if any of the five points of Calvinism the faculty of the Seminary now all accept. He answered courteously, but not pertinently. It appears that not one of these points which some years ago Presbyterians all professed to believe were true and important is now generally accepted in the school where Dr. Charles Hodge defended them so valiantly.

Another problem which Dr. Hodge addressed was the question of slavery as it existed in the United States in the first part of his career. He joined slave-holding with alcohol drinking as liberties for Christians and he explained why. This explanation he presented to the public in his *Retrospect of the History of the Princeton Review,* written in 1871. His words on this subject include the following:

> The conductors of the Review have always endeavored to adhere faithfully to the principles that the Scriptures are the only infallible rule of faith and practice. Therefore, when any matter, either of doctrine or morals, came under discussion, the question with them was, 'What saith the Lord?' Nothing that the Bible pronounces true can be false; nothing that it declares to be false can be true; nothing is obligatory on the conscience but what it enjoins; nothing can be a sin but what it condemns. If, therefore, the Scriptures under the Old Dispensation permitted men to hold slaves, and if the New Testament nowhere condemns slave-holding, but prescribes the relative duties of masters and slaves, then to pronounce slave-holding

[4] *Encyclopedia of Temperance and Prohibition,* New York, Funk and Wagnalls, 1891. Article, "Stuart, Moses," p. 621.

> to be in itself sinful is contrary to the Scriptures. In like manner, if the Bible nowhere condemns the use of intoxicating liquors as a beverage, if our Lord himself drank wine, then to say that all use of intoxicating beverage is sin, is only one of the many forms of the infidelity of benevolence. It is as much contrary to our allegiance to the Bible to make our own notions of right and wrong the rule of duty as to make our own reason the rule of faith.[5]

It is interesting that Dr. Hodge either did not know of the philologically and exegetically sound treatment of the question of alcoholic beverages done by Dr. Stuart or chose to ignore it.

He could not with consistency say that Dr. Stuart was *cajoled* or *driven* to his position by others.

It is important to examine the grounds on which Dr. Hodge justified slave-holding, for if these are inadequate it makes the task of refuting his position on alcoholic beverages all the easier.

Dr. Hodge was a humane man. He believed that slaves had a right to be taught to read the Bible, to have their conjugal rights respected, to own property, and that parents should not be separated from their minor children. But then, without apparent serious searching of the Scriptures he assumed that the type of slavery practiced in parts of the United States much of his lifetime was the same in principle as the slavery of the Bible.

Biblical slavery differed in a number of important particulars from American Negro slavery. The Bible provided that prisoners taken in lawful war might be enslaved (Numbers 31:30), but it does not follow that the Blacks brought to America were taken prisoners in lawful war. They were rather seized by powerful and cruel slave raiders who were often Black chiefs. These tyrants and terrorists made raids on unprotected people, killed some to terrorize the others, then bound such as they chose to enslave and led them in bonds to slave markets on the coasts of Africa. There they sold them to white traders who brought them to America.

The law of Exodus 21:16 condemns to death anyone who steals a man and sells him. If God's law had been enforced the slave

---

[5] Alexander A. Hodge, op. cit. p. 334.

raiders would have been executed. Anyone who bought these captives would be guilty of receiving stolen property. If Bible law had been enforced Christians in America could not buy these captives unless it could be proved they were taken in lawful war, had lost their liberty because of debts they could not pay, or had committed crimes for which they could not pay lawful fines and penalties.

Dr. Hodge apparently overlooked the fact that probably none, or very few, of the Black slaves brought here had lost their freedom in any way the Bible would recognize as just.

Biblical slavery provided for the release of a Hebrew slave after six years of service if the slave so desired (Ex. 21:2).

The Bible did not provide for keeping in slavery generation after generation of the slave-holders' coreligionists, but American Negro slavery did exactly that. A Christian Black slave could look forward to slavery for himself and his descendants to any generation, with no promise of future release.

By reason of the above mentioned dissimilarities between Biblical slavery and American Negro slavery it seems that Dr. Hodge erred. The rules governing Biblical slavery and American Black Slavery were so dissimilar that sound exegesis would have declared that Americans had no right to buy Blacks from traders who almost certainly had no Biblically authorized right to their possession.

Having written things which some may think are too critical of Dr. Hodge, it is only fair to show from his own writings that he was not what is now called a *racist*, or what is now called a *male chauvinist*.

He wrote:

> It may be objected that if slaves are allowed so to improve as to become free men, the next step in their progress is that they will become citizens. We admit that it is so. The feudal serf first became a tenant, then a proprietor invested with political power. This is the natural progress of political society, and it should be allowed freely to expand itself, or it will work its

own destruction.[6]

He did not, however, believe that the right to vote should be given universally. He wrote to his brother:

> It is true that Maryland is going with the administration?!! It is beyond all comprehension, and affords another proof of the ascendancy of the rabble. If we could have a Republic with the right of suffrage restricted to householders, who can read and write and have at least ten years in the country, we would get along grandly. But a democracy with universal suffrage will soon be worse than an aristocracy with Queen Victoria at the head. I feel such an interest in that youthful sovereign, that I could acknowledge her authority with far more complacency than that of Martin Van Buren.[7]

While Dr. Hodge erred in considering that American Negro slavery qualified as a legitimate form of deprivation of freedom according to Biblical standards, it is to be noted that he would not withhold citizenship and the vote from Blacks on the basis of race. Blacks and whites alike should earn the right to vote.

On matters not within his special area of competence, which was the central ideas of theology, Dr. Hodge was apparently inclined to take the opinion of others as true whether it was or not. Thus, on slavery the norm of the social group with which he was associated determined his understanding of Bible teaching, and the same was true of alcohol. If people of his group (Old School Presbyterians) thought American Negro slavery and the manufacture, sale and consumption of alcoholic beverages were Christian liberties only subject to such restrictions as *they* could perceive in the Bible, then, by a typical human frailty, he did not take up the tools of Biblical exegesis he had at his disposal. Dr. Stuart on the contrary *did* undertake Biblical exegesis on alcohol. In fairness to Dr. Hodge it is probably necessary to admit that Dr. Stuart, being a specialist in Biblical languages was better prepared to do this work, but with all due respect to Dr. Hodge's memory, it is impossible to understand him to have been altogether

[6] Op. cit. p. 336.
[7] Op. cit. p. 233.

excused merely on the basis of comparative lack of skill.

Readers with a high level of loyalty to the one-wine theory, who hold with great conviction that the beverage use of alcohol is a liberty to be cherished, may cling to the idea that Hodge was right and Stuart wrong on the wine question. To do so they must say that on the point of Stuart's excellence in Biblical philology Hodge was wrong, but on his adherence to the one-wine theory Hodge was right. They may say,

> Never mind that this is a question of Biblical philology and that Hodge praised Stuart's ability in this field of study, I have a feeling that Hodge is right on whether words usually translated wine always means an alcoholic drink or not.

Any person who would think along the lines of this hypothetical one-wine loyalist ought to consider what a great orthodox successor of Hodge said about him. This is Benjamin Breckenridge Warfield whose excellent scholarship is known to all Reformed theologians.

Warfield's estimation of Hodge may be found in his *Selected Shorter Writings*, vol. I, page 438.

> He had, however, no taste for the technicalities of Exegesis. He did not shrink from them in his lectures, indeed; but on such points he was seldom wholly satisfactory. His discussion of disputed grammatical or lexical points had a flavor of second-handedness about them. He appeared not to care to have a personal opinion upon such matters, but was content to accept another's without having made it really his own. He would state, in such cases, several views from various critical commentators, and then make a choice between them; but I could not always feel that his choice was determined by sound linguistic principles. He sometimes seemed to be quite as apt to choose an indefensible as a plausible one—guided, apparently, sometimes by weight of name, sometimes by dislike of what seemed to him over-subtlety, and sometimes, it seemed by theological predilection.
>
> He made no claim, again, to critical acumen; and in questions of textual criticism he constantly went astray. Hence

it was that often texts were quoted to support doctrines of which they did not treat; and a meaning was sometimes extracted from a passage which it was far from bearing.

Such was the considered opinion of Dr. Warfield. In view of this should we attach weight to Dr. Hodge's opinion that to denounce the manufacture, sale and use of alcoholic beverages is *infidel in its spirit and tendency*? On theology in general Hodge was good, but in exegesis rather weak.

Prolepsis

Prolepsis (which may also be called anticipation) is the treating of a future event as though it had already happened, or the giving a name to something as though it existed before it came to be. This figure of speech is rare in the Bible and when it is used it is for a good reason. A good reason is lacking in the places where one-wine theorists propose it as an aid in upholding their position.

One place where it is to be found is in Hebrews 7:10 where we are told that Levi was yet in the loins of his father (meaning Abraham) when Abraham gave tithes to Melchisedec. Now this is a very special case. It is not intended to teach us that there was a little Levi hidden away somewhere in the body of Abraham. It may speak to the fact that Levi when he was eventually conceived, inherited some of the genes of his ancestor, but it is not like Psalm 139:13 and Jeremiah 1:5. In these passages the real David and the real Jeremiah are said to have existed in the wombs of their mothers. They could have been seen if x-ray photography had existed. Today real people can be seen shrinking from and seeking to avoid the abortionist's tool of destruction. These words of David and Jeremiah are not prolepsis.

Hebrews 7:10 speaks of Levi in the loins of his ancestor by prolepsis as a vivid way of saying that the Levitical priesthood was inferior to the priesthood of Melchisedec and that Christ's priesthood is superior to the Levitical priesthood because it is of the order of Melchisedec. There is a good didactic reason for this prolepsis which is lacking in Isaiah 16:10.

In Job 10:10 the great sufferer Job is thought by many

commentators to have described himself as having been poured out in the semen of his father. Not all commentators agree, but if this is the meaning of Job, there was a good reason from Job's point of view for this figure of speech. It is the anguished cry of a man who is weary of life and who calls on his Creator to remember the process by which God, working through Job's father, brought him to conception.

The one-wine theorists say that Isaiah 16:10 refers to alcoholic wine by prolepsis. This in the context does not make sense. The prophet is saying that in the time of dearth he predicts the Moabites who would normally tread the grapes to make *yayin* (grape juice) could not do so because there would be no grapes. Grape juice unfermented is called *yayin mi-gat* in Talmudic times and there is no reason it may not have been called simply *yayin* in Isaiah's time. If a modern grower of grape vines would say in a time when there was no harvest, "my presses are producing no alcoholic wine," we would think it strange. Even if he were in a poetic mood we would see no point in this remark. We might ask him, "why did you not say, they are producing no grape juice?" If he answered, "I was speaking by prolepsis," we would consider his talk truly absurd. What would he be trying to prove? That he despised unfermented grape juice and vinegar?

A rule of interpretation is to put ourselves in the setting in which the passage is found. The Moabites are seen to be starving. Whatever grapes there might have been would have been consumed at once. To believe that the prophet was thinking in poetical terms by prolepsis of the lengthy process of wine manufacture would be totally out of harmony with the situation—and very bad poetry.

What word do the one-wine theorists propose would have been used by speakers of Old Testament Hebrew if they meant grape juice (unfermented wine) fresh from the press? *Tirosh* and *'asis* are not suitable as some, perhaps all of them, admit. As far as we can tell speakers of Hebrew in Old Testament times used the same word for fermented and unfermented grape juice. This word was *yayin*.

The one-wine theorists do not say how these people would

distinguish between intoxicating and non-intoxicating grape juice. It is hard to think that they suppose that everyone, even little children, drank intoxicating wine and drank it to the exclusion of grape juice in an unfermented state.

Bringing prolepsis in as an explanation of why, even when the circumstances forbid us to imagine alcoholic wine, the wine of Isaiah 16:10 is alcoholic, is not sound thinking.

The English word cider is used of both the alcoholic and nonalcoholic varieties. If speakers of modern English are required to make a distinction they call the former *hard cider* and the latter *sweet cider.*

It is impossible for some of us to agree that *yayin* was always alcoholic, leaving speakers of Biblical Hebrew with no good words to distinguish the two when the context or situation did not make the distinction sufficiently clear. This writer believes that they probably used *yayin mi-gat* or something similar, meaning unfermented wine, and *yayin ki yith 'addam,* or *chemer*[8] when it was necessary to say, without fear of misunderstanding, that they were speaking of intoxicating wine.

Usus Loquendi (Usage of Speech)

To make use of the hermeneutical tool called *usus loquendi* is very difficult in interpreting the Hebrew Bible, because there is no contemporary literature surviving. If we had the writings of a large number of Hebrew contemporaries of Moses, and as many of David, of Solomon, of Isaiah and of other Biblical writers, we would be in a better position to understand the *usus loquendi* of their expressions.

In the Greek New Testament an example of what had become *usus loquendi* is in 1 Corinthians 15:5 where Paul refers to *the twelve* at a time when Judas was dead and his successor not yet named. We can infer from this that the term *the twelve* had become a fixed

---

[8] The word *chemer* is proposed as an expression for *alcoholic wine* or fermented grape juice. This proposal is based in part on *yayin chamar* which we have attempted to demonstrate means *the wine is alcoholic. Chemer* in Deut. 32:14 is best explained as *alcoholic wine.*

designation of the order of the Apostles. It was not changed when temporarily there were only eleven.

Since we have no contemporary literature, it is impossible to prove that at any particular time and place *yayin* meant fermented wine and nothing else. On the other hand, it cannot be proved that at any particular time it meant unfermented wine (which in our contemporary *usus loquendi* we call grape juice) and nothing else. Apparently the *usus loquendi* of the Hebrew language throughout the entire period of several centuries in which the Bible was being revealed in that tongue was that *yayin* could stand for either meaning. There is nothing strange in this. The word *'elohim* means (1) the one true God in Genesis 1:1 and many other places. It means (2) gods, that is, pagan deities in Exodus 12:12 and elsewhere. It also means (3) angels (Psalms 8:6—8:5 in English versions—cf. Hebrews 2:7). There are other meanings of *'elohim* which are thought to exist. Christian scholars may disagree over these special meanings with no feeling that their opinions show an *infidel tendency*. But the three meanings cited above and generally agreed on are enough to establish the fact that every word must be defined *according to its context*. As far as the *usus loquendi* can be established it should be used.

The term *rebel* may to an Englishman mean what an American would call a patriot of the American revolution. The same term *rebel* meant to many American northerners what their southern contemporaries in the war of 1861-5 would call a patriot. If these terms are used out of context, it creates confusion. So do the terms which have more than one meaning with regard to whether or not they have alcoholic content.

We (meaning all people) may properly and confidently affirm that as far as can be determined the *usus loquendi* indicates that *yayin* praised is nonalcoholic and where condemned is alcoholic. When it is neither praised or condemned it may refer to wine in general (both kinds included) or it may refer to one or the other in particular. In the latter case, there may be some difficulty of interpretation, but no problem of faith or practice arises from this. Users of the English language are able to live comfortably with the fact that the word cider may designate an alcoholic drink and also a nonalcoholic one.

But we should not accept gladly the opinion of those who say God both praises and condemns the same substance.

THE WORD *Yith' addam*: A MORE DETAILED EXPLANATION OF THE GRAMMATICAL EVIDENCE

For the benefit of those who are not familiar with Hebrew grammar it is necessary to give an explanation of the reason for understanding the word *yith'addam* as a reference to alcohol. This interpretation may seem innovative and therefore suspect. Such a reaction is to be expected, but an effort should be made to remove the suspicions of all who are genuinely seeking the truth.

Such persons are invited to read the following statements written to help those who know nothing of the grammar of the Hebrew language as it was in Bible times. (As many as can do so, and who wish to know whether the things proposed in this paper are true or not, are urged to enter into the study of Biblical Hebrew and Biblical Greek in some depth).

The Hebrew language differs from English and other Indo European languages in having verb forms called *stems,* by which the meaning of a verb is modified by prefixes, vowel changes and by the doubling of the middle consonant of the root. Thus *'azar* means *to gird,* but if the prefix *hith*– is put before the root and if the middle consonant is doubled, the form is *hith'azzer* and the meaning is *to gird oneself.* This is called *hithpael.*

Hebrew also differs from English in that ideas which we express by adjectives and a verb, such as *to be, to make,* or *to make itself,* etc., are in Hebrew often expressed by verbal forms alone. Thus Hebrew not only has an adjective *'adom,* meaning *red,* but a verb which is also *'adom,* meaning *to be red.* This verb has a stem (*pual*) meaning *to be made* or *dyed red* as in Exodus 25:5 et al. It also has the *hithpael* stem as in Proverbs 23:31, where *yith'addam* (imperfect of *hith'addam*) means *it* (the *yayin*) *makes itself red.*

There is no justification at all for saying that in Biblical Hebrew this stem gives the simple meaning of the adjective *red* with the verb *is* before it. To express the idea *when it is red* the inspired writer could have written *ki 'adom* using the simple or *light* (*qal*) verbal form, or he could have used the adjective *red* with a form of the verb *to be* —*ki yihyeh 'adom*. Either way the expression means *when it is red*. The verb *yihyeh* (*it is*) could be omitted and the expression would still mean *when it is red*.

To sum up, the verb form *hith'addam* can only be explained as meaning *to make itself red*, and *ki yith'addam* as *when it makes itself red*. Other possible senses of the *hithpael*, such as reciprocal action, as in *hithra'ah, to look at one another*, cannot be applied to *hith'addam*.

Taking the whole counsel of God into account, that is evaluating carefully the general consensus of Scripture, and knowing that God does not make senseless commands, we are drawn inevitably to the conclusion that God is not speaking of color literally, but in a figure of speech. What God is saying is that we cannot look at *yayin* when it makes itself into such a drink as brings on all the evils so vividly described in Proverbs 23. This can only mean that we should not look on (and afterwards consume) *yayin* after it has fermented itself with the alcohol-producing yeast. The idea of alcohol is evidently connoted by this stem of the root *'adom*.

It is puerile to suppose this command is not to be taken seriously and that the prohibition is not absolute. All the prohibitions in Proverbs 23 are absolute. The God who will punish those who move boundary stones (verse 10), will not spare those who understand what verse 31 means and scornfully disobey. To claim not to understand when sound evidence is presented, is sinful.

THE ORIGIN OF THE MODERN CHRISTIAN TOTAL ABSTINENCE MOVEMENT

Dr. Paul Woolley, a noted Orthodox Presbyterian Church historian (now deceased), whom I knew and respected, and who stood on the side of Christian orthodoxy in the first part of the twentieth century, attributed the rise of the total abstinence movement to *Fundamentalism.* He used this term not as the doctrine of the five fundamentals of Christianity, but in the narrower sense of a system of rules for personal conduct.

A rather lengthy quotation follows and this is included to show one (and I believe incorrect) view of the origin of modern total abstinence in Christian circles.

> Machen (Dr. J. Gresham Machen) had expressed his opinion about fundamentalism on various occasions. If all Christians were to be classified as either *fundamentalists* or *modernists* then, obviously, he was a fundamentalist. But he disliked the term and what it usually represented. It stood for a limited number of *fundamental* doctrines, while Machen stood for the importance of the whole, rich system of doctrine which was found in the Scriptures and which he believed to be summarized in the Westminster Confession. He wanted no less than all the wealth of that system.
>
> Fundamentalism also stood for a system of rules concerning personal conduct which it had inherited from the Methodist Holiness Movement and, ultimately, from the German Pietism of Philip Jakob Spener and his followers. The rules of this movement were not to be found directly in Scripture. Their proponents thought them to be deduced from Scripture. But this was a very dubious proposition. What Buswell (Dr. J. Oliver Buswell, Jr.) seemed to have as his most immediate concern was an emphasis on total abstinence from alcoholic beverages. This was obviously not a proposition set forth in the

Bible.[1]

This last sentence is the one which most needs to be refuted, but as a matter of less importance, this historical treatment of the origin of total abstinence in Christian circles should be opposed.

I must admit being grieved by those who say total abstinence may be permissible as a personal position, but who deny that it is a Biblical command to abstain from the beverage use of what the Bible condemns so strongly in Proverbs 23:31-35.

Those who agree with the opinion that total abstinence is obviously not set forth in the Bible will of course seek to pin the blame for this supposedly pernicious idea on the culprit. Those who believe that total abstinence is the Bible's very own doctrine will be glad to trace the origin of the modern revival of Christian total abstinence and will honor those who are on record for taking a stand for Christian orthodoxy which demands abstinence from the beverage use of alcohol. This inclusion of abstinence from alcohol must not displace or supplant or do away with the orthodoxy of the historic creeds of Christendom or of the doctrine of the inerrant Bible. It is rather an orthodoxy which takes the Bible as a deadly serious book in all its parts, deadly, that is, to those who misuse it. It is a life giving Book to those who are willing to be nourished by its total truth.

Jerome (c. 346-420) the translator of the Bible into Latin (the *Vulgate*) was a master of the languages in which the Bible was originally written and was therefore qualified to speak on matters of Biblical interpretation. His theology has not been seriously questioned as to its orthodoxy. He wrote: "If experience gives me a right to advise, or clothe my words with credit, I would begin by urging you and warning you, as Christ's spouse, to avoid wine as you would a poison."[2]

This is as strong a statement for total abstinence from alcoholic beverages as those Fundamentalist total abstainers whose views

[1] Woolley, *The Significance of J. Gresham Machen Today*, Nutley, N.J., The Presbyterian and Reformed Publishing Co., 1977, p. 42.

[2] Letters, p. 25, vol. 6, *Post Nicene Fathers*. These remarks of Jerome are quoted at greater length elsewhere in this book.

Dr. Woolley repudiated might wish.

Unfortunately other Christian theologians, not as thoroughly trained in Hebrew as Jerome, abandoned his teaching (perhaps many of them did not even know it) that wine should be avoided as one would avoid a poison.

It seems from the evidence that Spener or the Holiness Methodists ought not to be thought of as the originators of the modern Christian total abstinence movement. Some Christians may reproach them for having made total abstinence a Christian requirement and others may honor them for having done so, but in either case it would be assigning too much blame or credit to them. What they did was to make moderation a requirement and not total abstinence.

As for the Holiness Methodists, the rules formulated by the Wesleys for the United Societies of Methodists in 1743 declared that all

> members were expected to evidence their desire for salvation, first, by doing no harm; by avoiding evil of every kind, especially that which is most generally practiced such as...drunkenness, buying or selling spirituous liquors, or drinking them, except in cases of extreme necessity.[3]

It is to be noted that this rule, good as it is, has no prohibition of wine or beer, but only of *spirituous*, that is, distilled alcoholic beverages.

Later (in the Methodist Episcopal Church in America in 1790) the rule of Wesley was modified so as to read, *drunkenness or drinking spirituous liquors, unless in cases of necessity,*—the words *buying or selling* and *extreme* being omitted. This less aggressive attitude of the church continued for a number of years, and in 1812 the General Conference voted down the following resolution:

> Resolved, that no stationed or local preacher shall retail spirituous or malt liquors, without forfeiting his ministerial character among us.

---

[3] Methodist Episcopal Church, *Encyclopedia of Temperance and Prohibition*, p. 45.

It is rather startling that the Methodists (called Holiness because of their belief that perfect holiness is possible for a Christian to attain in this life) thought by some to have wrongfully begun the movement to require total abstinence from all alcoholic beverages to all their members, were as recently as 1812 unwilling to censure their preachers for retailing distilled or malt liquors.

The credit (not blame!) for being the driving force of the total abstinence movement among Christians in the United States seems to go to the Rev. Dr. John Marsh (1788-1868). *The Encyclopedia of Temperance and Prohibition* says of Dr. Marsh:

> Born in Wethersfield, Conn., April 2, 1788; died in Brooklyn, N.Y., Aug. 5, 1868. At a 4th of July celebration he became intoxicated, but one such experience was sufficient to make him an abstainer. Upon finishing a course of study at Yale College he fitted himself for the ministry, and in 1809 he began preaching. In 1818 he was installed pastor of the Congregational Church at Haddam, Conn., where he remained for fourteen years...A temperance speech delivered by him in Pomfret, Conn., Oct. 29, 1829, entitled 'Putnam and the Wolf,' was printed and 150,000 copies were sold. In 1831 he was employed by the Baltimore Temperance Society to conduct a three month's campaign in that city and Washington. He left his church in charge of another and gave his entire time to the new work. One of the developments of this engagement was the famous temperance meeting held in the Hall of the National House of Representatives, Dec. 16, 1831. It was presided over by Lewis Cass, and among the speakers were Daniel Webster, ex-President John Quincy Adams, Senators Theodore Frelinghuysen and Felix Grundy, and Representatives J. M. Wayne and Isaac C. Bates.

These statesmen of national importance were not predominately Methodist; so the thesis that Christian total abstinence comes from the German Pietists to the Methodists and thence into other denominations of Christians fails at this point.

Mr. Marsh continued his labors and was very active in promoting the National Temperance Society with headquarters in Philadelphia. The first National Temperance Convention met in

Philadelphia in May, 1833, and expressed the conviction that "the traffic in ardent spirit as drink, and the use of it as such, are morally wrong and ought to be abandoned throughout the world."

It is to be noted that this statement said nothing about wine and beer. Mr. Marsh seems to have felt that it was good, but that more was needed.

The second Convention at Saratoga, New York, in August, 1836, took the final step *under the direction of devoted men like Dr. John Marsh* extending the principle so as to cover *all intoxicating liquors*.

The importance of Dr. Marsh was expressed by a friend of the movement in 1865:

> Dr. John Marsh for the last 25 years has been the American Union—its body, its soul, its spirit, its President, its Executive Committee, its everything.

Since Dr. Marsh was a Congregationalist minister the theory that total abstinence is a product of Methodist activity must be abandoned. Those who love the movement must honor the Methodists for putting the weight of their splendid organization behind it in the early twentieth century. It is for this reason in all probability that Methodists are credited, by people who do not study the history of the movement, with being its founders.

It must be regretted that the Methodist Church in the U.S.A. and other *mainstream* Protestant Churches and the Roman Catholic Church have lost much of their zeal for the worthy cause of Christian total abstinence. The credit, however, should be given where it is due. Christian saints who struggled in the past for a worthy cause should not be forgotten. It is not their fault if their modern successors are not carrying on the struggle.

Roman Catholics and Total Abstinence

It may come as a surprise to many Christians of the late twentieth century to be informed that almost contemporaneously to the American total abstinence movement a very important movement of similar nature was springing up in Roman Catholic circles, having its origin in Ireland.

The leader was Theobald Mathew (1790-1856) a Roman Catholic priest, a member of the Capuchin order. His eloquent sermons and his wisdom won for him a wide popularity. Throughout the cholera epidemic of 1832 he was a faithful attendant in one of the largest hospitals of Cork, having requested *as a favor* that the hours of his service should be from midnight to 6 in the morning when he would be exposed to the greatest contagion. For several years he was one of the Governors of the House of Industry—the Cork workhouse—and in his frequent visits to the inmates he won the friendship of another of the Governors, William Martin, an old Quaker, who, with two associates (Rev. Nicholas Dunscombe, a Protestant clergyman, and Richard Dowden) enjoyed local prominence because of their fanatically persistent, but not very fruitful advocacy of total abstinence. In passing through the workhouse in company with the priest it was Martin's custom to point out some of the most wretched victims of intemperance, with the comment, "Oh, Theobald Mathew, if thou would but take the cause in hand!" After long deliberation Father Mathew sent for his Quaker friend one evening early in April, 1838, and requested him to assist in forming a temperance organization. A meeting was held in Father Mathew's chapel on the 10th of April, resulting in the formation of the Cork Total Abstinence Society, with 60 enrolled members, each of whom took the following pledge: "I promise to abstain from all intoxicating drinks, etc., except used medicinally and by the order of a medical man, and to discountenance the cause and practice of intemperance."

The number of pledge-signers multiplied with a rapidity far surpassing the fondest dreams of the most sanguine of the reformers. In August, 1839, the members numbered 21,780, and from this date the movement assumed huge proportions; the enrollments in August and September swelled the total to 52,707, and in October to 66,360.

The Excise returns showed a remarkable falling off in the consumption of spirits in Ireland and crime was greatly reduced.

At the close of the first three months of the year 1841 the

number of pledge-takers had reached a total of 4,647,000 and by the end of that year it is estimated that it must have been at least 5,000,000 in a total population of 8,175,124 (Census of 1841).

Father Mathew visited Glasgow in 1842 and many there signed the pledge and in 1843 he toured England with similar results. He came to the United States in 1849; so we see that he was not exclusively concerned about Ireland in a narrow sense, but Ireland was his first and abiding love.

He cherished the hope that Ireland would have the cause for drunkenness removed. He must have been aware that many pledgetakers relapsed with liquor readily available, so it is obvious what he had in mind was national prohibition such as later became the law, by constitutional amendment, in the United States.

The portion of his speech in which he spoke of his hope that Ireland would have the cause removed is as follows:

> The great temperance movement which we witness was not lightly thought of by me; it was not the result of hidden excitement; it was not the impulse of a moment that induced me to undertake the share I have had in it. I pondered long upon it; I examined it carefully; I had long reflected on the degradation to which my country was reduced—a country I will say, second to none in the universe for every element that constitutes a nation's greatness, with a people whose generous nature is the world's admiration. I mourned in secret over the miseries of this country; I endeavored to find out the cause of those miseries, and, if that were possible, to apply a remedy. I saw that these miseries were chiefly owing to the crimes of the people, and that those crimes again had their origin in the use that was made of intoxicating drinks. I discovered that if the cause were removed the effects would cease; and with my hopes in the God of universal benevolence and charity, reposing my hopes in the Omnipotent, I began the mission in Cork.[4]

---

[4] Maguire's Father Mathew, p. 86, quoted in Encyclopedia of Temperance and Prohibition, p. 418.

National prohibition not having been attained in Ireland, the drink evil remained and even increased during the famine years of 1845 and 1846 in spite of the fact that many were starving to death. Father Mathew was moved to say:

> Is it not a terrible thing to think that so much wholesome grain, that God intended for the support of human life, should be converted into a maddening poison, for the destruction of man's body and soul? By a calculation recently made it is clearly proved that if all the grain now converted into poison were devoted to its natural and legitimate use it would afford a meal a day to every man, woman and child in the land. The man or woman who drinks, drinks the food of the starving. Is not that man or woman a monster who drinks the food of the starving?

Father Mathew came to the United States in 1849 and his reception was attended by official honors rarely accorded to a foreigner. For example, at Washington President Taylor extended a banquet to him at the White House, and the Senate voted to admit him to the bar of the Senate Chamber—a mark of distinction that had been conferred on only one other foreigner, General Lafayette.

It is to be observed that although John Marsh and Theobald Mathew were both clergymen in their respective denominations, we have no record that they interested themselves in the search to see if the Bible itself, if studied in detail and as a whole in the original languages in which God chose to bring its inerrant truths to mankind, did not itself teach total abstinence from the beverage use of what we now know as alcohol.

The fact that the total abstinence from the use of all alcoholic drinks taught by the Rev. John Marsh and the Rev. Theobold Mathew was not accepted by all Christians may be accounted for by this fact. Yes, many said alcohol is dangerous, but temperance not total abstinence is the means to resist it. And then, of course, many failed to be temperant and became alcoholics.

The tool of Bible exegesis based on sound exegetical methods which could prove that there are two kinds of *yayin, oinos* and *shekar*, one alcoholic and the other nonalcoholic, was available.

Few seemed to care to search for it. Many who were active in the different churches were content to attempt to prove that alcohol caused crime, degrades its addicts in many ways, and hurts society. Although this convinced some people to be total abstainers, others were shocked and said, Jesus created an alcoholic drink for the wedding guests at Cana. What about my Lord! Do you condemn what He did?

We urge such people to search the Scriptures with the tools of sound exegesis. First they should convince themselves that Proverbs 23 prohibits alcoholic *yayin*. Then they should convince themselves that there is another sort of *yayin* which is permitted. Further study should lead to a similar distinction in the Greek word *oinos*.

The slowness of perception of Christians from the time of Jerome to the nineteenth century that all Christians should abstain totally from all alcoholic beverages is easily explained. It is partly tradition. They said, "My Christian parents always drank." But Christ had only contempt for tradition not based on the revealed, inerrant truth of the Bible. It is partly to be explained by the general (but false) belief that the intoxicating ingredient in wine and beer was one of the natural elements of fruit and grain.

When the chemistry of alcohol began to be understood, and when there was full knowledge that it is not a natural element of fruit and grain, the excuse (weak as it was) that alcoholic beverages are permitted to Christians should have disappeared. Wine (nonalcoholic) *makes glad the heart of man* (Psalm 104:15). Wine (alcoholic) whose effects are vividly described in Proverbs 23:29-35 is strictly prohibited (verse 31).

It is time that Christians accepted the idea that total abstinence from alcohol is directly derived from the Word of God. It is not merely indirectly derived as is the sound idea that we should avoid the use of opium for pleasure. No one should say we may use opium because it does not appear to be condemned by name in the Bible. It kills and the Bible condemns self-destruction. Nicotine kills too, a fact more widely known now than formerly. Christians who use it should ask themselves if they are not sinning against God by slow self-destruction. Alcohol, however, differs from opium and nicotine in that what is obviously an alcoholic drink, described by its effects on the user, is forbidden. From this it is easy to deduce that what is forbidden is not the grape juice in which the alcohol has formed but the alcohol itself.

WISDOM OR FOLLY?

A paper has been presented to the public entitled *All Embracing Wisdom* which is anything but wise. After a few correct statements it lays the groundwork for a house built on a foundation of sand, which cannot stand.

In this paper we find these words:

> In Scripture, there is no such distinction as unfermented and fermented wine. Of the 140 times yayin (Hebrew for wine) is used, in no instance can it be shown to mean unfermented wine...

Answer: In Isaiah 16:10 God says of a desolated area that "the treaders shall tread out no wine (*yayin*) in their presses." Unfermented grape juice is the only liquid possible as a result of the treading of grapes. Ancient Hebrew had no word restricted in meaning to unfermented grape juice, but there can be no doubt that they knew what it was, and grape juice was what was meant here. The word *yayin* for grape juice in an unfermented state was used, and this proves that the statement quoted above, on which the author attempts to build so much, is wrong.

The paper's next statement is also incorrect. It is: "Tirosh (Hebrew for new wine) also cannot mean unfermented grape juice."

Answer: A recent widely accepted authority (Koehler-Baumgartner's Dictionary) says that *tirosh* is archaic for *yayin*. If this is true, whatever may be said for *tirosh* can also be said for *yayin*, and no further proof is needed that *tirosh* may be free from alcohol. If, however, *tirosh* does have a different meaning from *yayin*, Proverbs 3:10 is proof that it (*tirosh*) also may be nonalcoholic. The expression is: "thy presses shall burst out with *tirosh*" (KJV and NIV—both translate *tirosh* as new wine). The press (*yeqeb*) was where the grapes were pressed. It could never burst forth with alcoholic wine. Fermentation to alcohol takes time and the grape juice passes immediately from the press in an unfermented state.

The paper says: "*Oinos* (Greek for wine) means fermented

grape juice of alcoholic content. For proof see its use in the *Septuagint*."

Answer: This is false, because *oinos* is used in the *Septuagint* to translate *yayin* in Isaiah 16:10 and *tirosh* in Proverbs 3:10 where, as has been demonstrated, the meaning *cannot* be *alcoholic* wine.

The paper says: "The Apostles did not forbid or condemn the wise use of wine and strong drink. 1 Cor. 6:12; 10:23; 1 Cor. 11:21, 22, 1 Tim. 5:23; 3:3 ."

Answer: These Bible citations are ineptly chosen. The point the paper tries to make cannot be sustained, but the citations show the poverty of thinking that brought about their selection. The first two are not intended to free believers from obedience to the moral law. No sound thinker supposes that they do. Proverbs 23:31, which forbids looking at a certain kind of wine, is a *moral* law and has never been abrogated. It is a *moral* law (not a *ceremonial* or *judicial* law) and is of precisely the same grammatical form as the *moral* command in verse 10 against *stealing land,* verse 17 against *envying sinners,* and verse 20 against *associating* with *drinkers* of (*alcoholic*) wine. All these prohibitions stand in all ages and people disobey them only at their peril. The freedom Paul refers to in these Bible citations has to do with freedom from the ceremonial law.

1 Cor. 11:21, 22 does not support the view the paper is trying to make. Paul is condemning the drunkenness of the Corinthians who came to the church not to eat a[1] Lord's Supper, but to consume their own supper, which contained intoxicants. They were not interested in the canonical Lord's Supper which had to be explained to them in verses 23-34. When the true Lord's Supper is here described there is no word even suggesting an *intoxicant.* The liquid element is here referred to as *the cup.*

The new Christians of Corinth were perhaps attempting to transfer some crude pagan orgy to the church. They had houses where they were at liberty to eat or to drink nonalcoholic substances.

1 Timothy 5:23 does not prove that Paul commanded Timothy

[1] The definite article is not in the original Greek.

to drink a little alcoholic wine for his stomach's sake. Nonalcoholic wine (grape juice) is good for weak stomachs, alcohol is not.

1 Timothy 3:3 (cited in the paper in favor of drinking alcoholic wine) *opposes* being given to wine (being addicted to it). A command against addiction does not abrogate a command not even to look at a forbidden substance.

The paper says: "The apostles condemned those who sought to impose total abstinence upon the conscience, 1 Tim. 4:1-4; Col. 2:20-23."

Answer: The inerrant Bible must be interpreted by sound rules. An important rule is that we examine the context and see what the inspired writer wishes to say. In 1 Timothy 4:1-4 there is no reference to drink of any kind, but that is not the reason, or at least the principal reason, for rejecting this alleged proof text. It must be rejected because the people condemned were hypocritical liars who were teaching a particular system of doctrine which prohibited marriage and abstinence from foods. It should not be understood to mean that every prohibition of marriage (e. g. of incestuous marriages) or command concerning abstinence from food is a doctrine of demons. The Rechabites and Nazirites were taught, with God's approval, to abstain totally from all products of the grape vine. For G. I. Williamson to propose that a Christian who teaches that Proverbs 23:31 forbids alcoholic wine is teaching a doctrine of demons is invective and nothing more. A Christian who teaches total abstinence should not be dismayed at this, but should rather rejoice (Matt. 5:11-12).

1 Timothy 4:4 says that every creature (*ktisma*) of God is not to be rejected. This is singularly inappropriate as a proof text for the beverage use of alcohol, as this poison is not created by God, but is the excrement of a microorganism (a yeast). God created all living creatures, but the matter they expel as waste should not be dignified with the title *creature of God*. We may thank God for animal waste, for example as fertilizer, but we should not call it a creation of God.

Colossians 2 is written to oppose Judaizers, as scholars are agreed. In this context the drink referred to in verse 16 may be milk, which Orthodox Jews legislate against under certain conditions.[2] In no case may the passage be understood to abrogate the moral law of Proverbs 23:31.

---

[2] See the Talmud, Hullin 105a. Here we are told that Jews may not eat milk after meat in the same meal. Julius H. Greenstone in *Dietary Laws*, The *Jewish Encyclopedia*, vol. 4, p. 598 says, *not only meat, but also milk and cheese bought of a non-Jew are forbidden.* This was because a Jew could not be sure the meat, milk or cheese bought of a non-Jew had not been previously offered to idols. The non-Jew's word was not to be trusted. Anything (including liquids) previously offered to idols was strictly forbidden to the Jews. Colossians 2:16-33 may refer to the prohibition of milk after meat or to the prohibition of liquids offered to idols. Even if some prohibitions introduced by heretics from religions other than Judaism are in view here, Paul's opposition to these prohibitions in no way gives the Christian permission to drink a poison, of which alcohol is an example.

PERMANENT BRAIN DAMAGE AND THE MODERATE USE OF ALCOHOL

There are numerous Bible passages which teach that we should not damage the brain, the center of our thought processes in any way. For example, *thou shalt not kill* (Ex. 20:13). The brain is part of the life God has given, and we have no right to kill it. Another text is Proverbs 20:1, "Wine is a mocker, strong drink is raging and whosoever is deceived thereby is not wise." We are commanded to be wise (Matt. 10:16) and if we allow a drug to deprive us of wisdom we are sinning against God. When we see an advertisement saying *Clear heads call for* such and such a liquor, we should be wise enough to know that it is a lie.

One verse in particular strengthens the argument against damaging our brains through alcohol abuse, or in fact through any drug abuse. It is Isaiah 1:18a: "Come now let us reason together, saith the Lord" (KJV). The Hebrew word translated *let us reason, niwwakechah,* which is of the same root and stem as the verb in Job 23:7 where Job pleads that he may *dispute,* that is defend his cause before God in person. What Job sought from God in Job 23:1-17, God freely offers in Isaiah 1:18. He the Almighty, gives a free offer to rebellious children to reason with him, that is, to seek to reach an understanding.

To be invited to reason with God is an awesome invitation. Proud men do not reason with those they think of as their underlings, even though in flattery and when it suits their purposes they may call them friends. If they have come to believe that their opinion is right, their pride causes them to refuse to enter into reasonable discussion when a less powerful person seeks by reasonable arguments to convince them of a point of fact or theory.

Not so God! He invites men to reason (dispute) with Him!

There are some who say that God only invites people who are regenerate (born again) to reason with Him. The argument follows these lines: (1) Proverbs 9:10 says "the fear of the Lord is the beginning of wisdom"; (2) the fear of God is reverence for Him;

(3) only the regenerate revere God; and therefore (4) only they are gifted with wisdom in the theological sense. (5) Those who lack wisdom in the theological sense are fools, and God would not deign to reason with them.

But the first chapter of Isaiah refutes this line of reasoning. The people who are invited to reason are rebellious sinners whose worship is utterly rejected by God. They do not *know* God in the scriptural sense (1 John 4:6, 7). The first chapter of Isaiah teaches that even the vilest sinners may present their needs, even their doubts to God and then they may read the Bible to find God's answer. We are not told that men must have the mystical experience of being born again before they can reason with God. He is omniscient and His ways are past finding out, but He graciously meets man at his own level and whatever reasoning powers a human being has, he is invited to test them in disputing with God.

If we are invited to debate with a human antagonist we would probably prepare well, especially if the reward for winning is considerable, as for example the possibility of being elected to high office.

Since we are invited to reason with God (a kind of debate) we ought to try to see that our mind is as good as it is possible for us to make it.

What folly to do after the manner of many of our fellow men to destroy, not temporarily only, but permanently as well, the part of our brain where the highest degree of reasoning power is concentrated! Our eternal destiny is at stake.

All persons interested in the alcohol problem should be aware that modern science has made it possible to examine the brain damage caused by alcohol and the findings are not comforting either to social drinkers or to alcoholics. The new technique is the use of what are called CAT[1] scans, which show that brain cells,

---

[1] Acronym for coaxial tomography. A CAT scanner is a medical term for computed axial tomography, a diagnostic X-ray device providing a detailed three-dimensional view of a slice of the body by rotating the X-ray machine completely around the patient, taking pictures at various angles.

particularly those in the frontal lobes, are actually destroyed by the consumption of alcohol.

Drivers who drink and then refrain from operating a motor vehicle may congratulate themselves in thinking that all is well and that they can drive with perfect safety for themselves as well as others as long as the alcohol has oxidized so that it is no longer in their bodies. But they should think again.

Galen C. Bosley, D.H.Sc., has studied numerous medical reports published in journals in different countries showing that even moderate drinking of alcohol actually destroys brain cells which are never replaced. It is hard to see how anyone can contemplate the destruction of a part of his body with equanimity. When the part of the body first to be destroyed are cells in the brain controlling moral discernment the complacency of mankind about this wholesale destruction of human capacity is astounding.

Part of what Dr. Bosley has written, together with quotations from his sources, is included in the following paragraphs in the hope that concerned readers will be stimulated to pursue the matter further. It is to be hoped that once they are informed by competent authorities people will act in appropriate ways.

Dr. Bosley writes:[2]

> In Australia Dr. L. A. Cala and associates have for many years studied the effects of alcoholism on the brain and its ability to function.[3] To determine the point at which alcohol consumption begins brain damage, Cala examined heavy drinkers, using CAT scans and found brain shrinkage already in progress. Using the same CAT procedure, she then examined a group of individuals considered to be moderate to light drinkers. Of thirty-nine drinkers tested, thirty were found to have some brain shrinkage, with frontal lobes bearing the

---

[2] *The Effects of Small Quantities of Alcohol*, *Ministry, International Journal for Clergy*, vol. 59, no. 5 (May, 1986), pp. 24-27.

[3] L. A. Cala, *C.T. Demonstration of the Early effects of Alcohol on the Brain*, in M. Plenum, ed., *Recent Developments in Alcoholism* (New York: Plenum Press, 1985), vol. 3, pp. 253-264.

first signs.[4] Thus far the results of these studies indicate that the amount of alcohol intake to cause brain shrinkage is less than two ounces, or approximately four drinks. Research has also found an impairment of moral discernment with an intake of only one or two ounces of alcohol.[5]

It must be remembered that brain shrinkage and brain function impairment occur at an alcohol intake level of a light social drinker who may never have been intoxicated. 'It was found,' said one researcher, 'that the progression of the degree of cerebral atrophy in the social drinkers follows the same trend line as does that in patients with alcoholism, but the degree of atrophy was greater in the latter group.[6]

These well documented proofs of brain shrinkage as a result of drinking alcohol should convince every one, alcoholics, social drinkers and abstainers alike, that even what is called moderate use of alcohol is forbidden in the Bible.

---

[4] L. A. Cala, B. Jones, P. Burns, R. E. Davis, N. Stenhouse, and F. L. Mastaglia, *Results of Computerized Tomography, Psychometric Testing and Dietary Studies in Social Drinkers With Emphasis on Reversibility After Abstinence, Medical Journal of Australia* 2, no. 6 (1983): 264-269.

[5] F. Fincham and J. Barling, *Effects of Alcohol on Moral Functioning in Male Social Drinkers, The Journal of Genetic Psychology*, 134 (1979). pp. 79-88.

[6] Dr. Arnold Washton, nationally known substance abuse recovery expert, wrote: "Alcohol is America's biggest drug problem. It always has been and always will be. Because it's legal, that makes it confusing.

"Alcohol is more toxic to the brain than cocaine. It kills brain cells. Cocaine won't do that. Alcohol is more toxic than heroin. It rots the insides. Heroin won't do that

"If you needed a prescription to get alcohol, it would fail the approval standards of the Food and Drug Administration."

SUMMARY OF THE ARGUMENTS FOR THE PROHIBITION OF ALCOHOLIC BEVERAGES BASED ON PROVERBS 23:29-35

1. In this passage a substance is described in considerable detail.

2. Looking at it is prohibited (verse 31).

3. What is not to be looked at is, of course, prohibited for consumption. Not to look at a thing implies not to drink it. A prohibition of looking is just a forceful way of saying don't put yourself in the way of consuming the forbidden thing.

4. The forbidden substance is a specific kind of the juice of the grape (the fruit of the *genus vitis* when pressed and made into a liquid).

5. The description of the ill effects of this substance is such that it can only be alcoholic grape juice and not the nonalcoholic kind.

6. A recognized word for the noun *alcohol* or for the adjective *alcoholic* did not appear in any language until centuries after Proverbs was written, and after translators had attempted to render the book into other languages.

7. The word *yayin* can be demonstrated from Bible usage and the Talmud to include both alcoholic grape juice (commonly called *wine*) and that which is nonalcoholic commonly called simply *grape juice* in modern English.

8. The descriptive words *ki yith'addam* in this passage were not understood in early centuries to mean *when it is red*. The ancients understood it as referring to effects connected with intoxication, but not having a word for alcohol, did not and could not translate these words, *when it is alcoholic*.

9. The translation *when it is red* adds nothing meaningful to the passage, and it does not conform to the grammatical force of the *hithpael* stem in which it is expressed. All that it has in its favor is that the idea of *redness* seems to be in some way connected with the root.

10 When the translation *when it is red* first began to be widely

used it became almost universal. This is to be attributed to the tendency of translators to depend on earlier works, rather than on the merit of this rendering. An analogy in the physical world is that when water descends from the mountains to the plain it at first tends to spread out, but when a channel has been cut, it runs through the channel. This is called *the path of least resistance*. Translators should not follow it, but rather those who translate the Bible should be animated by a Spirit directed desire to tell the people what God is intending them to know. Paraphrases presented as though they were translations must be offensive to our God, the God of truth.

11 . Because the proposed translation *when it is alcoholic* is the only one which agrees with the ill effects described, and which agrees with the reflective sense of the *hithpael* stem, and with the way God instructs in meaningful ways, it should be accepted.

12. If *when it is red* is supposed to mean when it is beautiful, this idea fails in two ways. One is that other colored wines besides red ones are beautiful in a physical sense. The other is that such a command would not agree with the goodness of God. Just as He would not limit a command to us not to stare longingly at a *beautiful* prostitute, He would, because of His very nature, not limit the prohibition to a beautiful beverage.

13. The reasons cited above taken together point positively to the conclusion that *ki yith'addam* means *when it is alcoholic*.

14. Therefore, alcoholic wine is prohibited as a beverage.

15. Alcohol in all forms is by analogy prohibited. Common sense tells us that what is prohibited is what causes the ills so vividly described in Proverbs 23:29-35, not merely alcohol when formed by the fermentation of grape juice.

16. Passages which prohibit excess in the use of a drink do not permit the drinking of it in moderation, if it has previously been prohibited totally and if the prohibition has not been repealed. The whole includes the parts, which is a law of logic.

17. God is continually testing all people, including the elect, and has done so in all ages. People must do their best to pass all tests, the law of logic being one such test. It is not good enough for

us to say that this or that great Christian, as Calvin or Luther, performed in one way or another. We must search the Scripture (John 5:39) and study the evidence, and be tested on our individual performance.

18. When it happens that the law of logic if followed rigidly would lead us to live a more self-denying life, and by so doing avoid the possibility of acquiring a bad habit and setting a bad example for little ones, we should be all the more concerned to follow it.

CERTAIN BOOKS WRITTEN BY ONE-WINE THEORISTS REFUTED

In defending Biblically based total abstinence from attacks by those who propose that alcoholic beverages in *moderation* are a liberty God grants to suffering humanity, it may be proper to discuss particular books. Believing this to be the case, I am including three sections which appear in the form of book reviews.

Two have been written by myself, the author of this book, Stephen M. Reynolds and one is by the Reverend Robert E. Baxter, a minister of the denomination to which the author of the book criticized belongs. He has graciously given permission to have his *Preliminary Response* printed in this work. I do so not only because of the merit of the *Response,* but also because it shows that not all members of the denomination to which Mr. Gentry (the author of the book criticized) belongs share his view on the alcohol question.

Edward H. Jewett, S. T. D.

"The Two Wine Theory..." (New York, 1888)

This book is by an author whose knowledge of Latin and the languages in which the Bible was written is praiseworthy, but his conclusions and manner of reaching them are faulty. In spite of their many faults his writings met with great praise in his day, and the scorn he heaps on the opposition may have intimidated many who might otherwise have been convinced that alcoholic wine is forbidden in the Bible and that nonalcoholic wine is permitted and even praised. He flatly denies that there ever was any such thing as nonalcoholic *yayin* or *oinos.*

In passages where *yayin* is used in such a way as to exclude the possibility of alcoholic content he resorts to strange reasoning. Thus on page 121 he writes that the word *yayin* is used

> twice proleptically of the grape itself, as the material from which wine is derived, Jer. 40:10, 12; and twice of God's

judgments preventing its manufacture, Isa. 16:10; Jer. 48:33.

This is the type of reasoning of one who would say that the expression *gay person*, means and always has meant a homosexual. If anyone would point out passages where the word meant a happy or merry person, one who argues after the fashion of Dr. Jewett would say,

> the word here is used proleptically; when the word was used the person may not have been an overt homosexual but in anticipation of what he will become the word is used in this sense, and properly so.

The fallacy of Dr. Jewett's interpretation may be seen by noting that not all grape juice in the press becomes alcoholic wine. Some is drunk fresh from the press and some becomes vinegar.

Another unsound argument of Dr. Jewett is found on page 129. Here he quotes an advocate of Biblical total abstinence (the Rev. W. M. Thayer) as follows:

> it is not the abuse of wine that is called a 'mocker' but wine itself. Solomon does not teach us to avoid the abuse of wine or not to drink to excess, but not to look upon it.

The argument of Mr. Thayer is basically sound. Can it be refuted? Read what Dr. Jewett writes in an attempt to do so.

> We will leave Solomon to settle the point with each man's own reason and conscience. But if being among 'winebibbers' and 'riotous eaters of flesh' unto drunkenness and gluttony, and 'tarrying long at the wine,' do not imply 'abuse' we are utterly unable to comprehend what they do imply.

Dr. Jewett seizes on the fact that Mr. Thayer failed to write *only* and *but also* into his sentence about Solomon to try to make it appear that Mr. Thayer denied that Solomon taught that excessive drinking of wine was an abuse. It is certain that Mr. Thayer meant, "Solomon does not teach us to avoid *only* the abuse of wine, but *also* not to look upon it." Stated in this way Mr. Thayer's argument is unrefuted. Dr. Jewett did not even attempt to refute Mr. Thayer's argument that it is not the abuse of wine, but wine itself that is called a mocker.

Dr. Jewett does not hesitate to call a man *ungentlemanly* who asked a question (a rather reasonable one) which he resented (p. 108), and in the same book he attributed a *Manichean spirit* to some of his opponents. It is very improbable that he could prove that any of the people he so labeled had such a spirit.

In spite of its shortcomings the book has some merit. These are to be found largely in the author's quotations from writers who opposed his point of view. These are in some cases quoted without even an attempt at refutation.

For example, the author quotes a German pastor, H. Pohlmann, who pointed out that the German Bible of 1554 says in Isaiah 25:6 that in the feast which the Lord of Hosts will give for all people the wine will have no *Barme* (yeast or leaven). In the 1643 Bible the same idea is repeated with a different word for yeast or leaven (*Heffen*).

It may or may not be possible to follow Luther in his translation of the Hebrew word *mezuqqaqim* as meaning without yeast or leaven, but what is especially interesting is that Luther and the revisers saw nothing impossible in speaking of unfermented wine and that God would provide it for all peoples. It is a dogma of the American *one-wine theorists* that there is no such thing as unfermented wine. Pastor Pohlmann partly on the basis of this passage used unfermented wine in communion.

He also saw that Leviticus 10:9,10 legislates that alcoholic beverages are *common* and *unclean* and for that reason are not to be drunk by priests when going into the place of worship. He reasoned that if alcoholic wine was not fit to be associated with worship in the days of Moses, it continues to be unfit and should therefore not be used in Christian communion.

He asks,

> Why should God have called a 'woe unto him who giveth his neighbor drink, etc. (Hab. 2:15)' when he wants fermented wine even in the 'House of God?'

Dr. Jewett does not even attempt to refute these telling arguments. We should, however, be grateful to him for having preserved them by having them printed.

G. I. Williamson
"Wine in the Bible and the Church"
Phillipsburg, New Jersey, 1976

The author of this book assumes without proof that alcoholic beverages are not prohibited for human consumption in the Bible, and then following Dr. Charles Hodge, who also made this assumption without proof, he proceeds to attack the total abstinence movement as *infidel in its spirit and tendency* (p. 7).

Dr. Hodge, on whom Williamson relies too much, wrote in a discussion of slave-holding as follows:

> In like manner, if the Bible nowhere condemns the use of intoxicating liquors as a beverage, if our Lord himself drank wine, then to say that all use of intoxicating liquor as a beverage is sin, is only one of the many forms of the infidelity of benevolence.[1]

The main error in this sentence from which others follow is the assumption that there is no other wine (*yayin, oinos*) in Scripture than alcoholic wine.

Dr. Hodge accepts the truth that the Hebrew word *'elohim* has more than one meaning, for example, the one true God and pagan gods. If there is confusion on this point, theology becomes a shambles. Many other words are accepted as having more than one meaning, but not *yayin* and *oinos*. We must ask whether this is not because people are habituated to alcohol as a permitted beverage and are willing to accept the inconsistency that the one true, righteous God would say that a substance is not to be looked at and is a mocker, forbid priests to use it in connection with worship, and on the other hand call it a gift He has given man to make glad his heart and command its use in worship in Christian holy communion?

If the context determines how we interpret many words (e.g. *'elohim, theos,* and words sometimes translated *messenger* and sometimes *angel*) why are those called infidels by Dr. Hodge who

---

[1] *The Life of Charles Hodge* by A. A. Hodge. A quotation from Charles Hodge found on page 334.

affirm that *yayin* and *oinos* do not always denote beverages containing the poison of alcohol? The arguments of the latter scholars are either totally ignored or brushed aside with inadequate answers by the famed Dr. Hodge and by Mr. Williamson.

What has happened is that against the evidence some Christians have affirmed with unshakable conviction that *yayin* is always an alcoholic drink, that *oinos* is always an alcoholic drink, that *shekar* is always an alcoholic drink, and some, but not all, who say drinking is a Christian liberty say that *tirosh* is always an alcoholic drink. Since these drinks are sometimes not condemned it is argued (against the evidence) that their use is never condemned, only their abuse.

For example, Mr. Williamson says on page 9,

> strange as it may seem, the Bible does not condemn wine and strong drink. It does not say that these are inherently evil. It does not forbid the people of God to use them.

The facts are somewhat different. Proverbs 20:1 says: "Wine is a mocker, strong drink a brawler." This passage personifies the drinks and when personified they are shown to be inherently evil. This does not say the *abuse* of wine is a mocker, it is the (alcoholic) *wine itself.*

The *yayin ki yith'addam* (Proverbs 23:31) that all people are commanded not to look at is not *condemned* according to Mr. Williamson. Why not? He may attempt to explain that it is only forbidden to drunkards (alcoholics), but there is not a word in the context to indicate that this prohibition applies only to such as these.

Is this substance (*yayin ki yith'addam*) which at the last *bites like a serpent and stings like an adder* not inherently evil?

Although their motives may not be the same, is it not possible that people who give others alcoholic beverages may fall under the curse of Habakkuk 2:15? "Woe to him that giveth his neighbor drink." The evil person in this passage gave the drink deliberately to debauch his neighbor, but if a Christian gives his naive young neighbor alcohol to drink he cannot be sure that he is not giving it to a person (like Rabbi Judah of old)[2] who has no ability to resist its intoxicating effects. Even worse than that, the one to whom he gives this first drink may have no ability to resist becoming a drunkard and may totally ruin his life.

Mr. Williamson says on page 13,

> it is recorded in 1 Corinthians 11:21, that some of the Apostolic Church even went so far as to get drunk at the celebration of the Lord's Supper.

But the passage says definitely that this was *not* a Lord's Supper (verse 20). It was not an *imperfect* Lord's Supper; it was not one of *any* kind. It probably was not even intended to be one. Whatever the new and uninstructed Christians intended it to be, we may not use this text to prove the legitimacy of alcoholic wine in communion. The fact that Paul wrote: "What! Do you not have houses in which to eat and drink?" (v. 22) does not mean that Paul was conceding that alcoholic wine may be used in homes. Paul is rejecting the idea that the church is a place to have a substantial feast even with food and drink otherwise permissible. At this point he describes what the Lord's Supper is. The food and drink was no doubt provided by the officers of the church and was not brought by the uninstructed members of the congregation. There is no reference to *wine* (*oinos*) whether fermented or otherwise. The Supper was not intended to satisfy physical hunger or thirst, for if it had been the true meaning of Christ's atoning sacrifice would have been obscured as the people dined. The bread and the cup were probably received in small quantities, and when these were brought to the place of worship they were without yeast or leaven. This prohibition of yeast or leaven applied to both elements and for proof those who are able should read 1 Corinthians 5:8 carefully in the original language of inspiration.

Since Paul made this statement about unleavened *things* (elements) in connection with a reference to spiritual qualities (sincerity and truth) men quickly and *naturally* assumed that the expression *unleavened things* was a figure of speech only. They began using leavened bread and fermented fruit of the vine, but if

---

[2] *Talmud*, Nedarim, 49 b.

they had not taken the easy way, but had searched diligently they would have seen that Paul was commanding that the Lord's Supper be celebrated not only with sincerity and truth but with unfermented (unleavened) bread and wine. The reason is not hard to find. Leaven (yeast) is symbolically impure in the Bible. In bread it is wholesome, but it is fitting that it be excluded from the Lord's Supper because it is not the product of God's gift of grain but of a separate microorganism. In the case of beverages the microorganism produces what everyone agrees is a poison, that is, alcohol. It certainly is not a fitting thing that we should drink a poison when we honor Christ who died that we might have eternal life.

There may be some people who will attempt to say that *azumois* can only refer to bread and not to wine. The fact is that it can be used of either what we call unleavened bread (bread in which the microorganism we call yeast has not worked) or what we call unfermented wine or grape juice in which yeast has not worked to produce alcohol. In proof of this we can cite the great Greek dictionary of Liddell and Scott. In this work the root *zum* gives both *zume* leaven and *zumosis* fermentation.

If anyone suggests that Paul speaks of unleavened-unfermented things in the plural because he means unleavened loaves of bread on the assumption that at most communion services more than one loaf was used, there is a good answer to repudiate that. It is that the communion feast consists of two elements one solid (bread) and one liquid (wine). In a figure of speech a bad perversion of the Lord's Supper would have two elements, leavened bread and leavened (fermented) wine and these stand for two vices, malice and wickedness. A good Lord's Supper has two elements, unleavened bread and unleavened (unfermented) wine and these stand for two virtues, sincerity and truth.

Those who obscure the fact that *azumois* is plural, or who while agreeing that it is plural would say that it refers to two or more loaves rather than two elements destroy the beautiful symmetry of Paul's language.

Microorganisms do not all excrete poison, and they are all

creatures of God; but when God chose to select those microorganisms called yeast, which on the one hand cause bread to rise and on the other destroy the natural sugar of grape juice to create alcohol, He gave a symbol easy to understand. It is that sin begins as a little thing and, left without the intervention of divine grace, permeates the whole nature of man. The medicine for our soul (Holy Communion symbolizing divine grace mediated by Christ in his atoning sacrifice) should not contain these symbols of evil. One of them, leavened bread, is permitted on other occasions, and one of them, alcoholic wine is totally prohibited for beverage use as well as in the Lord's Supper.

On pages 13 and 14 Mr. Williamson's exegesis is quite bad when he discusses 1 Timothy 4:1-5 and Colossians 2:20-23 (not verse 33, an error in Williamson's printed text). In these passages Paul is commanding Christians about food. Alcoholic drinks are not mentioned in these passages, but Mr. Williamson falsely applies the expression *don't touch* to mean that it is wrong ever to say don't touch alcoholic beverages, or to say don't touch anything else. By taking this position he is making Paul contradict himself when he wrote, *touch not the unclean thing* (2 Cor. 6:17).

What we must do is seek to resolve the paradox that Paul says in Romans 14:14 that *nothing is unclean in itself,* and in 2 Corinthians 6:17 he says, *touch not the unclean thing*. If nothing is unclean then the command to touch not the unclean thing is meaningless.

Obviously we ought not without careful exegesis to accept Mr. Williamson's assertion that the words *nothing is unclean in itself* justify people in drinking alcohol. In the context of Romans 14:14 Paul is referring to food forbidden under the law of Moses (called *koinos*), and in 2 Corinthians 6:17 he is speaking of something connected with idolaters and idolatry (called *akathartos*). The context of the two passages is somewhat different and the words for unclean are different, but having determined that, we have not resolved the paradox.

One way, and probably the best, of doing so is to propose that in Romans 14:14 Paul is speaking of the flesh of beasts declared to be clean in Peter's vision (Acts 10:14) when Peter was commanded no longer to call them *koinos* (common or unclean). In 2 Corinthians 6:17 Paul is saying that some things are unclean in another sense, that is they corrupt morally those who touch them. Leviticus 10:8-10 suggests that alcoholic wine destroys the ability to make a distinction between the clean and the unclean. It has led to many sins from the days of Noah on through history and may therefore be called unclean (*akathartos*) in a moral sense. Therefore, Paul could without self-contradiction say that nothing is unclean (*koinos*) in a ceremonial sense, but that some things are unclean (*akathartos*) in a moral sense, and Christians are commanded not to touch the latter. So if God forbids in Proverbs 23:31 all persons to look at *yayin ki yith'addam,* should Mr. Williamson and Professor J. G. Vos, whom Williamson quotes, say it is a denial of the power of the Holy Spirit to affirm that God commands literal obedience to Proverbs 23:31, and to affirm that Christ also obeyed throughout his earthly life, including the wedding feast at Cana and the Last Supper?

The Pentateuch teaches that wine was forbidden only to certain classes (Nazirites and priests when they entered the Tent of Meeting). Others were permitted to drink it, although if they were wise they probably accepted the example of Noah as a warning not to indulge in wine after fermentation had run its course.

The prohibition at first imposed on Nazirites and priests while ministering at the altar and on them alone, was extended in Proverbs 23:31 to prohibit all people from even looking at *yayin ki yith'addam,* and certainly this implies that they should not drink it. Its unclean effects on people is vividly described in the latter part of the chapter in which this verse occurs. This is a moral law and is applicable to all people of every race in every subsequent period of history. It is not one of the ceremonial laws such as were the shadow of things to come (Col. 2:17), and which were abolished when Christ fulfilled all the things for which they stood.

Williamson says on page 24:

> To say that wine should not be used even at the communion table, out of supposed concern for the alcoholic, is therefore not the pious and innocent thing that is often pretended. No, it is really a practical application of a false doctrine of man, and of

sin.

The point he is trying to make is that on the assumption that Christ commanded all Christians to take alcoholic wine in communion, a Christian who is an alcoholic should take alcoholic wine and depend on the power of the Holy Spirit to preserve him from a relapse into alcoholism. The error is in the false assumption. In the first place, Christ never mentioned alcoholic wine in connection with the Lord's Supper, and in the second place, Paul while fully inspired spoke of the Christian's Passover (their Communion) as being with unleavened things or elements (not merely unleavened bread) (1 Cor. 5:8 in the original).

What the Holy Spirit *did* say is, *wine is treacherous* (Hab. 2:5).[3] Christ said, that we should pray *lead us not into temptation.* If a little alcohol is a temptation to an alcoholic how can we pray this prayer and then give him what threatens his health and even his life? The Holy Spirit is not promised as a Protector if we break God's law.

A total abstainer, one who teaches total abstinence, may be as staunch a defender of the doctrine of man's total depravity[4] as Mr. Williamson professes to be. Mr. Williamson denies this in his

---

[3] Not abuse of wine, or too much wine, or wine except in Holy Communion, but simply *wine*. Alcoholic wine is the only kind that has treachery. *Hayyayin boged* means "the wine is treacherous." (See, for example, C. F. Keil.) Most translations obscure the sense.

[4] Total depravity is defined, according to Reformed theology, as follows: "The whole human race, by their apostasy from God, are totally depraved. By total depravity, it is not meant that all are equally wicked; nor that any man is as thoroughly corrupt as it is possible for a man to be; nor that men are destitute of all moral virtues" (Charles Hodge, *Systematic Theology*, II, p. 233). Williamson argues from his understanding of total depravity that some people do not have to be shielded more from temptation than others. The doctrine, when properly understood, permits us to understand that while all men are constitutionally sinners, that some have a greater proclivity to certain sins than others, and that it is a sacred obligation for those who are able to do so to seek to protect such as have a proclivity to a particular sin from falling victim to it. Laws prohibiting the distribution of alcoholic beverages are just and in total conformity to Christian ethics. Biblical texts can be cited to prove all these points. Mr. Williamson's argument that alcoholics do not need to be protected from the temptation of alcohol in Communion cannot be supported by Biblical texts.

Chapter Five in order to disprove the idea that there are any *constitutional alcoholics*. It is hard to see any strength in his argument. If we agree that all men are constituted sinners (Rom. 5:19) why is it a denial of this doctrine to say that some are constituted with special proclivities to certain kinds of sin, that is, alcoholism, homosexuality, or any other particular sin? His case here is unproved.

Since Dr. Williamson proposes that teachers of total abstinence on the basis of the Bible do so because they ignore the doctrine of total depravity of man, it is not unreasonable at this point to suggest that it is because of his total depravity that mankind has generally failed to obey the command not to look at alcoholic wine. After Israel was delivered out of bondage they failed to circumcise their sons during the forty years of wilderness wanderings (Joshua 5:5). Why? Was it because they did not know it was commanded? No. It was because of depravity. The Israelites of Old Testament times failed to keep God's laws protecting the poor from exploitation. Was it because of ignorance or depravity? More probably the latter. Is it any wonder then if total depravity, which according to Reformed theology afflicts all mankind, regenerate and unregenerate, should affect the teaching of Christian theologians and they in turn should influence other Christians?

This is not to say that godly Christian scholars who have discerned the truth that God prohibits the beverage use of alcohol are necessarily holier or wiser on other particulars than Christians who do not discern it. Their exegetical skills may sometimes fail in particular instances.

It is not very good scholarship for Mr. Williamson and others to put in print weak arguments of the total abstainers and by so doing demolish a *straw man*. As guilt by association is an unethical device in controversy, so is stupidity by association. Every writer and speaker should be judged on his own merit. Of those who dealt with the Scripture as it relates to alcohol, Moses Stuart and Ernest Gordon were not in their day stupid men. Why are they ignored and unscholarly total abstainers quoted?

This book is not recommended. It may do great harm.

Preliminary Response to Kenneth Gentry's Paper, "The Case for Moderation," by Robert E. Baxter[5]

Kenneth Gentry in his paper, *The Case for Moderation,* attempts to justify the beverage use of alcoholic beverages on Biblical grounds. The subtitle of his paper is, *The Bible on the Christian and Alcoholic Beverages.*

The two most prominent errors in his paper are:

1. That the Biblical words for *wine* always mean *fermented wine.*

2. That the abuse of fermented wine is drunkenness, which is what the Bible prohibits.

The first proposition above is historically, scientifically, objectively, and verifiably false. This basic error undermines all the rest of Mr. Gentry's arguments. He says on page 20, "Those who attempt to argue that there were two types of *yayin*—one fermented and the other unfermented—fare no better." Mr. Gentry then launches into a long discussion of how freshly pressed grape juice can be called fermented wine because of the *effecta pro causa* principle of incipient seed-beginning. He argues that poetic license *allows the eventual end-product to stand for the seed-beginning.* He concludes this rebuttal against Dr. Reynolds on page 24: "The critical argument put forward by Reynolds is not established at all."

If we accept the idea that the whole may be expressed by the part, and the end by the beginning, that concept might eliminate any clear way of determining from the words themselves whether or not unfermented wine was used by the ancients. The lack of linguistic proof would not refute the historical proof however.

From the quotations which Mr. Gentry gives on page 20 with approbation, we see that he believes *yayin* means *fermented grape juice.* His arguments indicate that he also believes *oinos* means the same. "OINOS, which means 'fermented grape juice,' i.e., alcoholic wine" (page 47). "The Last Supper was instituted with

[5] Published with the knowledge and consent of the author.

wine—not grape juice." Also, on page 42, he says, "It has been shown that this word indicates fermented-quality grape drink, i.e., wine." He also quotes another commentator, "...the wine had to be fermented. The grape harvest had been collected over six months earlier in September." This is simply ignorance as to the many methods the ancients had for preserving their unfermented wine.

The second proposition above is a subjective opinion as to what constitutes ABUSE. Mr. Gentry thinks that drunkenness is the abuse of alcohol. I believe that the USE of alcohol for non-medicinal purposes constitutes its ABUSE, just as it does for any OTHER DRUG. Alcohol IS a drug, the drug which causes the most deaths. Alcohol is a drug that kills brain cells as well as causing much other destruction. If there were NO scriptural passages prohibiting the USE of alcohol, as there are no passages prohibiting the use of marijuana or cocaine, there would still be sufficient Scriptural deductions against the beverage USE of this drug. Its USE *is* its abuse. Drunkenness is simply one *result* that often follows its use.

Proverbs 20:1 states the case against wine itself, and not just against drunkenness. It says, "Wine is a mocker, strong drink is raging: and whosoever is deceived thereby is not wise." Many HAVE been deceived by wine, and not only the people who drink it. I have observed in 30 years of ministry that the people whose children drink alcoholic beverages, sometimes resulting in great tragedy, are usually the children of adults who drink alcoholic beverages. That is not surprising. We also know that the children who successfully resist peer pressure to drink usually have parents who do not drink either, with one notable EXCEPTION. Parents who hold to the position of moderation, who do not drink themselves but who teach that it is a matter of Christian liberty to drink, often find that their children choose to exercise that *liberty*.

Evaluation of Mr. Gentry's Paper

Mr. Gentry argues in circles. The reasoning goes like this: *Wine* in the Bible is always fermented. When the Bible speaks negatively of wine, it is referring to the ABUSE of wine, not its

USE. Therefore we are free to drink fermented wine as long as we don't abuse it by getting drunk. A variation on this argument is often heard, that a person is free to drink alcoholic beverages as long as he doesn't offend *weaker* brethren who don't know as much or can't control their drinking.

The circular argument evades all Scripture warnings against wine by simply saying that such warnings pertain to its ABUSE, not its USE. Those passages which deal with the RESULT of drinking wine are thus neutralized by saying that they merely condemn drunkenness. This position finds support for the beverage USE of wine from those passages which refer to unfermented wine which Gentry denies existed.

Gentry argues in such a way as to disqualify all that is in opposition to his point of view on the basis of his own interpretation of the words. For instance, any mention of sweet *wine* must possibly include its vintage stage of hard *wine*. Yet any evil usage of *wine* in the Bible must imply its RESULTS of DRUNKENNESS, These are subjective assumptions.

To break the circular reasoning of Gentry it is only necessary to show that he is factually in error concerning the generic nature of the word *wine*. If, indeed, wine was enjoyed by the ancients in an unfermented form, then the context will have to determine whether the word is referring to fermented or unfermented wine. Then to LOOK on fermented wine so as to be tempted to drink of it, which can lead to drunkenness, becomes sin as well as to look on a woman with lust can lead to adultery. The adultery is the more serious sin than the lust which leads to it, and the drunkenness is the more serious sin than is the drinking of the wine. Nevertheless, mortification of indwelling sin requires killing the root cause of both drunkenness and adultery.

Proverbs 23, of which Mr. Gentry makes so much ado, deals with other sins too, besides drunkenness. Immediately before this passage, it deals with whoredom. Is it to be argued that this passage is addressed only to harlots, as the final verses of the chapter are supposedly addressed only to drunkards? Mr. Gentry sees verses 29-35 as relative rather than absolute, but Dr. Reynolds correctly observes that *all the prohibitions of Proverbs 23 are absolute*.

Earlier in the chapter when removing the ancient landmark is prohibited (verse 10), this is not a relative matter of degree, meaning "don't move it too far; don't cheat the fatherless too much!"

Proverbs 23:30 says, *They that tarry long at the wine,* in describing the drunkard. This passage is NOT addressed exclusively TO drunkards, but is describing the sinful result of drinking alcoholic wine. It is not second person, but third person at this point. After describing this in verses 29-30, the warning is given in the second person, "look not THOU upon the wine when it is red." Here the sober person is addressed, warning him not to drink it, lest he experience what follows in verses 32-35. What kind of exegesis is it that suggests this passage is addressed only to drunkards?

The progression of the passage is from looking at, to drinking, to lingering long over it, to drunkenness. It is not merely the final result that is prohibited, but the entering in to the first temptation.

If this circular reasoning were used concerning lust, we could say that it is not the look of lust that is evil, but only its RESULT; namely, the ABUSE of lust, which is adultery. Furthermore, it could be denied that *lust* has two meanings, just as it is denied that *wine* is a generic word which can refer either to fermented or unfermented grape juice. Thus when Deuteronomy 14:26 says, "And thou shalt bestow that money for whatsoever thy soul lusteth after;" if *lust* is always evil lust, then such a Scripture could be twisted to show that *lust* in itself is not prohibited but only its abuse.

Why would anyone want to defend the use of alcohol? Distilled liquors were completely unknown in Bible days, so we cannot justify their use by any appeal to Scripture. To attempt to justify the beverage use of fermented wine from Scripture requires clever manipulation of the facts and circular argument.

Mr. Gentry's reasonings fail completely if he is factually in error about the Bible words for wine not being generic words. His arguments about these substances being used in offerings, etc., carry no weight if he is wrong at this vital, factual point. We have the historical writings of the ancients themselves which attest to the popularity of the non-intoxicating wines and the method of preserving them from fermentation.

I do not write this article with animosity toward Mr. Gentry himself, nor do I question his sincerity or his persuasion that the Bible is the Word of God. I believe Mr. Gentry to be a godly man, holding to the Reformed Faith and sincerely seeking to understand what Scripture teaches on this issue. Nevertheless, I find him in error; and it is a dangerous error for any Church or community.

"THE BIBLE AND ITS WINES"
By Charles Wesley Ewing, D. D.

Charles Wesley Ewing, D. D., has written a book, *The Bible and Its Wines*,[1] which deserves the attention of everyone.

It is only right, with all due respect to the fine scholarship of Dr. Ewing, that I should meekly and humbly point out that if *tirosh* never means anything fermented, as Dr. Ewing affirms, and if he is right that whenever any drink is recommended in the Bible it is nonalcoholic, then the inspired writers would have used *tirosh* and not *yayin* in Psalm 104:15 and in certain other passages. There would be no reason to use a word ambiguous as to whether or not it had alcoholic content if there were a perfectly good Hebrew word meaning, as Dr. Ewing, following the original Hebrew-German dictionary of Wilhelm Gesenius and the *New Schaff-Herzog Encyclopedia of Religious Knowledge,* says it does, *newly extracted grape juice, ungegorener Wein* (unfermented wine).

As the use of the word *tirosh,* if that were its meaning, would remove ambiguity, the reasonable deduction would be that *tirosh,* in Bible times, did not always mean unfermented wine. It can easily be demonstrated that it did not always have that meaning in Talmudic times.

It is probable that the dictionary of Koehler and Baumgartner is correct in defining *tirosh* as archaic for *yayin*. If so the words could be used interchangeably and each of them could be either alcoholic or nonalcoholic, the context alone being the guide to determine the precise meaning with regard to alcoholic content.

While etymology is an uncertain guide in determining what a word may mean at various stages in the development of a language, a few remarks on proposed etymologies of *tirosh* and *yayin* may be proper at this point. Dr. Ewing does not discuss the etymology of *tirosh,* but many scholars think it comes from *yarash, to take possession of.* If so, the idea of the ancient people who gave the beverage that name may have been to call it *that which takes*

[1] Published by the National Prohibition Foundation, Denver, Colorado.

possession. If this understanding is correct, the idea would be that a person who has taken a considerable quantity of this drink is no longer the same as he was before. The ancient inventors of the word may have seen the drink as a mysterious, even supernatural power which possesses the mind and body of the user.

All who have studied Hebrew know that the letter *tau* (*t*) is frequently put before a root word, originally a verb, to make a noun. The noun is connected in some way in meaning with the verb. Thus we have *Torah* (law) from *yarah,* one of the meanings of which in the *hiphil* is *to teach.* The underlying idea is that the Law of God is taught by Him. We have *tiqwah, hope,* from *qawah, to wait for,* because hoping is associated with waiting. Many other examples could be cited.

It is important to know that there is nothing in the etymology of *tirosh* to suggest newness. Some two-wine theorists think that because *tirosh* is sometimes translated in the English Bible as *new wine,* the idea of newness is embedded in the word. This has led some of them to become heated in reproaching others who see other meanings derived from other etymologies in the word *tirosh.*

The etymology from the verb to *possess* makes reasonable the idea that when *tirosh* first came into use it was associated with the idea of taking possession of the mind and body. If this is accepted, it must also be clearly understood that the idea of the alcoholic quality of *tirosh* did not keep another idea, namely that nonalcoholic grape juice could also be called *tirosh,* from becoming a part of the language. Practically all scholars admit there was a nonalcoholic *tirosh.* Even most of those who deny that there was a nonalcoholic *yayin* do so. Thus most *one-yayin* theorists who consider *yayin* to be always alcoholic are not *one-tirosh* theorists. It is to be regretted that a number of *two-yayin* theorists are not *two-tirosh* theorists. By refusing to admit that there are two kinds of *tirosh* they weaken rather than strengthen their case for Biblically based prohibition of alcoholic beverages.

If the word *yayin* came into the Hebrew language from some unknown source in prehistoric times, it may have quickly taken on both of the meanings already established for the earlier word *tirosh.* Dr. Ewing quotes Fausset as saying that *yayin* is from a root *boil up* This etymology of Fausset is not supported by strong arguments, nor do writers of standard dictionaries approve of it. Gesenius says it is from a root of unknown meaning, regarded as a loan-word. Koehler and Baumgartner say it is un-Semitic. No etymology for it can be found in Indo-European languages. This is enough for now as to the thus far unsuccessful search for the origin of the word *yayin*.

As for *tirosh*, an idea of Koehler and Baumgartner should at least be brought to the attention of the thoughtful reader, even though the evidence for it is weak. This is that *tirosh* comes from a meaning of *yarash* which is supposed to have existed, signifying *to press* (grapes). The principle alleged evidence for the existence of this supposed meaning is arrived at by amending or rather changing the Hebrew text of Micah 6:15 where *tirosh* is made to be *tirash*, understood to be a verb meaning *thou shalt press* (grapes). There is no basis for this proposed change in the Hebrew text, for if *tirosh* is taken in the sense of *grapes*, the verse makes very good sense and no change in the Masoretic text should be considered. That *tirosh* may mean grapes has been demonstrated elsewhere in this work. In Joel 1:10 as well as this passage the meaning grapes is indicated. To propose a change in the Masoretic text when such a change is not necessary is not usually the best exegesis. The thoughtful reader should weigh in his own mind the Koehler and Baumgartner suggestion and the reasons and then determine for himself what he thinks it is worth.

As for Hosea 4:11 where Dr. Ewing sees *tirosh* as *fresh grape juice* (page 22), it seems that Hosea is best understood if we propose that *tirosh* here explains *yayin*, and that these words both refer to the same (alcoholic) drink. As is known to Hebraists *waw* may mean *that is*.

Hosea, guided by God, may have known that the readers to whom he was primarily addressing his prophesy did not all know the word *yayin*. Some would have to have it explained to them as meaning *tirosh*. The latter was probably an archaic word in some parts of the Holy Land, but current in the area where Hosea lived and wrote.

Whatever readers who are convinced of the two-wine theory

may think of the above, I respectfully ask them to consider the arguments presented. I believe that any who have previously thought that *tirosh* was always unfermented should rethink their position, and conclude that it does not serve their cause well to insist on a one-*tirosh* theory, that is, that *tirosh* means the unfermented juice of the grape and never the fermented kind. They should consider that the ancients did not have modern chemistry to guide them in making distinctions based on alcoholic content.

I commend Dr. Ewing's book. It is my modest wish that those who read it may make use of mine as well. We who are convinced of the two-wine theory should be supportive of one another, each rejoicing in the work of others of like faith and practice.

APPENDIX ON TRANSLITERATION

The arguments in this book are derived from the meanings of Hebrew and Greek words. Since the Bible in the original languages is the only rule of faith and practice on doctrinal matters for evangelical Christians, it is important that every such person equip himself as far as possible to search the Scripture for himself and not depend totally on others.

It cannot be expected that Christians in general will acquire even a slight knowledge of Bible languages, but in our day we see a decline in interest in their study even in Christian denominations which used to require them for ordination to the ministry. One minister of more than usual intelligence wrote recently concerning Hebrew and Greek:

> I had no special talent for languages and had no intention of using either of those languages in any effective way. As soon as I obtained the necessary credits, I closed those books and scarcely ever opened them again. I believe that in actual practice at least nine out of ten students have the same experience. As for myself I knew full well that I could never in the world make more accurate or more beautiful translations than those which competent Greek and Hebrew scholars already had made in the KJV or the *American Standard Version* of 1901.[1]

It is necessary to ask how does this fine Christian teaching elder tell which is right when his two favorite versions disagree?

For example in Hosea 7:5 the KJV says, "In the day of our king the princes have made him sick with bottles of wine," and the *American Standard Version* of 1901 says, "On the day of our king the princes made themselves sick with the heat of wine." The *American Standard Version* has a footnote, "Or, *him*" as an alternative reading to *themselves.*

How would this minister answer an earnest inquirer who would ask which reading is right? He is a scholar who was once

[1] Loraine Boettner, *Presbyterian Journal*, vol. 45, no. 4 (July 9, 1986), p. 28.

trained in Hebrew grammar, and probably many of his hearers and readers suppose he has retained some of his ability. I believe he has not lost it all and could in necessity go to his Hebrew Bible and with the aid of a dictionary give an answer to the inquirer, but by his letter he encourages candidates for the ministry who wish to specialize in communication skills to avoid the languages of the Bible as a *terrific waste of time*.

Far more serious than this difference between the KJV and the *American Standard Version* of 1901 are the variations in meaning introduced by more modern versions. Some of these modern translations introduce words not at all to be derived from a sober reading of the inspired original. They are paraphrases, not translations, and often give an entirely wrong idea to the uninstructed reader.

Are all but a very few ministers and practically all laymen to say, I am incompetent to judge so I will trust a particular version and reject all others, or, I will read different ones and in particular passages choose the one that appeals most to my particular taste and prejudices?

These uninformed and only partially trained ministers are as inadequate in this matter as is a medical practitioner who has forgotten everything he learned in medical school but his specialty. If someone tries to point out to the Bible teachers that the word translated by the KJV as *bottles* (a rendering which can easily be proved to be incorrect), and by the *American Standard Version heat*, can also mean *poison*, they will resist the idea. They have no competence to decide wisely; so they will hold firmly to the version they believe is best. This they may do not only because they are emotionally committed to a particular version, but also because they have probably been trained to resist the idea that alcoholic wine is a poison. Alcoholic wine, they fondly think, is God's gift to man to make him rejoice.

Many other examples could be given to show that the ordinary pastor of a congregation should not only have once studied Greek and Hebrew, but should spend enough time in Bible study in the original to retain a reasonable competence, not perhaps to read extensive passages by sight, but to be able to refer, with the aid of dictionaries, to what God really and truly said to His people of all tongues and in all historical periods.

Those really facile in the languages of the Bible will find no problem in understanding the words used in this book, even though the transliteration is not according to the system they may be used to. To those who have studied the languages, but who do not read and speak them with ease the following scheme is presented.

In this book Hebrew *aleph* is represented by ', *beth* by b, *gimel* by g, *daleth* by d, *he* by h, *waw* or *vav* by w, *zayin* by z, *heth* by ch, *teth* by t, *yodh* by y, *caph* or *kaph* by k, *lamed* by 1, *mem* by m, *nun* by n, *samek* by s, *ayin* by ', *pe* by p, *tsade* by ts, *qoph* by q, *resh* by r, *sin* by s, *shin* by sh, *tau* with *dagesh* by t, *tau* without *dagesh* by th.

It is apparent that according to this system *teth* and *tau* with *dagesh* are both transliterated t, and *samek* and *sin* are both transliterated s. Where this might cause difficulty in identifying Hebrew words used in this book, an explanation follows:

The t in *tirosh* is *tau*. The t in *mi-gat* is *tau* without *dagesh*; the spelling with t rather than th is because the expression is a quotation from another writer who chose to transliterate this way. (Modern Israeli Hebrew makes no distinction in pronunciation between t with *dagesh* and t without it.)

The T in *Tanakh* is *tau* and the kh is *kaph*. (Hebrew makes a spirant of *kaph* without *dagesh*. This word is taken directly from the title of the Book.)

The examples of s in *'asis, Kesil, mesappeach* and *sammekuni* are all sameks.

The s in *Kir-hareseth* is *Sin*. This word is not transliterated according to the system used in the rest of the book because the place name *Kir-hareseth* is known to English Bible readers in this form. If it were transliterated according to the system it would be *Qir-chareseth*.

Shawas when they are vocalic are represented by full vowels. Thus *chateph-segol* and simple vocal shewa are both represented by e. This is true of *tsere* and *segol* as well.

Transliterations from Greek are usually not difficult to trace back to the original, but a problem exists in that e represents both *epsilon* and *eta,* and o represents both *omicron* and *omega.* In this book it may be of help to some readers to point out that the e in *brosei, gluekos, en, eytheos, methuo, methu* and *neos* stands for *epsilon.* In *suneideseos* the first and third e's are *epsilon* and the second is *eta.* In *teganou* and *chrestos* the e is *eta.* In *chrestoteros* and *sterisate* the first e is *eta* and the second *epsilon.*

The o in *amoriten, oinos, gleukos, neos, azumois,* and *palaios* is omicron, while that in *brosei, eutheos* and *suneideseos* is *omega.*

The guidelines given above are intended to make it easier for a student to look up in Hebrew or Greek dictionaries the comparatively few words in these languages cited in this study. It is hoped such searching as to the meaning of words may convince doubters and confirm in the minds of others the truth of the arguments presented.

APPENDIX ON SYLLOGISMS

An advocate of the idea that drinking alcoholic beverages is a liberty all people, except alcoholics, ought to have, has sought to prove it syllogistically. This supposed proof has apparently been received by some Christians as convincing and must therefore be examined and refuted. The illustration presented to the public is as follows:

1. Scripture, condemns drunkenness.
2. Drinking can lead to drunkenness.
3. Therefore Scripture condemns all drinking.

1 Scripture condemns gluttony.
2. Eating can lead to gluttony.
3. Therefore Scripture condemns all eating.

1. Scripture condemns sexual perversion.
2. Enjoyment of sex can lead to sexual perversion.
3. Therefore Scripture condemns all sexual enjoyment.

The intention in presenting these premises (1 and 2) which it is presumed the public will recognize as true, followed by the conclusions numbered 3 which it is presumed they will recognize as false, is to prove the case for drinking alcohol in moderation, or, as some *moderationists* put it, that abuse and not use of alcoholic beverage is condemned.

The fact is that the analogies presumed to exist, do not. This is because truths in the Bible are ignored. The second premise in the first column does not even state accurately what can lead to drunkenness. It is not *drinking,* which word could include water or other nonalcoholic beverages. By leaving out the idea that it is not drinking in general but drinking alcoholic beverages in particular that causes drunkenness, the maker of the syllogisms attempts to lead his readers to the false assumption that all beverages, all foods and all sexual relations are in the Bible placed on exactly the same footing.

Alcoholic beverages are excluded in the Bible from the classification of wholesome, permitted things. Of course chemical analysis of substances was unknown and inspired writers could not speak of alcohol, which must be defined chemically. The Bible makes absolutely clear that it is speaking of an alcoholic beverage in Proverbs 23:29-35 and it does it by describing the effects of the beverage in question. It is forbidden, not merely to alcoholics, but to everyone.

Food and marital sex are not treated as something forbidden.

Readers are invited to consider these propositions. Are they not true according to the Bible?

1 Scripture condemns looking at alcoholic beverages.
2. Looking at alcoholic beverages leads to drinking them.
3. Therefore scripture condemns drinking alcoholic beverages.
4. A corollary to this is that other beverages are permitted if taken in moderation.

1. Scripture condemns gluttony.
2. Eating without restraint leads to gluttony.
3. Therefore scripture condemns eating without restraint.
4. A corollary to this is that eating all foods is permitted if done in moderation.

1. Scripture condemns sexual perversion.
2. Treating sex without Biblical restraints leads to perversion.
3. Therefore scripture condemns indulging in sex without regard to Biblical restraints.
4. A corollary to this is that sex in marriage is permitted if done in moderation and with the consent of the marriage partner. The marriage partner should not withhold consent without good reason.

THE END

SUBJECT AND PROPER NAME INDEX

SCRIPTURE REFERENCES

About the Lorine L. Reynolds Foundation

The Lorine L. Reynolds Foundation was founded by Dr. Stephen Reynolds in memory of his late wife who has preceded him into the presence of the Lord.

The Foundation is dedicated to issues of Bible Translation, especially where these issues impact the ethics and morals of the Lord's people. It is dedicated to the purpose of providing a translation of the Scriptures where many of the extant errors of previous translations have been corrected. To that end in the year 2000 it published *A Purified Translation* of *The New Testament.* It is currently engaged in producing *A Purified Translation* of *The Old Testament.* The Foundation publishes books and articles relevant to its purposes, as well as its translations of the Holy Scriptures. It also maintains a website at **llreynoldsfoundation.org**, where much of this material is available free of charge in an electronic format.

To inquire more fully about the Foundation, to correspond with us on any issue, to order books, translations, and other literature please contact the Foundation at...

The Lorine L. Reynolds Foundation
702 Custis Road
Glenside, PA 19038-2016
llreynolds@llreynoldsfoundation.com